Introduction to Inter

Introduction to International Business

Sonia El Kahal

Senior Lecturer
Coventry Business School

McGRAW-HILL BOOK COMPANY

London · New York · St Louis · San Francisco · Auckland
Bogotá · Caracas · Lisbon · Madrid · Mexico
Milan · Montreal · New Delhi · Panama · Paris · San Juan
São Paulo · Singapore · Sydney · Tokyo · Toronto

Published by
McGRAW-HILL Book Company Europe
Shoppenhangers Road, Maidenhead, Berkshire, SL6 2QL, England
Telephone 0628 23432
Fax 0628 770224

British Library Cataloguing in Publication Data

Kahal, Sonia El
Introduction to International Business
I. Title
338

ISBN 0–07–707871–3

Library of Congress Cataloging-in-Publication Data

The CIP data of this title is available from the Library of Congress, Washington DC, USA

12345   CL   97654

Typeset by Computape (Pickering) Ltd, North Yorkshire
Printed and bound in Great Britain at the University Press, Cambridge

If you give a man a fish, he will have single meal.
If you teach him how to fish, he will eat all his life.

Kuan-Tzu

For John, Diala and Khaldoun

CONTENTS

PART III: THE GLOBALIZATION OF BUSINESS OPERATIONS AND MANAGEMENT

PART FOUR: BUSINESS IN THE SINGLE EUROPEAN MARKET

PREFACE: TOWARDS A POLITICAL ECONOMY
OF INTERNATIONAL BUSINESS

The recent globalization of competition, the rapid expansion of Japanese multinationals, the Free-trade Agreement between the USA, Canada and Mexico, the awakening of China (the sleeping giant), the creation of a unified Single European Market, the dramatic political and economic changes that have occurred in Eastern and Central Europe in their process of liberalization and transition to free-market economies, and the development now of Third World multinationals, have together confirmed the importance of 'international business' as a definitive field of study, which can no longer be understood in terms of the traditional, established concepts and methods of the discipline of 'business studies'.

Today, more and more managers, besides those employed in already established international firms, are realizing that their businesses cannot be located or conceived of as operating within national boundaries only. Domestic firms are increasingly facing external competition within their own domestic markets. Business activities can no longer be considered as external and separate from the global environment within which they operate, or as subject only to the conditions of national political economies. Considerable socio-economic and political relations located at the global level are increasingly influencing business decision-making, even at the most local, domestic or regional levels. To compete successfully, or simply to survive, in such a challenging and dynamic environment, firms are realizing the need for their managers to look for opportunities abroad as well as in local domestic markets. To do this, they need to understand and take account of relevant international aspects of their business and the international political and economic environment within which they operate.

This growing awareness of, and demand for, international business knowledge has also prompted many universities and colleges to introduce a number of general and specialized courses in international business. Many courses, such as International Marketing, International Finance, International Strategic Management or International Human Resource Management, have been added to the traditional business curricula with the underlying assumption that a combination of a wide range of practical international business courses and detailed knowledge of empirical and observable political and social aspects would constitute a coherent international business studies programme.

As with traditional business studies, students are now being technically equipped with sets of principles, prescriptions and strategies to follow and apply in an 'international context', where the latter dimension is taken as given, and is still conceived of as external to the domestic business context. Such an approach, by concentrating only on the normative and prescriptive nature of the discipline, neglects the issues and factors which underlie global developments, and the movement towards 'internationalization and globalization'. This provides only a limited understanding of the political, economic, social and cultural challenges now facing multinational firms within the new global political economy. Business activities can no longer be evaluated and understood in terms of international economics or international finance only, but increasingly need to be related to the way in which the world is politically organized, for example, the nature of capital, problematic relations between states and markets and the underlying structures and dynamics of information technology, economic and political instability, and contradictory trends in international trade. As important is the increasing management of the international system by international organizations which are attempting to establish international rules of conduct, and are actively mediating privatization, deregulation and the internationalization of private sector management and budgetary practices.

Consequently, it is not sufficient in today's world to train students or managers simply to acquire academic or practical technical skills and methods to apply within an international context which might become rapidly obsolete, or inappropriate for successful rapid decision-making in a constantly changing economic, political, legal, sociocultural and technical environment. There is a need to develop critical ways of thinking, and methods of analysis, on the basis of which they can address unfamiliar situations, and relate global factors to their specific business and management tasks.

It is the recognition of such a crucial and increasing need to understand global changes in the world political economy, in order to meet the challenge of global competition in the 1990s that inspired the writing of this textbook.

THE STUDY OF INTERNATIONAL BUSINESS

The study of international business is very broad and complex, and various different views have been developed and adapted within the discipline. Economists traditionally refer to the study of international business in terms of the fields of international trade and finance, and focus primarily in their analysis on the flow of commodities among nations. Domestic and international business, they argue, are undertaken for the same ends. In most cases, profit is the driving force behind each transaction. Both domestic and international business, in their view, consist essentially of the production and distribution of products and services and the financing of such activities. International economic relations therefore are the source of key concepts in their approach. Any change in the world economy could create enormous challenges for business firms in their overseas markets. Even companies that have not ventured into overseas production frequently find themselves dependent on a worldwide production system and market place (Davidson, 1991).

Others consider the multinational firm as the key figure and leading actor in international business and focus mainly on the firm in their analysis, as it looks outwards at an assumed external economy. They closely examine the functions and operations of the firm and ask how it operates and what motivates its management to act as it does in world markets and in the increasingly competitive global environment. Although the basic principles behind any of the functional areas such as Marketing, Management, Finance and Accounting are much the same whether business is carried on domestically or internationally, the practices themselves must be altered in a functional way when operating across national borders to correspond with different variables present abroad (see, for example, Grosse and Kujawa, 1992; Rugman et al., 1985; Vernon and Wells, 1991; Wortzel and Wortzel, 1990; Drucker, 1990; Welch and Luostarinen, 1990).

International business however, is not limited to international trade and international finance, or to specific theories of the multinational firm. Environmental conditions hugely influence international business operations. An understanding of the environmental variables that affect international business is crucial to the survival or success of the firm in foreign markets (see for example, Asheghian and Ebrahimi, 1990; Matusura, 1991; Khambata and Ajami, 1992; Daniels and Radebaugh, 1992). A great emphasis, for example, is placed upon the role and influence of cultural variables, such as linguistic diversity, religion, values and attitudes, education and technology, on international economic activities (Terpestra, 1978, 1985, 1991).

Along with the knowledge of environmental variables, and in addition to the basic functional business field, the study of international business, by operating within the broad context of the world environment, also draws heavily on the contributions of a number of other basic disciplines, such as geography, history, politics, law, culture, sociology and anthropology.

However, international business cannot be conceived of as a simple geographic expansion where the international is simply tacked on to the domestic, and constructed in terms of territoriality and space. International business cannot be simply abstracted from the global political economy and explained in terms of separate units, but needs to be related causally to the international system within which it operates (El Kahal, 1992). The changes in the global political economy since the mid 1980s have not only altered the relationships between states and firms but have also changed the 'name of the game' for both states and firms. Increasing global competition has pushed governments to realize their increased dependence on the scarce resources controlled by firms. Firms, on the other hand, aware of the need for security as well as the pursuit of profit in their international operations, are now seeking corporate alliances with the state to enhance their capacity to compete with others for world market shares (Strange, 1991). This mutual interdependence between states and firms and the efforts to reunite politics and economics within international business cannot be realistically achieved without locating both states and firms within the ever-changing structures of power within the global political economy (Stopford et al., 1991).

DISTINCTIVE FEATURES OF THE BOOK

A review of the literature dealing with this field indicates a major omission of textbooks directed towards HND/BTEC and first-year undergraduate business students. Most textbooks published in this area assume a significant body of prior knowledge of business, and are aimed primarily at advanced level undergraduates and MBA students. This book has been developed to fill this gap and respond to the growing demand for a comprehensive yet accessible introductory text on international business.

The book should also be valuable to first line managers and junior managers who want to get quickly to the heart of the subject, or as a reference material for managers' bookshelves. It could also be useful to senior executives wishing to update their international business knowledge and to enhance their international managerial skills. It should also be of interest to managers of companies planning to remain national or local, but who wish to know what developments can be expected in their own markets as a result of the recent movements towards globalization.

A second distinctive feature of this book is that, while maintaining the traditional coverage of the subject in terms of substantive content, practical concepts and so on, the overall approach or framework adopted is different. It provides a new and fresh insight into the field of international business by relating core features of the contemporary global political economy to the traditional business context. This is certainly not a 'radical' or 'controversial alternative' to the conventional study of international business in some fundamental way, but it does seek to capture more fully aspects of recent developments of the discipline, in particular the rapid and dramatic growth of global competition in the 1990s.

A third distinguishing feature of this textbook is that it deals with many relevant and practical applications of theoretical concepts and managerial policies, in such a way that students can test their understanding of the material covered through an 'experiential learning process'. This is consistent with the recent BTEC Common Skill Policy established in September 1991, which requires that a significant proportion of the student learning process takes place through some form of personal learning activity. Seminars and practical exercises at the end of each chapter have been specifically designed to meet those requirements, which could also be valuable to practising junior and middle managers as well. The main objectives of these exercises are to:

1. Encourage in students a critical analysis of facts and events.
2. Provide an opportunity for concrete experiential learning of international business within the classroom.
3. Develop the students' ability to update their normative knowledge and to adjust their practical skills towards rapid decision-making in a constantly changing economic, political, social, legal and technological environment.

Finally, no book embracing international business would be complete without looking at the speed of change within Europe. This book adds a new dimension to the specific study of European Business. The year 1992 has become the subject of a considerable increase in publications and academic research. The creation of a Single European Market has fuelled the publication of books prescribing various models and techniques for direct application in Europe, as well as guides for conducting business in Europe, or what has often been referred to as a 'European Management Cookbook'. It is not enough to teach students and European managers only what they need to know in order to handle various practical situations within the Single European Market. They also need to understand how the global political economy has developed in the way that it has, and what consequences and implications this might have for both the study and practice of business and management in contemporary Europe. A stark example of the need for this larger global approach to the nature of European business is clearly illustrated by the recent complex and fundamental changes occurring within Central and Eastern Europe. In this respect, this book should provide a vital background resource for introductory courses in European business, and for anyone interested or contemplating doing business in the European Community and in Central and Eastern Europe.

OVERALL STRUCTURE OF THE BOOK

The field of international business is very complex and broad. There are several possible ways of organizing the analysis of such an interdisciplinary subject. There is no unique starting point and no prominent linear sequence in which we can simply deal with one process at a time. Consequently, there is no given order in which the process should be examined.

The book starts by adopting a systemic analysis by dividing the study into separate units and explaining them in their relative simplicity. The analysis is then extended further to show how these units interact, not only in terms of action and reaction, but also how they determine each others functions and operations – that is to say, how these apparently separate units (state, firm, international organization for example) exist also in sets of complicated relationships. Figure P1.1 shows the interaction of individual sections, and the mutual relationship between individual chapters.

Overall, the textbook is organized into four main parts, subdivided into five chapters. Key concepts and substantive subject areas in the field are introduced in a way that makes them accessible, understandable and thought-provoking to students and managers who may be encountering this subject for the first time. Each chapter begins with a statement of the main learning objectives and concludes with practical advice to business managers on how to improve their international business skills, followed by a number of review questions and discussion topics and practical exercises. Each chapter also has a carefully selected up-to-date list of

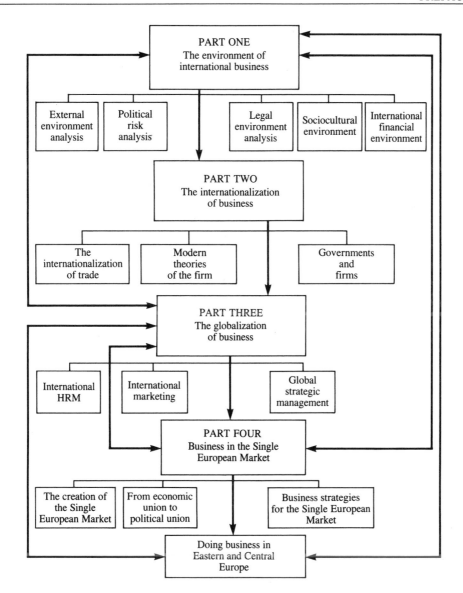

Figure P1.1   Overall structure of the book

recommended further reading to guide readers' next steps in international business should they wish to study further. Short case studies taken from existing multinational firms and global firms are also included to illustrate more concretely international business incidents.

Part One (The Environment of International Business) sets out the conceptual framework within which international business may be studied. Its main objective is to present a full understanding of the main features of the global political economy by establishing the relationships between the economic, political, legal, sociocultural and financial dimensions of international business. International business is seen here not as an external factor, but as part of the domestic environment in which it operates and simultaneously helps to constitute. The framework developed here is then applied in an interdisciplinary manner throughout the remaining sections of the book.

Part Two (The Internationalization of Business) attempts to trace and explain the historical context of the internationalization process of business within the global political economy. It covers the key concepts of traditional international trade theories, modern trade theories, theories of the firm, and the changing relationship between governments and firms, and outlines their practical relevance for the 1990s.

Part Three (The Globalization of Business) reviews each of the management functions and operations of international business, including international marketing, international business operations, international human resource management and global strategic management, and finally focuses particularly on the recent movement towards 'globalization' and 'global competition' showing clearly what distinguishes the 'internationalization' of business and 'globalization' of business.

Part Four (Business in the Single European Market) provides a detailed empirical study of European economic and political integration, and shows how the theoretical concepts and international business practices developed in Parts One, Two and Three may be applied within a specific, in this case European, context. Particular consideration is also given to contemporary issues related to the current changes in Central and Eastern Europe, and their implications for international business.

FURTHER READING

Bergsten, F. C., Keohane, R. O. and Nye, J. S., International economics and international politics: a framework of analysis, in *World Politics and International Economics* (eds. Bergsten, F. C. and Frause, C. G.), Brookings Institute, Washington, 1975, pp. 3–36.

Maclean, J., Interdependence. An ideological intervention in international relations, in *Interdependence on Trial* (eds Willets, P.), Frances Pinter, London, 1986.

Maclean, J., Marxism and international relations: a strange case of mutual neglect, *Millenium*, **17**(2), Summer 1988.

Rosecrance, C., *The Rise of the Trading State*, Basic Books, New York, 1986.

Spero, J. E., *The Politics of International Economic Relations*, 4th edn, Unwin Hyman, London, 1990, pp. 1–17.

Strange, S., Firms and world politics, *International Affairs*, **68**(1), January 1992, pp. 1–16.

Walter, R. and Blake, D., *The Politics of International Economic Relations*, 4th edn, Prentice-Hall, Englewood Cliffs NJ, 1991.

ACKNOWLEDGEMENTS

It is a real problem for any author to recognize specifically and acknowledge properly the significant contributions of all contemporary writers that go into the making of a textbook. A bibliography has been prepared at the end of the book to partially compensate for this shortcoming. This also contains a selective list of relatively recent texts, which I believe make a useful contribution to our understanding of international business.

I owe an immense debt to Dr David Morris, head of Coventry Business School, for giving me the opportunity to teach at Coventry University and for his encouragement and support with this project. I owe very special thanks to my dear friend and doctoral supervisor John Maclean of Sussex University for his thorough review of the manuscript. His insight and critical comments have been invaluable. It was he who made me believe I could write this book in the first place. I would also like to thank the internal reviewer at McGraw-Hill for useful comments and Brendan Lambon, Editor (Business and Economics) and Lavinia Porter, Production Editor, for their patience and tolerance – particularly when deadlines were getting tight. My thanks also go to Carol Humphreys at Coventry Support Services for her expert knowledge and assistance with the use of information technology.

Above all, I am grateful to my children Diala and Khaldoun. This book would have been difficult to complete without their understanding, patience and forbearance – they gave up many outings and holidays without complaint.

THE ENVIRONMENT OF INTERNATIONAL BUSINESS

The secret to success in all industries today is to be extremely sensitive to the international events and forces reshaping the business environment. (Davidson, 1991, p. 5)

A business firm's decision to internationalize its operations does not simply mean expanding into new geographical areas. It involves moving into and operating in different economic, political, legal, sociocultural and financial environments. The ability of the firm to identify these environmental differences, understand their implications for its business and adapt its operations and products accordingly, will be important in determining the success or failure of its international expansion (Weekly and Aggarwal, 1987, p. 19).

Chapter One introduces the environment of international business and provides guidance on how to conduct a business environment analysis. Chapter Two focuses on the political risk involved in conducting international business. Chapter Three examines the legal environment of international business. Chapter Four analyses the overall sociocultural environment of business. Chapter Five introduces the international financial system and aims to provide useful guidance to business managers on how to understand and deal with foreign exchange risks, how to evaluate international money markets and how to benefit from them.

ANALYSING THE ENVIRONMENT OF INTERNATIONAL BUSINESS

Business firms do not operate in a vacuum. They are neither self-sufficient nor self-contained. They cannot be isolated from the external environment within which they operate. No matter how efficiently managed internally their survival, success or ultimate failure is largely dependent upon their relations with their external environment. External environmental factors can lead either to positive opportunities or to negative constraints. It is therefore important for a business manager to recognize all the relevant factors in the international business environment, understand their influence on the firm's operations and assess their weaknesses and strengths.

The contrasting experiences of General Motors (GM), Ford and Chrysler during the 1973 oil embargo illustrate the difference between companies that fail to monitor their environments and those that do and plan accordingly.

In 1972, General Motors executives began discussing the potential economic effects of an oil shortage on the price and supply of gasoline in redesigning its products. As a consequence, GM was able to respond quickly when the embargo began. Ford and Chrysler had failed to perceive the potential implications of such an event and their reaction was characterized by confusion and internal turmoil. By responding promptly, GM gained two years on Ford and Chrysler in redesigning its products. This edge enabled it to withstand the 1979–1982 economic slump in much better financial shape than either Chrysler or Ford (Zammuto, 1982, pp. 126–42).

The external environment of business consists of direct and indirect action elements (Stoner and Freeman, 1989, p. 70). Direct action elements are those elements that directly influence the firm's activities either in its attempts to attract or acquire needed resources or to market profitably its products and services. Direct action elements together constitute what is also called the 'task environment'. The elements of the task environment include customers, suppliers, resources, competitors, market conditions, creditors and labour markets (Asheghian and Ebrahimi, 1990, p. 203). Indirect action elements of the external environment are those elements that affect the climate in which a firm's activities take place, but that do not necessarily influence the firm directly (Stoner and Freeman, 1989, p. 70). Indirect action elements are known as the 'remote environment' and consist of economics, political, legal, sociocultural, technological, physical, geographical and natural factors (Asheghian and Ebrahimi, 1990, p. 203) (these are discussed in Chapters Two, Three and Four).

It is often assumed that the firm has little or no reciprocal influence on the remote environment. Demographic changes, cultural norms and political movements are, for example, seen as the results of profound changes in society over which the firm has no control. Business firms, however, can (and many have been able to) manipulate some of those external factors to suit their private purposes by influencing government policies, or by determining the rate of technological change, or by imposing their own international culture (Part Three deals with these issues in detail).

LEARNING OBJECTIVES

- Introduce the concept of the environment of international business
- Understand the relationship between the environment and business operations
- Learn how to conduct a global environment scan

ELEMENTS OF THE ENVIRONMENT OF INTERNATIONAL BUSINESS

The environment of international business is composed of three major elements:

1. The domestic environment, which includes all the elements of the remote and task environment of the firm's home country.
2. The foreign environment, which includes all the elements of the remote and task environment that are encountered in the domestic environment of the host country.
3. The international environment, which refers to the interaction between the domestic and foreign environments and includes international economic and political forces, international relations, international organizations such as the United Nations (UN) and its agencies, the International Monetary Fund (IMF) and the World Bank (WB), international trade agreements such as the General Agreement on Tariffs and Trade (GATT), the Organization for Economic Cooperation and Development (OECD), and other multinational firms.

Figure 1.1 shows the relationship between these environmental factors in abstract and diagrammatic terms. The central question here is, given the complexity of the modern international environment, how much should a manager know about the international environment of business, how can a manager analyse it, and what constitutes an appropriate starting point?

GLOBAL ENVIRONMENTAL ANALYSIS

There is no single or universal formula for analysing the international business environment. Economic situations vary widely, political conditions can and do change dramatically, and technology is constantly and rapidly developing. In addition, people in different cultures hold different values, beliefs and attitudes, which need to be understood and brought into planning.

Global environmental analysis is the systematic identification and analysis of the domestic, foreign and international environments that may face a business firm in its international activities. It involves the collection of information about the international business environment and an assessment of its impact on the present international operations of the firm and its future global planning.

There are many ways of conducting a global environmental analysis. The simplest, easiest and quickest way is to watch where the firm's competitors are going and follow them, on the assumption that they know what they are doing and that by following them abroad you will receive the same benefits they might get by locating abroad (Garland *et al.*, 1991, p. 41).

International firms, since the mid-1980s, have become much more sophisticated in their global environmental analysis. A majority of them now employ more than one permanent

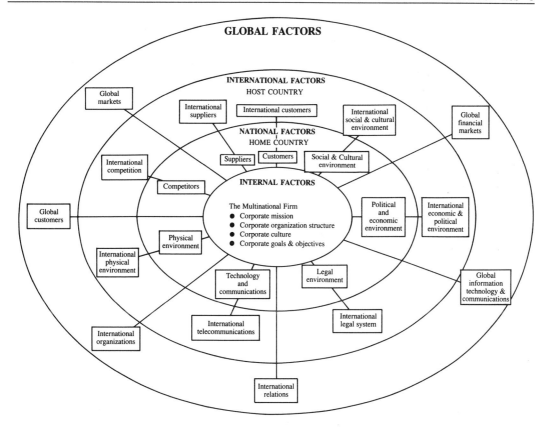

Figure 1.1   The environment of international business

executive to monitor the international business environment. Sears, for example has a Corporate Monitoring Unit that continuously tracks some 100 publications and research reports to identify potential environmental changes (Bedelian, 1989). Japan's Mitsubishi has several hundred employees in New York whose task is to gather information about American rivals. Mitsubishi Trading Company employs over 60 000 market analysts around the world whose principal job is to conduct environmental analyses and feed the information back to the parent company. Environmental analysis, also commonly referred to as 'country analysis' varies from informal information gathering to much more elaborate mechanized programmes, depending on the purpose of the analysis, the type of information needed, the depth and details of the analysis required, the firm's objectives and position and the time frame being considered.

Various methods of environmental analysis are used by international firms. If the firm has a local subsidiary in the foreign country under consideration, and if the purpose of the analysis is to assist in the planning for further expansion or diversification into new industries, a two-tier analysis is usually carried out (Khambata and Ajami, 1992, pp. 187–8). At the first tier the local subsidiary collects all the relevant local data and passes them, along with its own assessment of the situation and future prospects, to the home office headquarters. The home headquarters office will then examine the information received and the recommendations of the subsidiary, and makes its own assessment.

If the international firm has no subsidiary already established and the country considered is totally unknown the firm has three alternatives.

1. It might consider hiring consultants who are experts in that particular field and ask them to conduct a comprehensive country analysis. It is often better to use local consultants in such cases because of their deeper understanding of the local environment and better access to relevant local data.
2. It might purchase reports already prepared by commercial firms such as Ernst & Ernst: *International Business Services*; Barclays Bank: *Country Profiles*; Price Waterhouse: *Information Guide*.
3. It might subscribe to newspaper clipping services such as the International Clipping Bureau. Many companies have recently linked their computers to a number of on-line services and global database files which offer information on economics, business and political conditions as well as important factors on health risks, transportation and so on. Reuter *Country Reports*, for example, collect data for 190 countries and territories and offer an in-depth information on political, economic and social/cultural factors. The Official Airline Guide (OAG) *Electronic Edition Travel Service* covers customs, business, social conventions and social customs. *Kaleidoscope: Current World Data* from Nexis provides information on 185 countries and major international organizations. Other databases offering global information, include Predicasts, ABI/Inform, Political Risk Services and Dow Jones International News (Noreen, 1991, pp. 40–7).

Information collected in this way may be exhaustive, complex and too general. Business executives thus need to identify the relevant data, classify them and construct a concise country profile specifically related to the firm's objectives and particular needs. Different approaches and methodologies have been developed for this purpose. Various approaches have so far been adopted by many scholars in analysing the environment of international business in relation to Country Profiles (Viza Yakumar *et al.*, 1991, pp. 102–6). In this chapter we will focus only on three major approaches: the analytical approach, the systems approach and the holistic approach.

The analytical approach

According to this method a complex whole is better understood by studying its elements in their relative simplicity and by observing the relationships between them. The external elements of the environment of international business are disaggregated and classified into the remote environment, the task environment and the international environment. These elements are then re-combined or aggregated to re-make the whole of the country profile. Such an approach is purely descriptive and is limited to the analysis of observable elements of the environment of business.

The systems approach

Like the analytical method, the systems approach starts by identifying the various elements of the environment of international business, classifies them into separate structures and studies each element in detail within its own structure. The aim of systems analysis is to show how the different levels or structures operate and interact (Waltz, 1979, Ch. 3). In addition to the description of the various elements of the task, remote and international environments provided by the analytical method, a systems approach would include a closer examination of the firm's interaction with those elements within each structure. However, such a system of positing levels, although capable of identifying the natural properties and the observable effects of interacting agents, fails to explain the causal status of the structure itself (Maclean, 1988).

The holistic approach

In a holistic approach, the analyst seeks to understand the total system as a whole by dividing it into its elements to make a detailed study of these elements, but where the relationships among those elements are the focus of analysis. Their interactions can then be analysed in relation to the structure of the environment of international business, and their combined effects understood as a whole. A country profile adopting such a method of analysis would not only provide a detailed description of the various elements of the international environment of international business and their interactions with the firm in its international operations, but would also assess the combined impact of those elements on the overall international business operations of the firm, particularly its global strategic planning and global expansion.

BASIC STEPS IN CONDUCTING A GLOBAL ENVIRONMENTAL ANALYSIS

Figure 1.2 traces all the steps necessary to conduct a global environment analysis and to construct a country profile.

REVIEW QUESTIONS

1. Identify six elements of the environment of international business and try to think how each might affect a business firm known to you.
2. What aspects of the environment of international business have to be taken into account by business managers, and what can safely be ignored?
3. How can a firm minimize the threats from the environment of international business and take advantage of the opportunities that may exist?

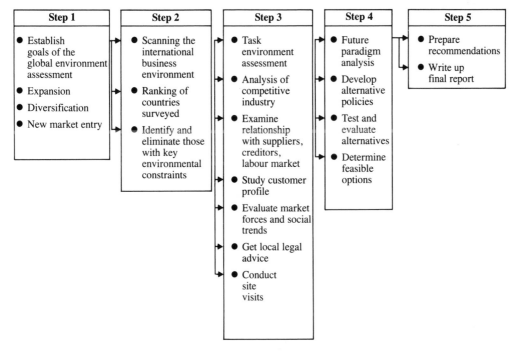

Figure 1.2 Steps in global environmental assessment

4. What is meant by 'global environment assessment'? What are the various approaches adopted in conducting an environmental scan? Discuss the advantages and disadvantages of each method.

EXERCISE 1.1: International business environmental analysis

Aim   This exercise intends to develop students' analytical approach in assessing global environments and global markets.

Assignment   Students are asked to put themselves in the role of a manager of a multinational firm that is planning to expand its operations overseas, conduct a global environmental analysis for the company and present their findings and recommendations to the class.

Skills   This exercise will not only develop students' analytical skills and methodology in assessing global markets and environments, but it will also develop their skills in analysing information gathered and putting this in the relevant format. This exercise therefore should be accompanied and supported by a written report highlighting all the data collected in the analysis.

Sources of information

Effective global environmental assessment requires extensive research, data collection and up-to-date information. Here is a list of the main sources of information that may be useful.

1. *International organizations*
    (i) United Nations
        — UN Economic Surveys
        — UN Yearbook of International Statistics
        — UN Survey of Research on Transnational Corporations
        — UN Center on Transnational Corporations
        — UNESCO Statistical Yearbook
    (ii) OECD
        — Statistics of Foreign Trade
        — Country Profiles
        — Economic Surveys
        — Financial Statistics
        — Eurostat
    (iii) IMF
        — International Financial Statistics
        — Balance of Payment Yearbook
        — Directory of Trade
        — International Trade Statistics
    (iv) World Bank
        — World Bank Encyclopedia
        — World Tables
        — World Bank Annual Report
    (v) Pan Arab Research Center
2. *Foreign governments*
    — Government Census, Statistical Services
    — Chamber of Commerce

    — International Trade Association
    — Consulates
    — Research Centres
    — Japanese External Trade Organizations

3. *Private agencies*
    — Business International Corporation NY
    — Master Key Index
    — Business Europe
    — Business Asia, Hong Kong/Asia/Pacific
    — Business Latin America
    — Business International Money Reports
    — Eastern Europe Report
    — Research Reports: periodic country and functional studies
    — Ernst and Ernst: International Business Services
    — Barclays Bank: Country Profiles
    — Price Waterhouse: Information Guide

4. *Companies*
    — Competitors:
        (i)   Company annual reports
        (ii) Speeches and public announcements of competitors' officers
    — Products
        (i)   Forecasts of competitors' sales
        (ii) Employment advertisements
    — Suppliers
        (i)   Firms catalogues
    — Professional associations and meetings
        (i)   Company displays
        (ii) Company brochures
        (iii) Scientific papers and speeches
    — Consultants management services and media
        (i)   Special-purpose reports

5. *Current periodicals and journals*
    — *International/European Marketing Data*
    — *Euro Monitor*
    — *Economist Intelligence Unit*
    — *Export Today*
    — *Euromoney*
    — *Middle East Economic Digest*
    — *Financial Times*
    — *Japan Economic Journal*
    — *Far Eastern Economic Review*

6. *Publications*
    — *Encyclopaedia of the Third World: Facts on File*
    — *The New Encyclopaedia Britannica*

7. *On-line databases*
    — Reuters: *Country Reports*
    — *The Official Airline Guide* (OAG)
    — *Electronic Edition Travel Service*

  — *Kaleidoscope: Current World Data*
  — *Nexis*
  — *Predicasts*
  — *ABI/INFORM*
  — *Political Risk Services*
  — *Dow Jones International News*

Sources

Montgomery, D. B and Weinberg, C. B., Towards strategic intelligence systems, *J. Marketing*, Issue 43, 1979, p. 46.

Asheghian, P., *International Business*, Selected Sources of International Business Data, pp. 223–224.

Noreen, K. Searching the online globe: best files for country profiles, *Database*, **14**(3), June 1991, pp. 40–7.

EXERCISE 1.2: Country profile

Aim   This exercise aims at improving students' awareness and knowledge of world geography, economics, politics and culture of different countries in the world, which is often very limited.

Assignment   A country profile assignment is useful to involve students in an active exercise where they are asked to choose a particular country of interest to them, investigate the various environmental factors that are crucial to the conduct of business in that country, and present their findings to the class.

Skills   This exercise will familiarize students with sources of country information and serves to ensure that they are able to locate current information from periodicals, journals and on-line databases. It will also help them to identify criteria for establishing what data is relevant for the purpose of their project.

Format   This should be used only as a guide to follow in writing-up the country profile, and students should not feel constrained by it. They may include any additional information they feel relevant; for example, any dramatic recent changes should be highlighted and explained.

Country profile format

1. *Geography*
   — Location
   — Area
   — Climate
   — Terrain
2. *Demography*
   — Population dispersion, density
   — Growth rate, death rate
   — Ethnic group minority
   — Education
   — Health
3. *Economic data*
   — Natural resources
   — Agriculture
   — Industry
   — Services
   — Economic and fiscal policies
   — Annual GNP

　　　— Per capita income
　　　— Currency and exchange rates
4. *Trading Data*
　　　— Trade policies
　　　— Trade statistics
　　　— Exports, imports
　　　— Major suppliers
　　　— International trade relations
5. *Government data*
　　　— Type of government
　　　— Political parties
　　　— National constitution
　　　— The legal system
　　　— The national flag
　　　— Membership of international organizations
　　　— International relations
6. *Infrastructure*
　　　— Banks
　　　— Insurance
　　　— Medical facilities
　　　— Communications media: telecommunication, telephones, satellites
　　　— Roads and transport
7. *Social/cultural data*
　　　— Social structures
　　　— Religion
　　　— Language
　　　— Lifestyle
　　　— Social norms and customs

Source
Punnet, B. J., *Experiencing International Management*, PWS Kent, Boston, 1989, pp. 121–290.

FURTHER READING

Davidson, W. H., The role of global scanning in business planning, *Organization Dynamics*, Winter 1991.

Stoner, J. A. F. and Freeman, R. E., *Management*, 4th edn, Prentice-Hall, Englewood Cliffs NJ, 1989.

Viza Yakumar, K., Pratap, K. J. Mohapatra, Environmental impact analysis: A synthetic approach, *Long Range Planning*, **24**(6), 1991, pp. 102–106.

Sumantra, G., *Environmental Scanning*, Doctoral Dissertation, MIT Sloan School of Management, 1985.

TWO

POLITICAL RISK ANALYSIS

Political risk forecasters are doomed to failure as crystal ball analysts.

(Grosse and Kujawa, 1992, p. 443)

In September 1989, *Euromoney* classified the USSR as the 23rd most stable country in the world out of a survey of 133 countries. Although Iraq was considered very unstable with a ranking of 101, Kuwait, on the other hand, was considered relatively stable, ranking 44th, and Saudi Arabia was ranked 37th in the world (*Euromoney*, 1989). Kuwait was even classified as the second safest country in which to invest out of a survey of 100 countries conducted by the Bank of America (Bank of America Information Service, 1986). This situation changed dramatically with Iraq's invasion of Kuwait in August 1990. The subsequent Iraqi attacks directed at company facilities, the detention of foreign citizens and executive kidnapping (Otis, 1990, pp. 33–45) are acute examples of what international business firms could face when operating in foreign countries, no matter how apparently stable and free from political risk these countries seem to be.

Although it is claimed that terrorism is becoming a significant factor in the life of multi-national firms (Maddox, 1990, pp. 48–51), it is, however, interesting to note that regardless of the political instability of the region, soon after the end of the Gulf War, a surge of business activity began in Kuwait (Cerami, 1991, pp. 11–15). A frenzy of business activity has also been taking place in Eastern and Central Europe since the opening up of the Soviet bloc countries in 1989, with many multinational firms tapping the vast new potential market of over 393 million consumers. (This is discussed in detail in Chapter Fifteen.)

In Hong Kong, the signing of the Sino–British Joint Declaration on the future of Hong Kong after 1 July 1997 has even triggered significant business investments by foreigners, led by the Japanese, despite the political and economic uncertainties of the local Hong Kong residents (Daniels and Radebaugh, 1992, p. 42; Sanger, 1990, p. A1). The full scope of issues involved in political risk analysis is so broad that it cannot be presented in detail here. The purpose of this chapter is to explain the importance of the concept of political risk, and its evolution in the 1990s, and to provide managers with strategies for dealing with it.

LEARNING OBJECTIVES

- To introduce the concept of 'political risk' and to describe the various causes of political risk
- To review and evaluate the existing methods used in political risk analysis
- To discuss the recent shift in political risk analysis and what business managers can accomplish in this area

POLITICAL RISK: EARLY CONCEPTS AND RECENT DEVELOPMENTS

Traditionally, the concept of political risk focused mainly on government interference with private investments. Political risk has been defined most commonly as 'the risk of loss of assets, earning power and managerial control due to events or actions that are politically biased or politically motivated' (Weekly and Aggarwal, 1987, p. 31). An example of this is the much publicized losses associated with the major confiscations of foreign assets which followed the Iranian Revolution in 1979 (Bassivy and Hrair Dekmejian, 1985, pp. 67–75).

Political risk has also often been referred to in terms of events in the political and economic environment of international business. Political risk accordingly is seen as a sudden or gradual change in the local political environment that is disadvantageous or counter-productive to the interests of foreign firms (Matsuura, 1991, p. 128).

According to Root (1972, p. 355), political risk is

> ... a possible occurrence of a political event of any kind (such as war, revolution, coup d'état, expropriation, taxation, devaluation, exchange controls and import restrictions) at home and abroad that can cause a loss of profit potential and/or assets in an international business operation.

These events it is stressed, however upsetting, are not political risks for a firm unless they can or do affect its operations. What we should be more concerned with is the impact of events which are political in the sense that they arise from power or authority relationships and which affect (or have the potential to affect) the firm's operations (Kobrin, 1979, pp. 67–80). Bata Ltd, the world's largest manufacturer of footwear, had some fascinating experiences in Uganda, for example when its local operations were nationalized by Milton Obote, denationalized by Idi Amin, renationalized by Amin and finally denationalized by Amin for a second time (Daniels and Radebaugh, 1992, p. 78). (A more detailed discussion of this case is provided in the illustrative case later on in this chapter.)

Others simply refer to political risk in their analysis as a source of risk for the firm (Dymsza, 1972; Brooke and Remners, 1970).

In the face of recent upheavals in the international political economy, multinationals have become more actively involved in political risk conditions, for example in dealing with inter-governmental negotiations over business executive arrests, kidnapping, assassination and terrorism. The case of Reebok and its influence on the Chinese government to free 211 prisoners in 1990, one year after the Tiananmen Square suppression, in return for negotiations with the US Government in an effort to prevent US actions and withdrawal of most-favored nation (MFN) status from China is quite illustrative of this development (Daniels and Radebaugh, 1992, p. 369; Ignatius, 1990, p. A8; Nathan and Wells, 1982, pp. 9–23).

FACTORS CAUSING POLITICAL RISK

There are three major sources of political risk that face the firm. These are: government actions within the domestic political economy, inter-governmental relations and external environmental factors. Each of these will be dealt with in turn separately. The categorization is analytical only – in practice, political risk may, and usually will, arise from overlapping combinations of each of these major sources. Figure 2.1 lists some of the conditions leading to political risk within each category.

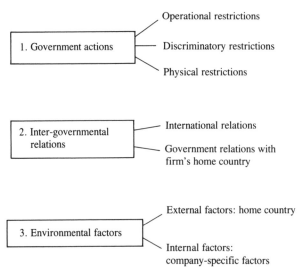

Figure 2.1 Steps in conducting political risk analysis

Government actions

Government actions leading to political risk can be grouped into three major categories: operations restrictions, discriminatory restrictions and physical actions (Matsuura, 1991, p. 138).

Operational restrictions are imposed both on domestic and foreign firms. These may include restrictions with respect to movement of employees across national borders. Passports and visas are common requirements, but some governments place rigid restrictions or prohibitions on persons entering or leaving the country. For example, expatriates working in Saudi Arabia are required by law to hand in their passports to their employer or sponsor upon entering the country, and are not allowed to leave Saudi Arabia without obtaining an exit visa, which is issued only upon the employer's request or with the employer's consent. Internally, the Saudi Government controls the movement of foreign workers by providing them with an identity card, which must be carried at all times.

Restrictions can also be imposed on the circulation of certain goods. The importation of certain products may be subject to heavy taxation or restriction. Economic sanctions, boycotts and embargoes might prohibit importation all together. The Arab Boycott established in 1948, when Israel was established, prohibits all Arab countries in the Middle East from trade with any foreign company that sells strategic tools or resources to Israel, or that has long-term agreements such as licensing arrangements or technical assistance with Israel. Marks & Spencer products and Revlon Cosmetics for example are blacklisted and banned from the Arab market and will be confiscated at the airport by Customs, even if they were bought for personal use.

Some countries often place restrictions on the amount of currency that a person, whether national or foreign, can carry when crossing its international borders, such as in Syria and Iraq. Countries with severe foreign exchange shortages might impose a blockage of funds by currency inconvertibility and exchange controls, as was the case in the Soviet Union prior to 1989. Countries like Brazil even put a ceiling on the amount of dividends that can be repatriated, whether domestic or foreign (Khambata and Ajami, 1992, pp. 290–1).

Discriminatory restrictions are imposed by governments on foreign firms and their subsidiaries. Some of these restrictions include taxation, tariffs and quotas and bring control on the prices that foreign firms can charge. Foreign firms may also face mandatory local subcontracting or minority ownership, so that local investors can gain a majority position. Such was the case during the 'Saudization' of Citibank in Saudi Arabia in the late 1970s, when Citibank had to sell 60 per cent of its share ownership to local Saudi investors to form the new Saudi American Bank (SAMBA).

Physical actions refer to direct seizure by governments of foreign assets and foreign operations through expropriation, confiscation or nationalization. Expropriation is the physical take-over and control of foreign assets by the host government, usually accompanied by some kind of compensation or reimbursement to the firm, the value of which is decided by the host government (Kobrin, 1984, pp. 329–48; Burton and Hisashi, 1984, pp. 396–414; Twitt, 1969, pp. 21–34).

Confiscation is similar to expropriation, but without compensation payments. Nationalization is the transfer of the whole industry from the private sector to the public sector. An example here is Iran's nationalization of Exxon and Mobil holdings after the expulsion of the Shah in 1979–1980.

Finally, 'creeping expropriation' (Weekly and Aggarwal, 1987, p. 32; Kobrin, 1980, pp. 65–88) is when foreign firms are subjected to demands to relinquish a large amount of ownership and management control of the business to the government and nationals of the country in which these businesses are located. Such was the case with the 'Saudization' of Aramco in Dhahran, Saudi Arabia, in the 1970s.

Inter-governmental relations

Deteriorating political relations between the host and home country governments could lead to political risk for a multinational firm operating in the host country. There are many historical examples of the risks faced by multinational firms arising out of inter-governmental conflicts, such as border warfare and geographical tension (Iran/Iraq, Arab/Israeli); economic warfare (economic sanctions on South Africa); trade warfare (USA, GATT and the EC); and civil war (Lebanon). More recently, the Gulf War illustrated vividly the case of multinational firms being caught between two governments' conflicting policies: Iraq's view of the oil production policies of the Kuwait Government and Kuwait's refusal to go along with OPEC production quotas.

CASE STUDY 2.1: Caught between government fire

Some years ago, Britain reduced its import quota for T-shirts as part of renegotiating the Multi-Fibre Arrangement. The Indonesian Government retaliated by putting an embargo on Davy International, a British firm whose contract was worth many times the value of the trade in T-shirts and who was at the time constructing a large chemical plant in Indonesia.

Another example is when Britain decided to raise the fees for foreign students in Britain, Dr Mahatir of Malaysia retaliated by issuing a 'buy British – last policy'. British exporters suffered a great deal as a result of this inter-government dispute, which originally had nothing to do with economics and trade

Source:
(Stopford *et al.*, 1991, p. 23).

External environmental factors

Individual government actions and inter-governmental relations are not the only sources of political risk. Several factors in the external environment of international business can lead to political risk, for example religious conflicts, social unrest, demonstrations and terrorism.

Other factors of political risk are company-specific and relate directly to the internal environment of the firm. Some of these factors which could be a source of political risk to the overall operation of the multinational firm include corporate culture and management philosophies conflicting with local cultures, beliefs and attitudes, corporate image and public relations. A good example here is the famous Nestlé case in 1974, where the company was subjected to serious allegations and criticisms both from activists in foreign countries where the company operated and activists in the home country against its synthetic infant formula feed. Critics argued that infant mortality increased in poor countries because mothers in Third World countries frequently over-diluted the formula, which caused an increase in infant mortality. Nestlé's image was associated with 'The Baby Killer' for a long time, even after a court case in June 1976 ruled that the cause of death was not Nestlé's product *per se*, but the unhygenic way it was prepared (*Wall Street Journal*, 1984; Freedman, 1989, p. B6; Terpestra and Sarathy, 1991, pp. 488–92).[1]

In the face of the extensive dangers and potential losses connected with political risk the question arises as to what strategies multinational firms can develop in order to reduce, manage or avoid such risks.

POLITICAL RISK STRATEGIC MANAGEMENT

Trade and investment have been exposed to expropriation, nationalization, war, terrorism and discriminatory government intervention since 'the first caravans ventured across the Middle East several millenia ago' (de la Torre and Neckar, 1988). Various approaches and strategies have been developed since then to assist multinationals in reducing or counteracting the detrimental effects of political risk upon their business. It is not possible to cover all the strategies developed. Selected strategies discussed in this chapter apply to a wide selection of countries in the industrialized and also less developed countries.

Political risk analysis

Large multinationals and banks have often employed a number of staff or ex-service officers and academic political scientists to analyse, assess and forecast political risk for their business. Texaco and Royal Dutch Shell, for example, maintain permanent corporate staff groups and political risk analysts whose assignment is to keep up with the political conditions in countries where the firm does business, and to try to anticipate important changes in those countries (Grosse and Kujawa, 1992, p. 343). Bankers Trust Corporation also employs 'Country Risk' staff that continuously track political and economic conditions abroad. Some multinationals rely on reports prepared by their own top executives following their visits or 'Grand Tours' to the host country and meetings with local business people and government officials. Other use profitability analysis, where the probability of various events occurring is estimated using a decision tree (Matusura, 1991, p. 143).

---

[1] Despite this ruling, Nestlé agreed in 1984 to cease advertising that would discourage breast feeding, to limit free formula supplies to hospitals, and to ban personal gifts to health officials.

Recent dramatic political and economic changes in most parts of the world together with new developments in information technology and international communications have recently contributed to a growing interest in and need for the use of more advanced statistical and computer modelling techniques in political risk forecasting.

In the political system stability index approach, for example, elements of the political system stability are grouped into three major categories: socio-economic characteristics index, social conflict index and government process index. Each element is then measured on a quantitative basis (Haendel *et al.*, 1974). Various computer models forecasting political risk have also been developed where responses are collected from overseas business executives and US Government officials to determine indices of economic and political stability, such as the Primary Risk Investment Screening Matrix (PRISM) (Simon, 1982, pp. 62–9).

A number of organizations are also now specializing in preparing political risk reports and forecasts that are made available to companies through a subscription arrangement. These reports rate the various countries of the world on the basis of some quantitative indicator of political risk. The ratings are developed by assigning weights to different political, economic and social factors that could lead to potential political risk. These weights are then added and averaged according to a particular formula to arrive at a final rating of the level of risk for a country (Khambata and Ajami, 1992, p. 213). These forecasts are called Business Environment Risk Information (BERI) reports and are prepared by companies such as Frost and Sullivan's Political Risk Services, Price Waterhouse, and Global Risk Assessments (Asheghian and Ebrahimi, 1990, p. 248). A Country Risk Assessment Service is offered by Business International while Comparative Surveys are conducted by the Bank of America. *Euromoney* publishes an annual list of countries ranked according to political risk based on bond assessment, in which political risk is based on comparative performance of the bond and money markets of the countries studied (for details, see *Euromoney*, October 1987). Multinational trading firms and security firms, such as Mitsubishi, Merril Lynch and Nomura Security Co., are also now offering professional assistance in political risk analysis and data gathering services on many foreign countries (Matsuura, 1991, p. 142).

All these methods, although useful and thorough in identifying various sources of political risk, have their shortcomings and limitations. First, the result of the analysis is often highly subjective and biased. Most of the weighting used is based on the arbitrary judgement of those experts who prepare the assessments and therefore may represent their own valuation and interpretation rather than representing an accurate analysis of reality. Second, it is very difficult to assess accurately sociocultural factors in quantitative terms. Third, all these methods of estimating environmental risk are 'macro-risk' orientated, and largely ignore the need of the individual firm (de la Torre and Neckar, 1988, p. 228). Fourth, most of these models are based on historical data that may be irrelevant for future conditions (de La Torre and Neckar, 1988, p. 228). Finally, all these approaches are limited in their analysis to the description of facts and events which are directly observable, without necessarily providing a causal explanation of the relationships between various factors.

Joint ventures and licensing

Establishing joint partnerships with local national firms and/or governments, or long-term contracts through licensing have been adopted by many multinationals as a way to reduce the political risk of their investment in foreign markets. The general assumption here is that once a local company is partnered, any adverse act against it will also affect the local partner. The decision to establish a joint venture with a local partner, it is believed, may free the subsidiary of various discriminatory restrictions (Vernon, 1990, p. 170), increase its bargaining position in relation to host governments (Stopford and Wells, 1972, p. 120) and can minimize the exploitative image of the multinational firm by sharing its profits and technical know-how with a local company (Khambata and Ajami, 1992, p. 295).

Localization and domestication

Localization involves placing local national managers in all key managerial positions and has been suggested as a means of altering the attractiveness of the multinational targets to terrorists with the underlying assumption that local firms are less attractive targets (Maddox, 1990, p. 35). This provides the multinational firm with relative security for its investment for that period of time.

Linkages

Developing strong linkages with local suppliers can minimize political risk by giving host country nationals a vested interest in the continuation of the international firm's activities (Weekly and Aggarwal, 1987, p. 35).

Integration with the host government

The company may develop positive local attitudes and support for their operations by integrating with the host government in promoting host country objectives, supporting social and charitable activities in the host country and also by explaining that they will be contributing to the country's economy as well as providing employment and job training (Souter, 1992, pp. 56–7).

Diversification

Another useful method for dealing with political risk is to diversify or spread the risk across national borders, so that problems in one country do not adversely affect the overall performance of the firm. Multinationals should not have all of their subsidiaries in one country. If operations in one country cease due to war, for example, facilities in another country will still allow the company to remain in business. Diversification therefore does not eliminate political risk but allows the firm to survive politically risky events (Grosse and Kujawa, 1992, p. 440). Multiple resourcing of the same components or products within the multinational system has been adopted by most Japanese multinational firms using world-scale plants and trading houses, thus avoiding the risk of having one of their subsidiaries held by a government and preventing them from taking advantage of its role as a sole supplier.

Political risk insurance

Terrorist acts during the Gulf War and the recent trends towards privatization of government-owned industries, especially in Latin America and in Eastern Europe, have considerably increased the demand for political risk insurance (Friedman, 1991, pp. 9–11). Political risk insurance addresses losses that occur because of politically caused crises. The loss of future earnings can now be covered by international profits insurance. The most important feature of such insurance is the possibility of covering against the risk of loss of profits due to a general political and economic deterioration with a foreign country. Under such a policy, the exporter or business operating in the foreign country does not have to wait for a political event to happen (Tavares, 1991, pp. 8–41). Many multinationals are now using kidnapping insurance, and consultants to negotiate ransoms, in order to minimize loss from kidnapping (Maddox, 1990, pp. 48–51). For example, claims submitted during the Gulf War to Chubb involved losses relating to increased consulting fees and employee salaries resulting from the detention of employees by the Iraqi government (Otis, 1990, pp. 3–34). The total premium volume worldwide of extortion coverage and kidnap/ransom bought recently by the vast majority of *Fortune* 1000 companies has been estimated at $60 million to $70 million (Otis, 1990, pp. 3–34). Agencies providing such insurance in the USA are the Overseas Private Investment Corporation (OPIC), Multilateral Investment Guarantee Agency (MIGA) (recently established by the World Bank), EXIM Bank, Chubb, America International Group and Professional Law Indemnity Agency (Poynter, 1991, p. 119). In the UK, similar policies are offered by the Export Credit Guarantee Department (ECGD) (Poynter, 1991, p. 132). This represents an interesting contemporary development in respect of the relationship between the public and private sector aspects of international business which will be discussed in further detail in Part Two.

RECENT DEVELOPMENTS IN POLITICAL RISK ANALYSIS

The rapid and often dramatic changes in the international political economy during the last decade have considerably altered the relationship between governments and multinationals (Stopford *et al.*, 1991, p. 1). Firms have become more involved with governments and governments have realized their dependence on multinational firms (Stopford *et al.*, 1991, p. 1). This 'mutual interdependence of states and firms' has also prompted a shift in political risk analysis. The traditional approach of assessing political instability no longer meets the needs of multinational firms (Poynter, 1991, p. 119). Political instability does not always lead to political risk. Even when civil riots, revolutions, war and similar shocks occur they do not necessarily affect all firms in the same way. Bata Ltd, the international footwear producer, is a classic example.

CASE STUDY 2.2: Shoes, not politics

Bata Ltd is a family owned business. It is the world's largest manufacturer and marketer of footwear and has factories in more than 90 countries. It employs over 85 000 employees worldwide, sells more than 30 million pairs of shoes annually and generates more than $3 billion in revenue from sales. This success is, however, not due to Bata's having investments only in politically stable and economically advanced foreign countries.

The company was originally established by Thomas Bata in Zlim, Czechoslovakia, in 1884. Its operations had spread into 28 countries by 1920. In 1945, the newly established Communist government took over Bata's operations, while elsewhere the Second World War had destroyed most of its factories and installations in Europe. Bata's operations in Uganda were nationalized by Milton Obote, later denationalized by Idi Amin, renationalized by Idi Amin and finally denationalized by Idi Amin. In Indonesia, Bata was nationalized in the early 1960s by the nationalist socialist government of President Subarto, and denationalized in the mid 1960s by President Subarto. Bata was also subjected to expropriation in Egypt in 1962, and in Iraq in 1964. The Lebanese war in the 1970s destroyed all its operations in Lebanon. In 1986, Bata Ltd had to leave its operations in South Africa, upon the Canadian government's general advice. Bata has not only operated in politically unstable environments; it also has production facilities in many different types of economies, from democratic regimes, such as in Europe and Canada and totalitarian regimes, such as in Chile, and many poor African nations. The secret of its success lies within its strategy for servicing a world market, regardless of the political and economic conditions of the countries where it operates. 'Shoes, not politics' are Bata's business. Bata's major concern, in all its foreign operations, is to contribute to the local economic development. All of its companies and employees are required to participate fully in local community affairs. Its basic strategy is to provide footwear at the most affordable prices, and its product is a necessity, not a luxury. The company tries to get most of its supplies locally and uses the maximum amount of domestically produced raw material inputs. Local supplies are therefore developed. The factories are labour-intensive, so many jobs are created, which increase consumers' purchasing power.

Bata Ltd transfers its technology, marketing and management skills to all its units in the world. Local management is trained to assume responsibility as quickly as possible so that each unit in each country becomes self-sufficient in production. Also, each unit only supplies the market in the country in which it is located. Bata's strategy is to service different national markets by producing in a given market nearly everything it sells in that market. Such a policy therefore protects the company's overall global operation against political risk in particular countries. Instead of relying on one main production plant and aiming to achieve economies of scale in production by producing as much as possible in the cheapest location and then servicing market worldwide from that single production facility, Bata has been able to avoid reliance on export and the political risk involved in the case of government interference such as trade restriction, nationalization or expropriation – which might result in a loss of market share – or riots, wars or terrorism – which might result in a loss of continuous production.

Sources

Case prepared by Professor Donald J. Lecraw at the University of Ontario and published in Beamish, P. W., Killing, J. P., Lecraw, D. J. and Crokell, H., *International Management: Text and Cases*, Irwin, Homewood IL, 1991, pp. 468–470.

Daniels, J. and Radebaugh, L. H., *International Business. Environments and Operations*, 6th edn, Addison-Wesley, Reading MA, 1992, pp. 77–9.

How Bata rules its world, *Canadian Business*, September 1990, pp. 28–34.

One man's multinational: Thomas Bata, BBC Television programme, produced for CBC by David Gerrard, 27 July, 1985.

The question that now arises is what can business managers do to deal with political risk in the 1990s? In addition to those aspects of traditional political risk strategy that are still potentially relevant, a number of new strategies have been developed in response to these changes.

POLITICAL RISK STRATEGIES FOR THE 1990s

Historically, many multinational firms have responded by reducing their assets exposure and speeding up profit repatriation. In recent years, assessing the vulnerability of international business operations has become much more important than assessing broad political shocks (Poynter, 1991, p. 119). International business managers are now advised to decrease their emphasis on choosing the appropriate political environment and to develop instead strategies to defend their international business operations (see Poynter, 1991, pp. 119–33, for a detailed analysis of defence strategies, implementation, and implications for multinationals, and the difficulties encountered).

A successful defence strategy is based upon four main activities:

1. Increasing a subsidiary's bargaining power.
2. Improving a subsidiary's political role.
3. Building local alliances.
4. Achieving a 'good citizenship' status.

Increasing a subsidiary's bargaining power

This is achieved by staying ahead of the technical and managerial capability of the host nation (Poynter, 1991, p. 123). The two most frequently used methods here are either to continuously introduce significant technological upgrading to existing product lines, or to introduce brand new products or highly complex technologies, which call for high managerial capabilities and technical skills not available locally.

Improving a subsidiary's political role

International business managers need to recognize the political role that firms increasingly have with their host government (Stopford *et al.* 1991, p. 224). A whole range of political strategies are available as means of enhancing that role. Firms in strategically important industries, such as natural resources, banking, insurance and public utilities have a high political profile. Government action against them provides greater public impact, greater opportunities for policy implementation (Poynter, 1991, p. 128) and, in some countries, trade union satisfaction. Very high profile firms are advised to establish joint ventures with firms from other countries and to use syndicated project finance (Poynter, 1991, p. 128). The creation of such a transnational web, by raising the political and economic cost of intervention, is the best deterrent against host government interference. (For further discussion of this type of deterrence see Moran and Maddox, 1981.)

Building local alliances

Smaller subsidiaries, on the other hand, are strongly advised to establish close links with their host government and become more politically involved. For example, a central department for managing political and administrative relationships with governments ought to be established. This department should be staffed by corporate 'diplomats' who have local expertise and knowledge and a broad experience of dealing with governments in other countries (Stopford *et al.* 1991, p. 224).

Additionally, international business managers should be able to analyse the local 'investment climate', understand the host government's development intentions, and set themselves an agenda for assistance. They should also act as diplomats and must be able to work with local politicians, understand them, search for areas of common goals and mutual interest, brief them on the company's contributions to the local economy and establish a long-lasting relationship based on mutual trust (Stopford *et al.*, 1991, p. 224). Such a relationship might help the firm in the future, for example in identifying proponents of intervention, and provide the opportunity to reach satisfactory arrangements between the government and the firm (Poynter, 1991, p. 129).

Becoming good citizens

Good citizenship involves much more than building contacts in the political society. It should include active contributions to local, social and economic goals of the host country. Business managers should not only be good diplomats; they should also be culturally aware and able to deal with local issues effectively, and cultivate many local allies from the social groups. To protect their overseas investments against political risk in foreign markets, international business managers therefore should become, first of all, good citizens. As IBM's President said recently: 'IBM cannot be a net exporter for every nation in which it does business, we have to be a good citizen everywhere' (Reich, 1990, p. 58).

REVIEW QUESTIONS

1. Define political risk and explain how it can affect international business operations.
2. What are the causes of political risk? Illustrate your answer with actual examples.
3. Explain how the political relationship between different governments could result in political risk for a multinational firm operating in a host country.
4. What strategies can a multinational firm use to avoid or reduce political risk?
5. The dangers and potential losses connected with political risk have prompted multinational firms to adopt various methods for assessing their political risk. Explain each method and evaluate the merits and shortcomings of each approach

EXERCISE 2.1: Political risk analysis

Aim　This exercise provides students with the opportunity to identify specific aspects of political risk, and to analyse strategies utilized by multinational firms to avoid, reduce or manage political risk.

Assignment　Students are asked to investigate a particular political event, government action or some factors in the external or internal environment of a multinational firm which resulted in political risk.

Examples of possible assignments

- *Company-related*
  - Pepsi Cola in India
  - IBM in South Africa
  - McDonald's in Moscow
  - Avon in Hungary
  - Adidas in Poland
- Political events related
  - The Gulf War and its impact on multinational firms operating in Kuwait
  - Terrorism, kidnapping and hostage taking and foreign multinationals
  - The Arab world boycott and its implications for international business
  - Foreign director investment in Eastern and Central Europe: problems and future prospects

Format　Students are asked to research fully the case and present their findings to the class.

Sources of information

To do these exercises refer to the sources of information for country profiles and company profiles listed in Chapter 1.

FURTHER READING

Kobrin, S., Political risk: a review and reconsideration, *Journal of International Business Studies*, Spring/ Summer 1979, pp. 67–80.

Poynter, T. A., Political risk: managing government intervention, in *International Management. Text and Cases* (ed. Beamish, P. W.), Irwin, Homewood IL, 1991, pp. 119–33.

Root, F. R., Analyzing political risk in international business, in *The Multinational Enterprise in Transaction* (eds. Kapoor, A and Grub, P. D.), Darwin Press, Princeton, 1972, pp. 354–65.

Simon, J. D., Political risk assessment. Past trends and future prospects, *Columbia Journal of World Business*, **XVII**(3), 1982, pp. 62–9.

de la Torre, J. and Neckar, D. H., Forecasting political risk for international operations, *International Journal of Forecasting*, **4**, 1988, pp. 221–41.

THREE

LEGAL ENVIRONMENT ANALYSIS

The previous chapter ended with a discussion of the different ways in which business managers can protect their investments and international operations against political risk. Political (and economic) risk is only one aspect of the risks involved in operating in foreign markets. Legal structures also present problems, and some of the legal problems that may be encountered by multinationals include the following:

- Differences in the regulations of collusion, competition, promotion and sales methods
- Differences in pricing regulations, profit margins, mark-up, loans
- Differences in dealing with breach of contract
- Differences in patent, trade mark and copyright protection
- Differences in determining corrupt practices and bribery
- Differences in legal compliance and implementation of international law

International trade and commercial law is too complex to cover in an introductory textbook. This chapter will explore only the most pressing legal issues and problems that business managers may face and suggest ways of dealing with them.

LEARNING OBJECTIVES

- To provide a broad understanding of the legal environment of international business
- To introduce the various relevant legal systems
- To examine relevant aspects of international law, and discuss their implications for international business
- To offer some guidelines for contract negotiations and methods for settling international commercial disputes

THE LEGAL ENVIRONMENT OF INTERNATIONAL BUSINESS

The legal international environment of business consists of the national legal structures of the many countries of the world, the international legal system and the relationship between them. When international commercial disputes occur they must be settled in one of the countries involved according to the laws and regulations of that country, unless the contract states otherwise. In some countries the national legal system provides only broad guidelines and the interpretation and application of the relevant laws are left to national companies. In others, the legal system prescribes and regulates every detail of business activity. It is therefore important for business managers to be aware of the host country's legal system and how it operates, and also to be familiar with the national laws themselves.

Most countries derive their legal system from one of the three traditional foundations: Common Law, Code Law or Islamic Law.

- Common Law is mostly practised in the UK, USA and Canada. This legal system is broadly based on previous court decisions, precedents or past practice.
- Code Law is practised in most European countries, Japan and Russia. Code Law is established by arbitrary methods and constitutes a comprehensive set of codes which clearly spell out the laws applicable in all possible legal situations. These are divided into three separate codes: commercial, civil and criminal. When dealing with business matters, commercial codes have precedence over other codes.
- Islamic Law is practised to a certain extent in more than 27 countries in the Arab world and most other Islamic countries. The legal system is derived entirely from the precepts of the Koran, which govern all aspects of life, individual behaviour, and social and economic relations. A unique feature of Islamic Law, which is important to multinationals operating in Islamic countries, is the formal prohibition against the payment of interest considered as 'ribba' or usury (Khan, 1988, pp. 1–3).

ENFORCEMENT OF NATIONAL LAWS

Multinational firms should be aware of how foreign laws are enforced or complied with. Some countries are more favourable to domestic firms and to local nationals over foreign multinational firms and their employees. In Saudi Arabia, for example, foreigners involved in car accidents are automatically arrested for 48 hours, whether guilty or not.

In international business matters many countries have established anti-trust laws and anti-corruption laws.

- *Anti-trust laws* are used to prevent foreign business firms from engaging in anti-competitive practices such as price-fixing, producer collusion, taking over competitors through illegal means, and other activities considered harmful to local competition.
- *Anti-corruption laws*. There is currently no international agreement regarding the control of corrupt practices. Governments and business firms have different definitions and interpretations of corrupt practices and policy standards. In the USA, for example, since the famous Lockheed scandal in 1977 it is illegal for companies to pay bribes to foreign officials, candidates or political parties under the Foreign Corrupt Practices Act. Heavy penalties are inflicted on those who knowingly accept bribery or authorize the payment of any bribery. In the Arab world, on the contrary, bribery is not illegal but the 'idea of giving and receiving is part and parcel of Arab history' (*Economist*, 1986). Bribery is considered as a 'fee' or a 'payoff' often necessary to get a contract or a business deal processed quickly and efficiently. Western European and Japanese firms are also allowed to use bribery in their foreign market operations (Terpestra and Sarathy, 1991, p. 141). In 1980 Italy even passed a law that bribery is to be considered as a legal way of doing business (Terpestra and Sarathy, 1991, p. 521).

Knowing the general features and basis of the legal system and how it operates is often not enough. It is also essential for business managers to be familiar with the laws themselves.

CASE STUDY 3.1: Implementing Islamic laws in Saudi Arabia

Islamic Law is the only legal system in Saudi Arabia. 'Al Sharia' regulates every aspect of life. Here are some examples that business managers ought to be aware of when doing business there.

Prayer times

Moslems are required to pray five times a day, preferably in the Mosque. Multinational firms operating in Saudi Arabia must make allowances for their employees to conduct their religious obligations. They usually allocate a special prayer room within their premises for that purpose. Shops, banks, restaurants, take-aways, even pharmacies are all required by law to close down for 10–15 minutes during prayer times at the risk of having their premises physically raided by the 'Mottawa', the religious leaders.

Ramadan

This is a holy month. All Moslems are required to fast (restrain from eating, smoking and drinking) from dawn to sunset. Working hours in government offices are reduced to four hours in the mornings only. Other business firms have to re-schedule their working hours to allow Moslem employees to observe their fast. Grocery stores and retailers close down their shops at 1 p.m. and do not re-open until 9 p.m., after the 'Iftar', and usually trade until the early hours of the morning. It is a public offence, even for foreign expatriates working during Ramadam, to eat, drink or smoke in public places during the day. Serving coffee, tea and even water in offices is also prohibited.

Pigs and pork meat

Pork meat or any food product containing pork fat is prohibited under Islamic Law for its impurity and the unhygenic eating habits of the pigs. The import of sausages, bacon and ham is therefore banned in Saudi Arabia. Many foreign meat producers have a special range of beef sausages, beef bacon and even beef pepperoni and ham especially made for those markets. Heavy censorship is also applied on all published books containing any reference to pigs. Children's books containing stories of pigs and illustrations of pigs are often covered with black ink or the offending material simply torn from the books.

Alcohol

Alcohol consumption is prohibited in the Koran because of its detrimental effect on health and social behaviour. Imports of alcoholic drink is therefore banned. Even home brewing is illegal. Expatriates can be sentenced with a one-year imprisonment and 100 flagellations – beating the bare sole feet with a hard stick – regardless of nationality or religious affiliation.

Physical appearance

The wearing of long hair and earrings for men is despised in the Koran because of the apparent similarity with women. Contrary to the general belief of new expatriates, wearing of the Arab national costume – the abbaya (white long robe) for men and the ghoutra (the head cover) as a sign of cultural acceptance in business meetings, is an offence to the Arabs and must be avoided.

The Royal Family

Unlike in the UK, where members of the Royal Family are often criticized by the press and even sometimes humiliated, in Saudi Arabia an expatriate who insults a member of the Royal Family in public, even if it is only verbal abuse, could be arrested and jailed for 90 days before being expelled from the country.

INTERNATIONAL TRADE LAWS

'The world cannot be permitted to act as though there is no such thing as International Law' (Behrman and Grosse, 1990, p. 233). There are a number of world trade policies that tend to regulate international trade and ensure uniformity in regulation. Some of these cover various aspects of the trading process including customs procedures, negotiations on tariffs, quotas, subsidies, retaliation for unfair trading practices, imposition of voluntary export restraints, assistance to labour adversely affected by imports, liability and insurance of foreign credits (for a detailed list of international trade laws, see Behrman and Grosse, 1990, p. 233). Enforcement of these laws, however, tends to differ from one country to another. Uniformity in regulation has not yet been achieved or fully enforced, for example in some less developed countries who claim that they were not party to such laws, being colonial subjects at the time (Lutz, 1992, p. 683). In addition there is no supranational institution that can implement decisions under it. States may still withhold their consent to the jurisdiction of third-party dispute settlement regimes (Lutz, 1992, p. 677). The International Court of Justice or the World Court can take jurisdiction only if national governments wish to bring a case before it. Its rulings, however, have been at one time or another either criticized for their partiality, ignored or defied (Lutz, 1992, p. 677).

Governments have taken different approaches to harmonize their international trade policies with each other with the assistance of international organizations such as the General Agreement on Tariffs and Trade (GATT), the United Nations Convention on Contracts for the International Sale of Goods (CISG), the International Union for the Protection of Industrial Property, the Madrid Union and the World Intellectual Property Organization, the Berne Convention for the protection of literary artistic works and the universal Copyright Convention. (This section draws heavily from Litka, 1991a, Chapters 7, 8 and 9.)

GENERAL AGREEMENT ON TARIFFS AND TRADE (GATT)

The general function of GATT is to establish a basic set of rules under which world trade can take place, to regulate international business conduct and to provide a forum for tariff negotiations, bargaining and international trade dispute settlements. It is discussed in detail in Part Three.

THE UN CONVENTION ON CONTRACTS FOR THE INTERNATIONAL SALE OF GOODS (CISG)

The Convention applies to the sale of goods between two parties signatories to the Convention but does not apply to consumer sales or to product liability. Many countries now participate in international conventions designed for mutual recognition and protection of international property rights. Some of these are:

- The International Union for the Protection of Industrial Property, also known as the Paris Convention. It is adhered to by the USA and has 94 members. The Paris Convention provides, for all members, protection of their trade marks, patents and property rights. One single registration in one member country ensures coverage in all member countries.
- The Madrid Union has 26 members in Europe. It ensures automatic trade mark protection for all members. Registration of trade marks is normally done at its International Bureau, which is part of the World Intellectual Property Organization located in Switzerland, but a specialized agency of the UN. This has superseded the Berne Convention, which is the oldest treaty for the protection of copyright and artistic works. It has 72 member countries, covering the European Community, Eastern Europe and Third World states. Under the Berne Convention there is no need for formal registration. Any publication in member nations is automatically covered. Authors need only to be citizens of a member country to enjoy protection.
- The Universal Copyright Convention (UCC) is administered by UNESCO. The UCC extends the same copyright protection to all citizens. It does not however recognize the moral right which is protected under the Berne Convention.
- The European Patent Convention was created by the Single Act in the European Community. It allows one single application for a European patent which becomes effective all over the European Community. This is discussed in more detail in Part Four.

INTERNATIONAL DISPUTE SETTLEMENT

When an international commercial dispute occurs, it has to be settled by the two parties involved in the host country where the multinational firm operates. The principal methods available in resolving international commercial disputes are mediation, arbitration, litigation or judicial settlement.

Mediation or third party settlements

When mediation is used as a method of dispute resolution, the assistance or help of a third party, known as the mediator, is used. The mediator should be an independent person and have no vested interest in the outcome of the solution. The mediator's decisions are not enforceable unless acceptable to both parties. Since the two parties involved in a conflict are not bound by the verdict of the mediator, mediation can become a long and tedious process. If the mediator fails to suggest a mutually agreed solution the two parties to a dispute may agree to resolve their conflict through arbitration.

Arbitration

Arbitration is more legally enforceable than mediation. In an arbitration both parties are required to submit their documents relative to the case to an outside agency for an independent arbitration, and to accept the judgement of the arbitrator. The arbitrator's decision is legally binding on both parties and backed by the national courts. Most arbitration for international commercial disputes is conducted under the auspices of the Chambers of Commerce of many countries in the world. The International Chamber of Commerce (ICC) has its own court of arbitration and its own rules are used in conducting arbitration (see Cateora, 1990, p. 189). Arbitration is not recognized or acceptable to the Japanese because it implies a failure to reach harmonious agreement between the two parties and the interference of an outsider to settle the dispute.

Litigation

Litigation is the most expensive and time consuming method of resolving international commercial disputes. In litigation, courts of the host country, home country and even of a third country could be involved in the settlement of the dispute. The enforcement of a litigation judgment is also very difficult, particularly when the court used has no jurisdiction over the losing party. Finally, litigation could create a poor image of the firm involved, and may damage its public relations with the host country and risk exposure of its confidential documents.

International Center for the Settlement of Investment Disputes

This method is particularly used when the disputed contract involves investments in foreign markets. Its main role is to provide a forum for disputing parties to resolve their difference.

LEGAL RISK ANALYSIS

The question arises as to what business managers should do to protect their investments and international business operations against legal risk. Business managers are strongly advised to conduct a legal risk analysis before signing any contract to start up a business in a foreign environment. The legal risk analysis should include (Asheghian and Ebrahimi, 1990, p. 249):

- A detailed examination of the legal system in operation in the country considered (Civil, Code or Islamic) and a thorough understanding of the laws themselves
- A historical review of any discriminatory practices against foreign citizens and firms practised by that country
- A familiarity with contract enforcement practices and appeal procedures
- A clear identification of arbitration practices available
- A study of the foreign country's consistency in implementing the law
- An understanding of the compensation award system and its procedures
- A current revision of administrative procedures
- A consideration of relevant international law and international conventions and codes.

REVIEW QUESTIONS

1. Why should business managers be concerned about the legal environment of the foreign countries in which they operate?
2. What methods are available for international commercial dispute settlements? Explain the differences between each method, and discuss their advantages and disadvantages.
3. Do you consider bribery a legal offence, or an efficient tool in conducting international business? Support your answer with examples.
4. To what extent does international trade law influence the conduct and operations of international business?

EXERCISE 3.1: International legal environment analysis

Aim   This exercise should assist students in familiarizing themselves with various legal systems available in the world. It should also develop their research skills in locating relevant materials and cases in international business law.

Assignment   Students are asked to choose a legal system of particular interest to them and fully research its characteristics and evaluate their implications for international business.

Format   A presentation to the class introducing the legal system chosen, followed by illustrative examples of its application in particular countries where it is operational.

FURTHER READING

Anderson, A., Managers' Journal: Why there are so few lawyers in Japan, *Wall Street Journal*, 9 February 1981.

Campbell, D. (ed.), *Comparative Law*, Yearbook of International Business, Vol. 12, 1990.

Ingo, W. and Murray, T. (eds.), *Handbook of International Business*, 2nd edn, Wiley, New York, 1988, Chs 7, 21, 25–28.

Litka, M., *International Dimensions of the Legal Environment of Business*, PWS Kent, Boston, 1991.

Litka, M., *Cases in International Business Law*, Kent, Boston, 1991.

Platto, C., *Obtaining Evidence in Another Jurisdiction. Business Disputes*, International Bar Association/ Graham and Trotman, London, 1988.

Schaffer, R., Earle, B. and Agusti, F., *International Business Law and Its Environment*, West Publishing, Minneapolis/St Paul, 1993, pp. 33–60.

Wilson, D., *International Business Transactions*, West Publishing, Minneapolis/St Paul, 1984, Chs 6, 10, 15, 16.

FOUR
THE SOCIOCULTURAL ENVIRONMENT OF INTERNATIONAL BUSINESS

There is no cultural right or wrong, just differences ... we must not make value judgements as to whether or not cultural behaviour is good or bad, better or worse.   (Copland and Criggs, 1985, p. 43)

Once upon a time there was a great flood, and involved in the flood were two creatures, a monkey and a fish. The monkey, being agile and experienced, was lucky enough to scramble upon a tree and escape the raging waters. As he looked down from his safe perch, he saw the poor fish struggling against the swift current. With the very best of intentions, he reached and lifted the fish from the water. The result was inevitable.   (Adams, 1969, pp. 22–4)

It is wrong to assume that people in different cultures think, feel and act in the same way. Ignorance of cultural differences could end with fatal consequences, as dramatized so vividly in the story of the monkey and the fish.

In international business dealings, ignorance of cultural difference is not just unfortunate, 'it is bad business' (Arwind, 1989, p. 25). Sensitivity to cultural difference is crucial to successful international business operations. Ignorance of cultural differences could end in disastrous business blunders. (There are many documented cases in which multinationals have failed to understand fully the foreign cultural environment. For an interesting account of such blunders, see Ricks (1983).)

The purpose of this chapter is to provide business managers with a better grasp of the impact of the sociocultural environment of international business, and suggestions for how to better conduct their business in a multicultural environment.

LEARNING OBJECTIVES

- To introduce the concept of culture and its role in international business
- To identify the various elements of sociocultural environment and evaluate their implications for international business operations
- To provide guidance to business managers on how to deal with the multicultural diversity of the international business environment and how to conduct cross-cultural negotiations more effectively

THE CONCEPT OF CULTURE: DEFINITION AND FUNCTIONS

Culture is an extremely broad concept and very difficult to define. Culture touches and alters every aspect of human life and embraces everything from 'food to dress, from household techniques to industry techniques, from forms of politeness to mass media, from work rhythm to the learning of familiar rules ...' (Guillaum, 1979, p. 1). There is no general agreement with regard to the definition of culture. To some, culture refers to the distinctive way of life of a particular group of people (Herskovitz, 1952, p. 17), or a complete design for living (Kluckholm, 1951, p. 86). Others refer to culture as a pattern of behaviour transmitted to members of a group from previous generations of the same group (Hall, 1977, pp. 16–17). Culture is not simply 'a product of conditioning' (Grosse and Kujawa, 1992, p. 322) acquired, learned or transmitted from one generation to another. Culture also shapes people's values, attitudes, beliefs and behavioural patterns (Terpestra and David, 1985). It is therefore crucial for business managers to understand fully not only how people in different cultures behave but why they behave in the way they do. Knowledge about culture is achieved by a combination of factual knowledge and interpretive understanding.

Factual knowledge is acquired through an accumulation of the characteristics or observable facts about a particular culture, for example learning the different meanings of colour, tastes and so on. Interpretive understanding requires a deeper insight and understanding of the 'nuances of different cultural traits and patterns, which require more than factual knowledge to be fully appreciated, such as learning the meaning of time, of life, of attitudes towards others (Cateora, 1990, pp. 69–70), of gender, and of business itself.

THE RELEVANCE OF CULTURE

Knowledge of culture is essential to conducting international business. It enables business managers (Dressler and Carn, 1969, p. 60):

- To communicate with each other through the use of language either commonly known to them or learned
- To anticipate how other business people and consumers in various markets are likely to respond to their actions
- To distinguish between what is considered right and wrong, reasonable or unreasonable, acceptable or offensive, safe or dangerous, beautiful or ugly, in various countries of the world
- To identify themselves in the same category with other business managers of similar background and provide the knowledge and necessary skills for meeting and negotiating with them

ANALYSING CULTURAL DIFFERENCE

There is no best method of cultural analysis that is appropriate for all business decisions. Assessing the cultural environment of international business depends largely on the type of business and the international activities involved. One practical approach is to break down the broad area of the sociocultural environment into its various elements and to study each element in detail. (Herskovitz (1952), for example, lists five dimensions to culture: material culture; social institutions; mankind and the Universe; aesthetics; and language and communication.) It should be noted, however, that culture is not simply a group of unrelated elements, but that the different facets of culture are intricately intertwined (Cateora, 1990, p. 81) and must be viewed as an integrated complex whole (Terpestra and David, 1985). An employee's behaviour, for example, or a customer's reaction cannot be fully explained by a simple reference to certain aspects of the cultural environment influencing their attitude such as language, religion, social structure and so on. It is essential for business managers to understand the reasons and motivations behind such a behaviour or reaction. A systems approach to the analysis of the cultural environment is one where culture is understood as a system composed of parts that are related to other parts which mutually influence and adjust to each other, through a process of cooperation, competition, conflict and accommodation (Parson, 1951).

Elements of the cultural environment of international business.

There are many elements to culture. To describe any one of them fully would require a discussion of far greater length and depth than we can reasonably attempt here. We shall therefore focus only on those dimensions which have been found to influence international business practices substantially, as shown in Figure 4.1.

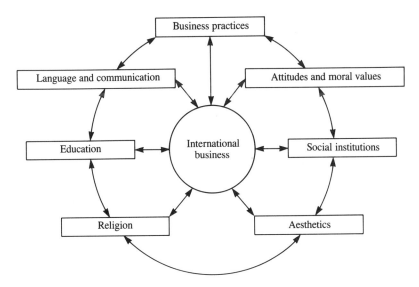

Figure 4.1   Elements of the cultural environment of international business

LANGUAGE AND COMMUNICATION

Of all the cultural elements of the international business environment, language is perhaps the most obvious difference between cultures and probably the most difficult to acquire and understand.

There are approximately 3000 different languages in the world with less than 300 nations and 10 000 different dialects. In some countries, several languages exist at the same time. Canada, for example, has two national languages, French and English. Belgium has three national languages: Flemish in the north, and French and German in the south. Switzerland has four dominant languages and India alone has 15 major languages and over 1000 dialects (Baldev, 1969, p. 26). Some countries, such as the former USSR and Yugoslavia, not only have different languages, but also have different alphabets (Daniels and Radebaugh, 1992, p. 91).

There has been an attempt by Dr Lazarus Ludwig Zamenhof to develop an international language, Esperanto, by combining many languages to form words that are easy to understand and remember, and where grammar, punctuation and spelling are simple enough to learn in about an hour (Asheghian and Ebrahimi, 1990, p. 263). Although Esperanto is nowadays spoken in some parts of Europe, it has not yet become a true language because there is no need for it. English has always been and still remains the dominant language of international business.

The ability to speak and understand the various interpretations of the language of a foreign country is essential for anyone planning a career in international business. The study of a foreign language should therefore include both the verbal language, or factual knowledge, and the non-verbal language, or interpretive knowledge.

Verbal language or factual knowledge

In addition to the formal learning of the verbal language and the ability to speak and communicate effectively in it, business managers must also acquire the competency to recognize the idiomatic interpretations of that language, which are quite different from those, for example, found in a dictionary. Matching words with identical meanings from one language to another, without being aware of the nuances of the local language, double meanings of words and slang and the various interpretations of the cultural terms and concepts, could lead to confusion, embarrassment and expensive mistakes.

CASE STUDY 4.1: Problems faced when conveying a message in another language

Pepsi Cola 'Come alive with Pepsi'

When technically translated in German the message conveyed the idea of coming alive from the grave, and in Asia of bringing your ancestors from the dead.

Parker Pens 'Avoid embarrassment, use Parker Pens'

The message meant to be transmitted was that a Parker Pen is a truly reliable fountain pen and could be worn in a shirt pocket without concern for embarrassing ink stains. But when technically translated into Spanish the same word for embarrassment is also often used to indicate pregnancy.

Eastern Air Lines 'We earn our wings daily'

The translation of this advertising campaign simply implied that its passengers often ended up dead.

CASE STUDY 4.2: Problems when establishing a brand name

Egypt Air 'Misair', when pronounced in France sounds like '*misère*', or misery

General Motors 'Chevrolet Nova'

After General Motors introduced its new Chevrolet Nova in Puerto Rico, it found out that although the word Nova means 'start' in Spanish, its pronunciation sounded also like '*no va*', meaning 'does not go', and had to change it to 'Caribe'.

Ford 'Fierra'

The low-cost truck 'Fierra' faced the same problems with its Spanish translation, where *fierra* meant 'ugly old woman'.

Rolls Royce 'Silver Mist'

Rolls Royce's new model, the 'Silver Mist', was not very popular in the German market where 'mist' is literally translatable into 'excrement'.

Colgate Palmolive 'Cue' toothpaste was not only offensive in the French market but also obscene, 'since '*Cue*' is a pornographic word in French meaning '*derrière*' or 'bottom'.

Schweppes tonic water Translation into Italian idiomatically means the bathroom.

CASE STUDY 4.3: Problems when communicating verbally

Former President Kennedy, in a major speech in Berlin, tried to say that he was proud to be from Berlin but actually remarked that he was proud to be a 'jelly-filled donut' (*ein Berliner*)!

Japanese 'Hai'   Many international business managers have been unpleasantly surprised to learn that the noddings of 'yes' responses of their Japanese counterparts did not mean that the deal was closed or that they agreed, because the word for 'yes', 'hai', can also simply mean 'it is understood', or 'I hear you'.

Sources

Ricks, D., *Big Business Blunders: Mistakes in Multinational Marketing*. Irwin Dow Jones, Homewood IL, 1983, pp. 80–84.

Ricks, D., International business blunders: an update, *Business and Economics Review*, January–March 1988, pp. 11–14.

Cateora, P., *International Marketing*, 7th Edition, Irwin, Homewood IL, 1990, p. 79.

Non-verbal language or interpretive language

Mastering a foreign language is not enough in itself, because not all communication is written or spoken. Non-verbal language, often referred to as the 'silent language' (Hall, 1960), can pose serious problems for international business managers. The study of interpretive language consists of six variables: the languages of time, of space, of things, of friendship and of agreements, and body language. The following draws heavily from Hall (1960).

Language of time   Each society has different attitudes towards time. These can have economic consequences for international business relations and be a source of frustration in conducting international business. Punctuality, for example, can cause confusion and misunderstanding in various cultures. In Western societies, arriving late for a business appointment could be interpreted as an insult, while in many Latin American and Arab societies waiting for up to two hours is quite often acceptable, and part of the business culture.

In the USA, time is money, Any delay in answering a communication could mean lack of interest or even a loss of potential business. Time for the Japanese belongs to nobody. It is at the disposal of everybody (Bairy, 1967, p. 15). A delay in communication does not mean that they have lost interest but that they might, instead, be building up to something big. In the Middle East, time is circular. If today is lost, there is no need to worry, it will return tomorrow. Time required for answering a communication is also directly related to its importance. Arabs therefore do not like to be rushed and dislike deadlines. However, once a discussion starts, there is no limit on the amount of time spent on it. A meeting scheduled for one hour could easily be prolonged in the Middle East to four or even five hours.

Language of space   Space here refers to the size of the offices and their location. In most US and Western firms the president and high executives of the company will have the largest offices, usually on the top floor. The Japanese, on the other hand, prefer to work together in an open area. In the Arab world, and in Saudi Arabia in particular, women are not allowed to work in the same offices as men.

Language of material things   Money and material possessions mean different things in different cultures. Americans often believe that money talks the same language all over the world. They use material things to reflect status and to ascertain it. The Japanese, on the other hand, take pride in inexpensive but tasteful arrangements, while the Arabs feel that family connections and friends are more valuable in reflecting their business status than the location or space or furniture of their offices.

Language of friendship   Americans regard friendship as a series of favours and obligations and often use it as a means towards getting ahead or at least getting the job done. In India, in contrast, the idea of reciprocity in friendship is unheard of. Friendship in the Middle East is based on real obligations and represents a sort of social security.

Language of agreements   The nature of contract negotiations and business agreements differs greatly from one country to another. Americans usually insist on spelling out all the details of a contract on paper and in formal texts. In the Middle East a verbal agreement is just as binding as a written contract.

   Contract negotiations often differ in various cultures. While Americans have the reputation of often being anxious to get down to business, the Japanese are more patient and prefer to take their time before committing themselves. The French, on the other hand, like to deliberate, discuss and engage in debate at meetings before signing a contract, while the Arabs would like to know you as a person before trusting you with their business and entering into a contract with you (see Graham *et al.*, 1988, pp. 49–62; Magnier, 1988; *Business International*, 30 May 1988, pp. 163–6).

Body language   The smallest details of body language can be extremely important to the conduct of international business. It is, however, difficult to generalize about differences in body language across different cultures. The ways in which people move their bodies, stand, sit, cross their legs, touch and walk differs from one country to another. Few gestures are universal in meaning. The following are a few examples.

   The joining of the index finger and thumb to form an 'O' means 'OK' in the USA, 'money' in Japan and 'I'll kill you' in Tunisia (Ferrieux, 1989, p. 39). 'Thumbs up' in the West is a form of acknowledgement in Ghana. Such a gesture is considered vulgar, and an insult in Iran. While a head shaken up and down in the USA means 'yes', the same motion in the UK is used to indicate that 'I heard you' but does not necessary mean agreeing. 'No' in the USA is conveyed by shaking the head from side to side, while the same gesture in Bulgaria means 'yes', in the Middle East the head is jerked in a haughty manner to mean 'no' and in the Orient a wave of the hand in front of the face is used. Folding arms is a show of respect in Fiji, but an insult and arrogance in Finland (Ricks, 1983, p. 17). Displaying feet on the desk in the USA is very common, but is considered an insult in the Middle East. One must never show the bottom of the feet in the direction of another person in Thailand, or cross your legs while sitting in the presence of an older person (Glover, 1990, pp. 2–6). While the traditional handshake in the West is mostly used for greetings and introductions in the East, bowing in front of your partner while placing the hands in a praying position is customary, and kissing on the cheeks is often practised in the Arab world – but not between opposite sexes. Kissing the nose of the King in Saudi Arabia is the customary salutation, showing the highest respect to the monarch.

PRACTICAL ADVICE ON HOW TO DEAL WITH LANGUAGE BARRIERS AND DIFFICULTIES IN COMMUNICATION WITHIN FOREIGN CULTURES

All we have done so far is to illustrate the magnitude of problems that business managers could face when operating in various foreign cultures. There are various techniques available for multinational firms to deal with language barriers and the difficulties of communicating effectively in foreign cultures. Some of these are: the use of professional translators and interpreters, employing bilingual executives and providing language training programmes.

Use of translators and interpreters

Multinational firms often employ skilled translators and interpreters to deal with their foreign written and oral communications. In the light of the various problems arising through translation errors and to avoid misunderstandings in interpretation, multinational firms are strongly advised to use translations by at least two different translators. The managers' words are first translated by a non-native speaker, then a native speaker will translate the first translator's words back into the original language (Khambata and Ajami, 1992, p. 257). The use of a native speaker is important given the cultural context of the spoken and written language, as discussed above.

Bilingual managers

The use of translators and interpreters is not only expensive but can cause several difficulties, especially when direct communications with customers, suppliers and often governments is needed. Many countries dictate that official communication with the government must be conducted in the national language of the country concerned. Instead of having to rely heavily on interpreters and communicate little with local employees and suffer indifferent relations with government officials, many multinational firms are now employing national bilingual managers at a high level.

Language training programmes

Language training programmes could prove as useful as various training programmes designed to improve employees' productivity. In Sweden, for example, language training has been mandatory since 1973 (*Business Week*, 31 March 1973, p. 107). Many European firms are now integrating language teaching with work, on-site.

In the United States Department of Foreign Services language training varies between a period of six months and may extend as long as two years for difficult languages such as Arabic and Japanese.

One company's approach to dealing with the language problem was to create its own work language. Caterpillar Tractor, in 1970 was facing severe language problems because its managers had to relate with many people in foreign countries who were not directly employed by the company but did serve the company or dealt directly with its customers, including local independent dealers and repair shops. To solve this problem and to facilitate the understanding of its parts, service and repair manuals throughout the world, without having to translate them into several languages, Caterpillar developed its own unique system of a one-way printed communication called Caterpillar Fundamental English (CFE) (*Business International*, 6 April 1973, p. 107) which does not need pronunciation or writing. CFE is a condensed, simplified and specialized form of English using a visual understanding of an 800 word vocabulary necessary to service Caterpillar products.

Other international firms, such as Philips, have instead adopted English as the official company language, even though its headquarters are in the Netherlands. When the Swedish Company ASEA merged with the Swiss company Brown-Boveri, English was also adopted as the corporate language. The problem is, however, much more complex in Germany, where workers come from as many as four different foreign countries. For example, at the Ford plant in Cologne three languages are used simultaneously by the workforce: German, Turkish and Spanish.

EDUCATION

Education is often restricted to the formal acquisition of knowledge and training within schools. Broader education takes place outside the classroom, and most people have been educated in this broader sense for the culture in which they live and work. A full definition of education should therefore include the process of transmitting skills, ideas and attitudes as well as training in particular disciplines. (The following section draws heavily on Terpestra (1978).)

The function of education

There are five major functions of education:

1. Instrumental education, or modern education, which enables individuals to earn a living.
2. Affiliative education, or socialization, which aims at teaching individuals to get along with others.
3. Political education is often included by national governments within the national curriculum to promote national integration, patriotism, respect for democracy, the creation of a sense of nationhood, and also the dissemination of political ideology and political indoctrination.
4. Mythopoetic education, which includes the study of myths, and folklore. It attempts to understand the human role in relation to the universe by providing a sense of ethics and conduct for people in their daily affairs (Terpestra, 1978).
5. Religious education refers to what types of behaviour are appropriate for adults, what goals they should aspire to achieve and what the meaning of justice is in their social order. Religious education is very important in Islamic countries. Primary schools concentrate on an intensive study of the Koran and on reciting various verses from the Koran from childhood to instil an attitude of obedience and respect for the elderly and parents and for ordered authority. It is interesting to note that the word for education in Arabic '*Adab*' is synonymous with politeness and '*Muadab*', or educated, simply means polite.

EDUCATION AND INTERNATIONAL BUSINESS

Understanding the educational environment in foreign countries is crucial to successful international business operations. Looking at the educational background of the foreign country in which a multinational firm is contemplating doing business could provide important information for the personnel manager in determining, for example, the quality of the local workforce available for employment. It is not just the level of literacy that is important, but also the nature of the educational systems available in order to determine on-the-job training needs and the development of skills required for the performance of certain business functions. Citibank, for example, when recruiting business graduates from the Middle East, often sends them to their MENA Office in Athens to attend a six months intensive in-house training programme in accounting and financial analysis, despite the fact that most of these recruits do already have a degree in finance and accounting, to meet the minimum requirements expected from Citibank international staff.

Understanding the level of education can also assist marketers in evaluating and assessing the levels of sophistication of local consumers, the nature of the media to be used and the kind of approach to be used in advertising. If, for example, the local consumers are largely illiterate, advertising and package labels would have to be adapted using more visual aids. Instructions may need to be modified to meet the educational level of the local consumers. Nestlé's experience in the Third World with its infant formula Similac, which led to a massive number of infant deaths due to the lack of proper instructions for preparing the formula is illustrative of the extent to which inattention to educational and cultural factors can have disastrous consequences (see, for example, Douglas (1978, pp. 60–4); *Business Week*, 23 April 1979, pp. 137–40; *Economist*, 9 May 1981, p. 50).

RELIGION

It is not enough for business managers to know *how* people behave in other cultures and *how* to do business with them. It is also very important to understand *why* they behave in the way they do. Religious beliefs shape many kinds of individual behaviour, whether economic, political, legal or social. Understanding the dominant religion of a particular foreign country, therefore, can provide business managers with a better insight into people's behaviour and cultural attitudes. Ignorance of differences in religious beliefs could lead to frustration and misunderstanding, poor productivity and a drastic reduction in the sales of products, or even cause the ultimate failure of a business.

The study of existing religions in foreign environments may also provide an indication of potential instability, division, social unrest and political risk. This aspect of business has generally been disregarded by many multinational firms. However, recent events, such as the Lebanese war between Christians and Moslems, periodic clashes in India between Hindus and Moslems and more recently the fighting in the former Yugoslavia between the Serbs, Croats and Moslems, have highlighted the importance of this factor in many foreign environments.

The following survey intends merely to identify and describe the core values of some major religions which may affect international business. The major religions surveyed are based on their importance in terms of number of adherents. Animism has 300 million adherents, Buddhism 310 million, Christianity 1900 million, Hinduism 700 million and Islam 900 million (*World Christian Encyclopedia*, 1983).

Animism

This is the oldest type of religion on Earth. It is dominant in Africa and the south Sahara and in some parts of Latin America. Animism is often associated with spirit worship, magic, casting spells, ancestor worship, taboos and fatalism. All of these religious beliefs lead to a conservative, tradition-oriented attitude in society. Business managers may face serious resistance from local consumers in accepting new products and reluctance from the local workforce in adopting new production methods or techniques. Introducing innovation could be a very demanding job, considering the high level of illiteracy, the belief in magic, the low level of newspaper circulation and the existence of various dialects. Business managers might have to educate potential adopters to a new way of thinking (Terpestra, 1984, p. 36).

Hinduism

This is, in some ways, more a way of life than a religion (Tandon, 1972, p. 80). It is a combination of ancient philosophies and customs, animistic beliefs, legends and more recently

Western influences including some elements of Christianity, or Islam and Buddhism. Many Hindu doctrines apply to the Indian situation only. Some key factors in understanding Hinduism, which business managers ought to be aware of when doing business in India, are the cyclical notion of time, the caste system, Bhadar and the veneration of the cow. The concept of time in Hinduism is cyclical (Radhakrishnan, 1961; Ross and Hills, 1986). For the Hindus, nothing is permanent. Life is a constant process of birth, death and reincarnation. The caste system refers to the specific place each individual has in society, which is determined by birth. Hindus are born into a caste which determines their job and work assignments, regardless of their ability or performance. There are 3000 castes and sub-castes in India. Each class (or Jati) has its own duty (or Dharma). Many restrictions exist between different castes, such as marriage outside caste, ideas of good and bad, personal purity and pollution. Since Indian independence successive Indian governments have sought to eliminate the caste system, but without complete success. Business managers must therefore be aware of some of the existing restrictions which could affect the internal management of the firm. It would be risky, for example, to appoint a lower caste person to a supervisory position over a member of higher caste (Terpestra and David, 1985, p. 89). The caste system could also have serious implications for employing women, particularly in relation to the restrictions on the freedom of women in Hinduism (Liddle and Joshi, 1986). Multinational firms also need to be careful in assigning women to executive positions in cultures dominated by Hinduism (Asheghian and Ebrahimi, 1990, pp. 269–70).

Baradari, 'joint family' or 'brotherhood', is another important concept of Hinduism which explains why there are so many family enterprises in India. Multinationals having joint ventures with Indian family enterprises must understand fully the Indian values and practices regarding Baradar, particularly when planning or staffing their international operations. A business manager for example may cause anger if he fires a family member. Baradari often leads to nepotism, favouring the employment of relations, which every business manager must understand to avoid frustration. Understanding Baradar is also crucial to marketing, because in India, the joint family, or Baradari, means a different consumer unit with a different income level and different decision-making processes with regard to consumer spending and consumption (Terpestra, 1978, p. 40).

Buddhism

This is a lifestyle affecting spiritual, cultural and political identity. It stresses tolerance and spiritual equality and focuses on wantlessness and contemplation rather than upon consumption and work (Theravaada, 1972). The ultimate goal of Buddhism is nirvana: the achievement of an ethical state marked by absence of desire and suffering. Human suffering for a Buddhist is caused by the desire for possession and selfish enjoyment of every kind. This suffering will only cease when desire ceases. It is therefore difficult for international business managers to motivate workers to increase their productivity and acquire greater wealth. Marketers will also face great difficulties in selling products because of the lack of enthusiasm for new products and material possessions.

Islam

This means 'submission to God'. Islam is not simply a religion but also a way of life promoting equality and brotherhood of every Moslem, of whatever race or colour. The political influence of Islam cannot be underestimated, particularly in the face of recent events in Iran, Lebanon and more recently Yugoslavia. Friday noon worship services, which all adult Moslems are required to attend, are often used by 'Ulamas' or religious leaders to speak about contemporary problems facing Islam and the Moslem World. During the life of the Prophet Muhammed (the spiritual founder of Islam), the political content of the Friday sermons was very high. Until today, in many Moslem countries such as Syria, Egypt, Jordan, and especially Saudi Arabia, prior governmental approval is required for all sermons. The political content of these sermons could provide useful indications to business managers about the internal stability of the country, social unrest and internal security, and what issues are high on the domestic, political and economic agenda.

The Koran and the 'Al Sharia', or Islamic Law, regulates all facets of life, including political, social and legal justice in most Moslem countries, particularly in Saudi Arabia and Pakistan, where there is a subordination of the state to Islamic tenets. Multinational firms must be familiar with the five pillars of Islam because of the serious implications some of these might have for the conduct of international business. These are:

- *Prayer* All Moslems are required to pray five times a day. Any work must be interrupted during these periods to allow individuals to conduct their religious duty. Work schedules, meeting times, sales calls and production schedules must be planned accordingly.
- *Ramadan* Moslems are required to fast for 30 days during the holy month of Ramadan. This includes complete absention from food, drink and smoking from dawn to sunset. This obviously reduces workers' productivity to a great extent. Working hours are drastically reduced. Public consumption of food during Ramadan is an insult. In Saudi Arabia this is even considered as a public offence. Drinking coffee, smoking in offices and even drinking water are forbidden. This applies to all employees, including foreign expatriates.
- *Zakat* Alms-giving refers to the sharing of wealth. It is an annual tax of 2.5 per cent collected from all individuals and used for charity.
- *Alcohol and pork meat* The consumption of alcoholic drinks is forbidden in Islam as well as eating pork meat. Many multinational firms have responded to this by producing all beef hot dogs, beef bacon and non-alcoholic beer, wine and even champagne to be sold in those particular markets.
- *Women's place in Islamic society* Saudi Arabia exhibits an extreme example of social and behavioural rigidity related to gender. Separation between males and females is strictly maintained not only in schools but also in public places and restaurants. Women's employment is restricted to the teaching professions and nursing. Islam, however, recognizes the economic role women can play in society. Citibank was quick in responding to such needs when it opened in 1978 its first Women's Bank entirely operated by women and providing banking facilities for women only.

Christianity

Two major branches of Christianity will be briefly introduced, Catholicism and Protestantism. In Catholicism, money-making is considered socially degrading and morally and religiously dangerous (Terpestra, 1978, p. 54). In recent years, however, Catholicism has adopted itself to capitalism much more than in the past. The Vatican itself may now be seen as a 'business' as well as the centre of the religious hierarchy of Catholicism. Protestantism, on the other hand, considers money-making not only acceptable but even respectable (Weber, 1952). Despite the claim that 'Capitalism in Protestantism has become synonymous with Christianity' (Griffiths, 1982), it is still the duty of Protestant Christians first of all to glorify God in all that they do. Glorifying God by working hard may lead to wealth accumulation as a by-product.

AESTHETICS

Aesthetics refer to the art, folklore, music, drama, myth, legends, sculpture and architecture of a culture. Understanding and interpreting the symbolic meaning of various aesthetics can be problematic for business managers. Use of symbols, for example, could have a distinctive meaning unique to a particular culture. The owl in the UK symbolizes wisdom, in France it is regarded as an ordinary bird with limited intelligence, while in the Middle East it is considered as a bad omen, or bad luck. It is no wonder then that a British firm which chose the owl as its logo to symbolize wisdom in its children's books experienced poor sales in France and especially in the Middle East. A product designer in Saudi Arabia was once arrested because the logo he designed of a snowflake for 'Snow White', a local dry cleaning plant, had six-pointed stars on the label with a strong visual similarity with the Star of David.

The use and meaning of colour is also of particular importance to international business, because in most cultures colour is used as a symbol that conveys specific messages. Colour perceptions vary greatly from one culture to another. Green, for example, is a very popular colour in Moslem countries, but is associated with disease in countries with dense, green jungles, while in France green is associated with cosmetics (Ricks, 1983, p. 33). Black is the colour of death in the USA, Europe and the Middle East. In Japan and Asia white is the colour of mourning, and black symbolizes power, luxury, prestige and high quality. For a detailed study of cross-cultural colour comparison, see Jacobs *et al.* (1991, pp. 21–30).

SOCIAL INSTITUTIONS

Social institutions, beliefs and values refer to the ways in which people in different cultures relate to each other. Elements of social organization include gender, age, family and kinship, class structure and social hierarchy. Some of these issues have been covered earlier. Discussion in this section will be limited to the values, beliefs and attitudes found to be critical to effective international business communications and operations. Some of these, which are particularly relevant to the conduct of international business, are attitudes towards work and achievement, attitudes towards change and innovation, attitudes towards material culture and technology and attitudes towards business ethics and practices themselves.

Attitudes towards work and achievement

These vary quite widely from culture to culture. People's attitudes towards work depends largely on their view of material gain and wealth and the level of economic development overall. Most people work to satisfy their basic physical needs of food, clothing and shelter. These human needs have been classified as a hierarchy of five needs (Maslow, 1970). According to Maslow's theory of hierarchical needs, starting with physical needs, each need must be at least partially satisfied before the individual's desire to satisfy a need at the next higher level emerges. Maslow's theory is useful in its capacity to identify people's various needs. The validity of the hierarchical classification, however, is questionable. People in different cultures attach different importance to various needs and even rank them differently. Workers in industrial societies, for example, may be unwilling to put in longer hours and work overtime in order to improve their own financial status. In some other societies, material wealth and monetary incentives may not be as strong as the need for spiritual well-being. Some countries have even developed other value systems and have come to value other needs. In Sweden, for example, social needs are more valued than personal esteem needs. In Germany, Japan, Switzerland, Italy and Australia security is valued over social and esteem needs (Hofstede, 1980, p. 42).

Attitudes towards occupations

Attitudes towards certain occupations vary among different countries. Certain occupations carry a greater perception of prestige, social status or independence than simply their monetary rewards. It is important for international business managers to be aware of these variations to be able to predict whether their firm would, for instance, have problems in hiring qualified local managers, how to approach them, and what incentive packages to offer them. In Japan, for example, to be a member of a prestigious large multinational appeals to a large number of college-educated professionals (Hofstede, 1983; 1980). In Europe, by contrast, and particularly in France and Italy economic independence is seen as essential for economic prestige (Matsuura, 1991, p. 55). In the Middle East, and in Japan too, the Civil Service is the most prestigious career and young graduates prefer to take governmental posts rather than pursuing a career in business or trade. In many underdeveloped countries, family businesses take precedence over any other career.

Attitudes to material culture and technology

Material culture is composed of three major elements: technology, economics and consumption. Technology refers to the techniques used in the creation of material goods, innovation, technical know-how and the ability to design and use things; economics is the name in which people employ these objects, use them and enjoy them. Material culture differs from one country to another due to tradition, status, climate, physical and geographic circumstances, economic infrastructures (Hofstede, 1983, pp. 65–70) and increasingly today, to the way in which the national political economy relates to the global political economy, for example as a site of diverse foreign investment, or as a market for consumption. It is crucial to evaluate these factors prior to making any foreign decisions because material culture could affect the level of demand for, and the quality and types of, products needed. It would for example, be extremely difficult to sell central heating units in Thailand or air-conditioning units in Iceland. At the same time, there is no doubt that materialism or the high evaluation of individual possessions and modern goods is a central part of the developing global culture in the modern globalized political economy.

Attitudes towards business practices

Business practices that are acceptable in one country could often be considered offensive or even immoral in another. There are so many different behavioural rules and various business practices that to describe fully any one of them would require a discussion of far greater length and depth than we can reasonably attempt here. The sources of information at the end of this chapter include some up-to-date guidebooks that have been compiled geographically based on the experience of many successful international managers to provide a basic set of rules and observations to which any business negotiator should adhere when engaged in cross-cultural negotiations.

GUIDANCE TOWARDS SUCCESSFUL, CROSS-CULTURAL NEGOTIATIONS

There are 12 basic rules for conducting successful cross-cultural negotiations (Herbig and Kramer, 1991, pp. 19–31).

1. Recognize that a foreign negotiator is different from you in perceptions, motivation, beliefs and outlook.
2. Identify, understand, and respect the other side's culture, protocol, social customs and beliefs.
3. Be aware that many of the rules taught and used domestically may not be culturally acceptable to the other party.
4. Familiarize yourself with the other side's decision-making process. Learn about their personal styles of negotiating tactics, and be ready to develop appropriate counter-negotiation tactics, which are not themselves in tension with, or offensive to, potential foreign partners or customers.
5. Patience is the key to success. Be prepared for the long term. Do not create self-imposed deadlines. The side that uses time most effectively usually wins.
6. Understand how people in each culture view time and value punctuality.
7. Establish good personal relationships. These are a prerequisite to building long-term business contacts with foreigners. Remember that very often written words are of less importance than personal ties.
8. Non-verbal communication is a key element in all negotiations. It is therefore vital that its ramifications are fully understood in cross-cultural settings.
9. Take the time to learn about the culture and language of the country in which you seek to do business.
10. Employ your own bi-cultural adviser and interpreter who can alert you to the peculiarities of the foreign culture before you commit a *faux pas* on a seemingly innocent matter, but which can have major consequences for levels of success or failure abroad.
11. Pictures are worth more than a thousand words. Plan to support your presentations by instructive visuals, photographs, drawings, diagrams, copies of key documents, catalogues, books and even samples of products.
12. Finally, the path to success in negotiation is 'prepare, prepare, prepare', technically as well as culturally. You should know sufficiently the country and the culture of those with whom you are planning to do business.

REVIEW QUESTIONS

1. To what extent does the cultural environment influence international business operations?
2. Why do multinational firms face greater cultural problems than firms operating within a single country?
3. Are local attitudes, for example towards time, work, wealth, material gain, etc. important for a firm setting up a factory in a foreign country?
4. Find a foreign language periodical with advertising, and translate a few into English. Discuss some of the problems of translation encountered, and how you have dealt with them.
5. As an assistant to the managing director of a multinational firm, you have been given the task of choosing a particular country known to you as a possible market for one of the company products. Outline the major cultural problems that the company might face and suggest steps that might be taken to overcome these problems.

EXERCISE 4.1: China the sleeping giant

Aim 'China will become a formidable economic and political power by the first third of the next century'. This exercise aims at improving students' research skills, updating their knowledge and developing their cultural awareness and tolerance of foreign cultures' attitudes, beliefs and values.

Assignment Students are asked to work in groups and to identify the major economic, legal, political, social and cultural obstacles for doing business in China, and provide guidance on how to deal with them. Students are also asked to support their presentation to the class with examples taken from various strategies adopted by multinational firms who are already operating in China, such as Kentucky Fried Chicken, Hewlett-Packard, McDonnell Douglas and General Electric Corporation.

China's open door policy provides foreign investors with fabulous opportunities. However, there are a lot of misunderstandings and misrepresentations about China in Western society because of differences in social systems, cultural traditions, the way of thinking, codes of conduct, the system of values and political organization. These misunderstandings and misrepresentations hinder some Western managers from really knowing China and objectively assessing Chinese markets, and prevent them from considering them as an important part of their global strategies.

EXERCISE 4.2: Multicultural diversity role play

Aim The aim of this exercise is to stimulate students' awareness of the problems faced by multinational firms while conducting international negotiations with foreign cultures, and to develop their skills in cross-cultural communications and negotiations.

Assignment The class is divided into various countries of the world. Students are asked to investigate fully the business practices, communications, negotiation tactics of their assigned country and become as familiar with them as possible.

Role play Representatives from each group are then given a deal to negotiate between two or three multinational firms and are asked to conduct a cross-cultural negotiation exercise in front of the class representing their own country and company. The rest of the class is then asked to comment on their performance, based on their knowledge of the cultural and business practices of those countries.

Sources of information

Japan

Magnier, M., Patience, dedication, key to succeeding in Japan, *Journal of Commerce*, 8 April 1988.
March, R. M., *Japanese Negotiations*, Kodanska International, New York, 1983.
No-nos in negotiating with the Japanese, *Across the Board*, April 1989.
Playing the game by Japanese rules', *Business International*, 30 May 1988, pp. 163–6.
Van Zandt, H. F., How to negotiate in Japan, *Harvard Business Review*, November–December 1970, pp. 45–56.

China

Banthin, J. M. and Stelzer, L., Ethical dilemmas in negotiating across cultures. The absence of universal norms, *Management Challenges: A Worldwide Perspective*, **29**(6), MCP University Press, Bradford, 1991.
Chambers, K., *The Traveller's Guide to Asian Customs and Manners*, Simon and Schuster, New York, 1988.
Helms, M., Taking the single step, *Management Decisions*, **30**(1), 1992, pp. 59–64.

Middle East

Badaway, M. K., Styles of Middle Eastern managers, *California Management Review*, Spring 1980.
Hall, E.T., Learning the Arab's silent language, *Psychology Today*, August 1979, pp. 45–53.
Hungton, I. K., *Doing Business in the Arab Middle East World*, Peat Marwick Mitchell Co., 1980.

Europe

Danton de Rouffignac, P., *How to Sell to Europe*, Pitman, London, 1990.

Graham, J. L., Campbell, N., Jobbert, A. and Meissner, H. G., Marketing negotiations in France, Germany, the UK and the USA *Jounal of Marketing*, April 1988, pp. 49–62.

Hall, E. T. and Hall, M. R., *Understanding Cultural Differences: Germans, French and Americans*, International Cultural Press, Yarmouth ME, 1990.

Eastern Europe

Danton de Rouffignac, P., *Doing Business in Eastern Europe. A Guide for the 1990s*, Pitman, London, 1991.

FURTHER READING

Hall, E. T., The silent language in overseas business, *Harvard Business Review*, May–June 1960.

Herbig, P. A. and Kramer, H. E., Cross-cultural negotiations: success through understanding, *Management Decision*, **29**(8), 1991, pp. 19–31.

Hofstede, G., *Culture's Consequences. International Differences in Work-Related Values*. Sage, Beverly Hills, CA, 1980.

Ross, F. H. and Hills, T., *The Great Religions by Which Men Live*, Fawcett, Connecticutt, 1986.

Terpestra, V. and K. David, *The Cultural Environment of International Business*, 3rd edn, South Western, Cincinnati OH, 1990.

THE FINANCIAL ENVIRONMENT OF INTERNATIONAL BUSINESS

A firm can face greater financial risks when operating at the global level than in domestic markets. On the one hand it must work within the framework of a more diverse international financial system than is found domestically, and on the other it must conduct its financial transactions in more than one currency. Given the recent moves towards floating exchange rates, deregulation, liberalization of capital and full globalization of international financial markets, it is now becoming imperative for business managers to be familiar with the basic principles and operations of the international financial system.

Many texts on international business, particularly when dealing with international financial management, presuppose a body of financial knowledge that most first-year business students or junior managers do not necessarily possess. The purpose of this chapter is simply to introduce the international finance system. It will explain how the foreign exchange market operates, and how other international money markets may be used in financing international business.

LEARNING OBJECTIVES

- To introduce the international financial system and explain how it affects international business
- To describe how the foreign exchange market operates and how it is used in commercial and financial transactions
- To explain the reasons for the rise and growth of Eurodollar markets and to provide guidance on how these can be used by business managers to finance international operations and to protect the financial value of the company's assets.

THE INTERNATIONAL FINANCIAL SYSTEM

In order to conduct international business an internationally accepted financial system must exist to provide a payment mechanism for settling international financial transactions arising from trade, to offer facilities for financing international business operations, and to help allocate funds for their use around the world.

The current globalization of the international financial system can be best understood within its historical context. There have been three principal types of international monetary regime (Argy, 1981, pp. 1–2), each representing an important stage in the gradual development of the process of globalization:

1. The gold standard (1880–1914 and 1925–1931).
2. The Bretton Woods system (1946–1973).
3. Deregulation and financial liberalization (1980s) to which we can now add an emerging stage which is the 'globalization of financial markets since the late 1990s' (O'Brien, 1992).

The gold standard

The first formal organization of international monetary relations was established in 1865 in Europe with the foundation of the Latin Monetary Union. This system was based on the use of bimetallic currencies which were acceptable to all members of the Union and against which the values of their own currencies were determined (Khambata and Ajami, 1992).

The bimetallic standard was replaced in 1880 by the gold standard until the outbreak of the First World War in 1914. Under the gold standard regime the accepted monetary standard for settling international business transactions was gold. A government could not create money that was not backed by gold. Three major rules were essential for the establishment of the gold standard (Argy, 1981, p. 11). The first rule required each participating country to fix the price of its domestic currency in terms of gold. Exchange rates were fixed against the value of gold. Members were not allowed to let their currencies fluctuate beyond the upper or lower gold point limits. The second rule was concerned with ensuring the free import and export of gold. The third rule provided participating countries with an automatic mechanism of adjusting their balance of payments, by allowing a country with a surplus (and hence gaining gold), to increase the volume of its money, and a deficit country (losing gold) to let the volume of its money fall.

However, with the beginning of the First World War large amounts of money were needed to finance the war. Legal restrictions were imposed nationally to limit the free flow of private gold. Private holders of gold were encouraged to sell their holdings to their national governments (Melvin, 1989, p. 48). Individual governments also began to issue their own currencies without gold backing. Local currencies were devalued according to national interests by arbitrary decisions, regardless of the current value of gold. The gold standard, as a result, was dropped. The USA left the gold standard in 1933, followed by France in 1936 and Britain in 1937. Many other countries followed, causing the international financial system to collapse. No universal international financial system prevailed during the inter-war period from 1918 to 1939. Instead, international monetary warfare prevailed. Countries devalued their currencies in an attempt to stimulate their domestic industries, leading to the great depression of the 1930s.

The Bretton Woods regime (1946–1973)

The reconstruction of the post-war financial system began at the end of the Second World War. The USA, UK and 42 other nations met at Bretton Woods, in New Hampshire, USA, in 1946. The purpose of this international conference was to put an end to the collapse of the international financial system and to create a new stable and internationally acceptable monetary system. At the end of the meeting it was agreed that:

1. Since the USA was then the strongest economic power in the world, the US dollar should be the key currency in the new international financial system.
2. The value of the US dollar should be fixed against its value in gold at $0.35 per ounce.
3. Each country should fix the value of its currency in terms of gold against the US dollar.
4. All currencies should be linked in a system of fixed exchange rates. In other words, no nation would allow its currency to fluctuate by more than 1% above or below the par value.

5. Central banks were required to buy and sell their currencies in the foreign exchange market.
6. Two international financial institutions, the International Monetary Fund and the International Bank for Reconstruction and Development (World Bank), should be created to monitor the operation of the new financial system, and to ensure the stability of international monetary relations among nations so that the international economic system as a whole should be more stable.
7. All nations committed themselves to trade liberalization.

The Bretton Woods Agreement operated successfully in the 1950s and 1960s, but collapsed in the 1970s. Several factors in the global political economy contributed to its downfall (De Vries, 1985) such as the US balance of payment deficit, the creation of Eurodollar markets, the oil shocks of the 1970s and Third World demands for a new international economic order. In the 1980s the impact of new trends towards computerization, deregulation and innovation, arising from developments in information technology and international communications, led to the removal of controls over the pricing of money, interest rates and deregulation (O'Brien, 1992, p. 18). One of the most important changes here is the information technology revolution and its contribution to the 'end of geography' thesis, thus putting an end to the relevance of location for financial markets (O'Brien, 1992, Ch. 2). Participants in financial markets today need not be in the same country or even on the same continent to be trading together. New technological developments now enable traders to develop 24 hour trading in more and more areas (O'Brien, 1992, p. 9). With improved communications, it has now become less and less necessary for market participants to congregate in a single place, or in a single financial market (O'Brien, 1992, p. 16; Meerschwam, 1991).

INTERNATIONAL FINANCIAL INSTITUTIONS

Two major international financial institutions were created at the end of the Second World War to regulate and monitor the international financial system: the International Monetary Fund and the International Bank for Reconstruction and Development, widely known as the World Bank. Business managers must be aware of these two institutions, even though they may not be involved in financing private international business in a direct way. Nevertheless, their existence and activities often affect multinational firms in their international business operations. The rules of international financial dealings for example are often set at the IMF, and substantial international loan decisions are made between governments and the IMF. The World Bank is the largest international lending institution in the world, and plays a major role in promoting global economic development by providing finance for productive purposes out of its own capital, and projects lending facilities and private investment by means of guarantees and finance from private banks.

The International Monetary Fund (IMF)

The International Monetary Fund commenced operations on 1 March 1947. It was set up initially to ensure first that a stable currency which could be used by all countries for international transactions was available, and that this currency would also provide sufficient world liquidity to facilitate the non-inflationary expansion of world trade. Second, it was to ensure that all countries would abide by an agreed set of rules to regulate their money relations with other countries. Third, it would make available some form of financial assistance to countries with short-term balance of payments difficulties so that they would not have to resort to protectionism, which was seen generally as bad for international trade growth, and by some as a contributory factor to the outbreak of the Second World War. International trade liberalization was seen as the best way to increase global wealth, and consequently, of enhancing global peace.

The objectives of the IMF are clearly stated in its original Articles of Agreement agreed on 27 December 1945 at a meeting attended by representatives of the Allied governments in Washington. Briefly, the Fund's purposes, as laid out in Article I are:

1. To promote international monetary cooperation.
2. To facilitate the expansion of international trade and thus to contribute to the maintenance of high levels of employment and income.
3. To promote exchange stability, maintain orderly exchange arrangements and avoid competitive depreciation of exchange rates.
4. To assist in the multilateralization of payments and in the elimination of foreign exchange restrictions on current transactions.
5. To give confidence to members by making the fund's resources temporarily available under adequate safeguards, thus providing them with the opportunity to correct maladjustments in their balance of payments without resorting to measures conducive to recession.

The IMF's primary responsibility was to provide its members with financial aid to cover short-term gaps in their balance of payments (Korner, 1986, p. 48). Its overall aim was to facilitate the growth of world trade by providing loans to those countries that were unable to earn enough foreign currency to pay for the imports they needed (Killick and Bird, 1984).

Initially, the IMF had 40 members, but now it has more than 150 members, including Russia and countries in Eastern and Central Europe. Membership is based on subscription in the form of a quota. A member's quota is equal to its subscription to the Fund and determines largely its voting power. The USA controls 20 per cent of the voting power and the European nations hold about 28 per cent of the votes, while Third World countries cannot hold more than 35 per cent, although they represent nearly 75 per cent of the total population of IMF countries. With an 85 per cent majority requirement for major change in IMF policy, it is evident that developing countries exercise only a very limited influence on the decision-making process, because of their lack of voting strength.

The IMF was reasonably successful in the 1950s and early 1960s in terms of its stated objectives. From the late 1960s, however, changes in the global political economy began to undermine its success, particularly as a result of the growing US balance of payments deficit, the oil crisis in 1974, the creation and rapid growth of the Eurodollar markets, and demands for massive automatic transfer of resources from Third World countries.

The IMF and Third World countries   In the late 1970s and early 1980s, the IMF was heavily criticized by developing nations. Many demands for changes in the international monetary system and in the Fund were made. These demands may be divided into two categories: those aimed mainly at reforming the system itself, and those aimed at a greater transfer of resources.

Falling into the reform category were demands for a new monetary and financial system. The purpose of this new system would be to substitute a more democratic system of decision-making and control to ensure that the economically powerful industrial countries would no longer be able to impose their will upon the majority of countries (Rweyemamu, 1980, pp. 75–91; Korner, 1986, p. 154).

A new international currency was also called for by Third World countries to take over the role played by the US dollar and gold. This new currency was proposed not only as a means of exchange and reserves, but also that it be distributed among developing countries on a preferential allocation basis to boost their reserves and to end the dominant role of the US dollar (Korner, 1986, p. 154).

The second category of demands made by Third World countries were essentially oriented toward additional resource flow, and transfers to the underdeveloped countries, such as the creation of Special Drawing Rights (SDRs) to be issued for the development of the Third World (Bird, 1984, pp. 198–232), to be linked to the development needs of nations. An increase in the quotas attributed to less developed countries was proposed and the creation of at least 15 000 million SDRs per annum to be allocated to developing countries to allow them to exchange them for any hard currency, thus giving them greater access to foreign exchange with no strings attached (Korner, 1986, p. 155).

Reforms of IMF conditionality and its debt-rescheduling procedure with longer repayment periods were also called for. Finally, a request was made to the IMF for a 300 per cent increase in the Fund's Compensatory Financing Facility to compensate fully for the export-related loss of earnings due to defective policies imposed by the IMF.

The IMF response to Third World demands   Initially, the IMF tried to respond to pressures from the Third World by enlarging the range of its facilities rather than by changing its policy conditions. But with the energy crisis of the 1970s, and the collapse of the Bretton Woods Articles of Agreement, potentially significant changes took place within the IMF, such as the establishment of the Oil Facility (OF) to assist countries to cope with the payment implications of the increased cost of oil – a subsidy account to assist less developed countries that had been seriously affected by the Oil Crisis. The Extended Fund Facility and the Trust Fund were established to provide assistance to members to meet their balance of payments deficits for longer periods, together with larger amounts of low conditionality and concessionary balance of payments assistance. An increase in members' quotas was also approved in 1975, as well as the sale of one sixth of the IMF's gold to be used solely for the benefit of developing countries.

Despite these institutional reforms, many countries today are reluctant to use the IMF as a source of finance due to the high conditionality it attaches to its loans, especially where connected commercial loans are concerned. Three major crises provide an insight into the consequences of IMF conditionality.

In the Jamaican experience (1972–1980), despite the sacrifices they implied for the majority of the Jamaican people, IMF policies failed to solve the crisis of the Jamaican economy, precisely because their analysis of the problem, rising imports and falling exports caused by excessive wage rises, proved to be incorrect. The experience of Chile (1965–1970) under the government of General Pinochet is another example of the failure of the IMF policies to work, despite their implementations by a government ideologically attuned to the IMF economic view. The Peruvian case (1968–1974), like that of Jamaica and Chile, illustrates the tremendous social cost that IMF policies bring with them. (For a detailed case study see De Vries (1973). A more comprehensive account can be found in Killick (1984), where the author analyses in detail three individual case studies dealing with economic management and the role of the IMF in Indonesia (1966–70), Jamaica (1972–80) and Kenya (1973–81). He also deals with Latin American cases, such as that of Chile (1965–70), the Velasco administration in Peru (1968–75) and the Allende administration in Chile (1970–73). It is argued from these case studies that, for example, the Velasco period in Peru and the Allende period in Chile both ended with the economies suffering major payments crises. In the case of Chile (1975–79), it is argued that combining fiscal and monetary restraint with major reforms in trade and financial fields seriously exacerbated the stabilization problems. Other case studies have been analysed in Korner (1986): the Brazilian crisis (1983–85), the Portugal experience (1977–83), Zaire (1974–85) and Jamaica (1977–80). These all reflect the failure or the impotence of IMF stabilization policies.) Current borrowers from the IMF include a number of highly indebted countries like Mexico, Venezuela and Eastern European Countries such as Poland and Hungary, as well as the world's poorest countries, like Ghana, Nepal, Madagascar and Togo.

The International Bank for Reconstruction and Development (IBRD)

The World Bank is the largest international lending institution in the world, and began its operation in 1946. The World Bank's original purpose was to assist in the reconstruction of war-devastated Europe, and to provide loans for economic development and project lending.

The main functions of the World Bank, as stated in its Articles of Agreement are:

1. To promote private foreign investment by means of guarantees and participation and if necessary to supplement this investment by providing finance for production purposes out of its own capital, funds raised by it, and other resources.
2. To promote trade and balance of payments equilibrium by encouraging international invest-ment for the development of productive resources.
3. To ensure that priority projects are dealt with first.
4. To conduct its operations with due regard to the effort of international investment on business conditions in its member territories.

The World Bank has three main sub-agencies:

- The International Development Association
- The International Finance Corporation
- The Multilateral Investment Guarantee Agency

World Bank operations

In some ways, the World Bank operates similarly to an ordinary investment bank. It borrows funds in the international capital markets, and lends the proceeds to developing countries. The World Bank offers long-term lending facilities at a fixed interest rate. The standard terms of the bank's loans are between seven to ten years grace and twenty five years maturity, repayable in annuity form.

During the first fifteen years of its operation, the World Bank operated basically as a project lender, taking a very 'banker-like' attitude to loans, financing only specific projects that promised to generate sufficient profits to enable repayment of the loan (MacBean and Snowden, 1981, p. 215). The Bank initially treated all borrowers alike with respect to interest rates, giving no special treatment to selected countries either on the basis of differences in credit-worthiness or on the size of shareholdings or size of loans (Mason and Asher, 1973, p. 154).

In the 1970s, however, under the Presidency of Robert McNamara, the Bank's approach became more oriented towards a basic human needs approach to development, at least in respect of the very poor Third World countries (Ayres, 1983, p. 10). This was reflected in the changes in the Bank's lending activities for development. In fiscal year 1968, for example, Bank lending for agriculture and rural development amounted to only $172.5 million, 18.1 per cent of its total lending. By fiscal year 1981, it had risen to $3.8 billion, or 31 per cent of total lending (World Bank Annual Report, 1968). Bank lending for agriculture and rural development in the single fiscal year of 1981 was almost four times as much as total bank lending during the period from 1946 to 1968 (World Bank International Development Association Annual Report, 1968).

Over 50 per cent of the Bank's lending for agriculture and rural development in 1974 to 1978 was accounted for by 210 rural development projects, in which more than half of the direct benefits were expected to accrue to the rural poor. From 1972, when the Bank made its first housing loan for a project in Dakar, Senegal, through to the end of fiscal year 1981, the Bank undertook 52 basic urbanization projects, representing total loan commitments of $1.6 billion. Approximately $202 million were committed for health components of projects over the fiscal years from 1976 to 1981. In addition the Bank approved 23 population projects by the end of fiscal year 1980, involving bank lending of $421.9 million.

This trend however, did not continue into the 1980s, because first, as is the case with the IMF, the World Bank's lending policies often forced borrowing governments to adopt harsh domestic austerity programmes which were disastrous for the people of the country which the Bank tried to help. Evidence in support of this claim is found in several cases where the Bank has interfered with the development policies of the countries to which it has extended its loans.[1] Second, despite the fact that under its Articles of Agreement the Bank is instructed to be non-political in its operations,[2] evidence of political pressure by the Bank is overwhelming.[3] Third, the rapid development and growth of the Eurodollar markets in the late 1970s and 1980s have made international financing through private banks more accessible to Third World countries, although such lending is very often tied to World Bank approval.

Regional development banks

In addition to the World Bank and the IMF, there are other official financial institutions, but these are limited to particular geographic areas and are known as regional development banks. Their aims are:

1. To foster economic and social development within their geographical area.
2. To provide loans and technical assistance to industrial, agriculture and infrastructure projects.
3. To formulate regional development plans.
4. To encourage private investment from both within and outside the region.

---

[1] Details of case studies may be found in Prayer (1982), where the author illustrates in detail how the Bank's development projects have adversely affected the interests of the poor. Such projects are listed as road construction, dams, agricultural reforms, exploitation of mineral resources and forest resources. See also George (1976) for more empirical evidence about the failure of the Bank's development projects. Hayter (1985) argues further that Bank projects do not help the poor but increase poverty and inequality.

[2] Articles of Agreement: Article IV Section 10: 'The Bank and its officers shall not interfere in the political affairs of any member, nor shall they be influenced in their decision by the political character of the members concerned. Only economic considerations shall be relevant to their decision and these considerations shall be weighted impartially in order to achieve the purpose of the Bank'.

[3] One can site, for example, the case of the Bank's minimal operations in Peru following the nationalization of the International Petroleum Company by the Government of Juan Velasco in 1969, or the case of Chile, where the Bank made no new loans to Salvador Allende from 1970 to 1973. Nor did it lend to Peronist Argentina from 1973 to 1976. In the case of Vietnam, following the domestic political controversy in the USA attendant upon an IDA credit to that country in fiscal year 1979, McNamara finally agreed that there would be no additional lending to unified Vietnam (Ayres, 1983, p. 57).

Some of the more important of these banks are:

- The Inter-American Development Bank, founded in 1959 in Washington DC to provide loans for economic and social development in Latin America. It also raises funds for development projects, and provides technical assistance to Latin American countries.
- The Asian Development Bank, established in 1966 in Manilla, Philippines, to provide development financing and technical assistance to Asian regions.
- The African Development Bank, also created in 1966, in Abidjan, Ivory Coast, to help reduce the economic dependence of African nations on their former colonial rulers, and to support joint economic projects among these nations.
- The European Investment Bank, established in 1958 in Luxembourg to fund investments projects in the European Communities.
- The Islamic Development Bank, created in 1975 in Saudi Arabia to finance foreign trade and provide loans for economic development projects, and the Arab Investment Corporation, which is an association of all Arab nations established to finance development projects in Islamic countries.

THE FOREIGN EXCHANGE SYSTEM

If money is the language of business, foreign exchange is the language of international business.

(Buckley, 1990)

The major difference between domestic and international business, besides cultural diversity, referred to in Chapter Four, is the use of different national currencies. While in domestic transactions only one currency is used, nearly all international business transactions require two or more currencies. The exchange of foreign currencies is more difficult and complex than the exchange of goods and services. The values of foreign currencies fluctuate daily, and can often affect international business firms quite dramatically. Even companies that operate purely within the domestic market are affected by international currency fluctuations because their foreign competitors will be affected by these fluctuations, and this is one clear sign of the increased globalization of international business in the modern world.

International business managers must be aware of these fluctuations, which can make a company lose operating profits for the year in foreign exchange losses, or increase its profits through exchange gains. It is therefore important to understand how foreign exchange rates are determined, how the foreign exchange market operates, and how best to use it in commercial and financial transactions.

The foreign exchange market

The foreign exchange (FX) market is a market where financial institutions, commercial banks, business firms, governments or their central banks, and individuals, tourists, speculators or investors buy and sell foreign currencies. The total world foreign exchange market is the largest of all markets in the world. Foreign exchange deals worldwide averaged $850 billion per day in 1989 (Buckley, 1990, p. 1).

The foreign exchange market does not refer to any specific geographical location. Since all transactions are done through a complex communication network of telephones, faxes, telexes, cables and communication satellites, the location for the foreign exchange for the US dollar, for example, could be anywhere in the world where the specific currency is purchased or sold. This could be in Hong Kong, London, Frankfurt or even Bahrain. Due to the variation in time zones between one location and another, and the technological revolution in communications and information processing which has reduced the time between transactions (Watchel, 1986, p. 18), foreign exchange markets now work around the clock. Instantaneous electronic communication via satellite enables vast sums of money to be moved anywhere in the world in a matter of seconds: 'The sun never sets on these financial empires' (O'Brien *et al.*, 1980). Citibank, for example, advertises that it never sleeps. 'As evening comes to America, US Bank deposits are, in a sense, released from duty, because no transactions take place for which their tutelary presence is required. Consequently, the out of service deposits are loaned over-night by Citibank and all other big banks to financial centres such as Hong Kong or Singapore, where the business day has just begun. There the deposits play their formal role of backing credit transactions until the sun sets in the Orient and the time comes for the funds, like Cinderella, to return to work in America' (Heilbroner, 1983).

Structure of the foreign exchange market

Transactions in the foreign exchange market can be classified into three areas:

- *The customer or retail market* is where individuals or companies buy and sell foreign currencies to commercial banks dealing in foreign exchange. Participants include importers, exporters, portfolio managers, central banks and foreign exchange brokers.
- *The interbank market* is where commercial banks deals with each other. Banks purchase and sell currencies from and to one another. Interbank transactions are usually very large sums between $1 million and $50 million per transaction, with a daily volume in excess of $100 billion (Levi, 1990, p. 30)
- *The central banks market* is where central banks engage in foreign exchange transactions in order to control the value of their currencies (Asheghian and Ebrahimi, 1990, p. 141).

The foreign exchange market performs a number of functions that are essential to international business. On the one hand, foreign exchange markets assist multinationals in making and receiving international payments and in paying and receiving royalties from licensing partners. On the other hand, foreign exchange markets facilitate the use of credit transactions through the use of Bills of Exchange and Letters of Credit.

Instruments used in the foreign exchange market

There are various instruments used by multinational firms in the foreign exchange markets (Asheghian and Ebrahimi, 1990, pp. 141–6). These are:

- Cash in national currencies
- Deposits in commercial banks
- Cable transfers
- Bills of Exchange
- Bank Drafts
- Letters of Credit
- Export documentary drafts

Cash in national currencies is payments made in the national currency, such as bank notes circulating in particular countries.

Deposits in commercial banks are when the monetary payments are made through transferring ownership of bank deposits from one company to another.

A cable transfer is an order transmitted by one bank to another bank in a foreign country with instructions to pay a specific amount to a designated person or account.

A Bill of Exchange is a written order to pay a certain amount of money specified in the Bill to a specified person or company. These are mostly used in the financing of export–import transactions. If the Bill of Exchange is payable on presentation it is called a Sight Bill. A Time Bill is when the payment is to be made at a certain date in the future. The most common credit periods are either 30 days, 90 days or 180 days.

A bank draft is similar to a Bill of Exchange, except here the Bank is the drawee instead of an individual or a company.

A commercial Letter of Credit is issued by a bank upon the request of an importer, declaring that payment should be made to an exporter regarding a specific shipment of commodities upon the presentation of shipment documents. A Letter of Credit guarantees payment, and reduces the possibilities of delays in payments.

A document draft is used to pay for an export transaction. These are usually accompanied by documents showing the price of the goods traded, such as the commercial invoice, the bill of lading (to provide evidence of shipment), and the marine insurance certificate. An importer cannot secure the possession of the imported goods unless these documents are released to the importer. These documents are normally released only after the importer accepts to pay the draft (Asheghian and Ebrahimi, 1990, pp. 114–5).

Types of foreign exchange market

There are two types of foreign exchange markets: the spot exchange markets and the forward, futures and options markets (Levi, 1990, p. 27–74)

The spot market involves the exchange of currencies in the form of cheques drawn on different currency-denominated bank accounts bearing an immediate delivery or value, or in the form of cash where payments of one currency into the other is completed on the same day. The advantage of using the spot market is the immediate delivery of the foreign currency at the current exchange rate, thus avoiding the risk of fluctuations in the exchange rate which might result before the delivery of the foreign currency at a later date.

The forward contract market is an agreement between two parties to exchange one currency for another at some future date at a fixed rate mutually agreed upon. The time and the actual exchange of currencies can range from two weeks to more than a year. The main advantage of using the forward markets is that the firm can negotiate a fixed rate in advance with their bank. The bank, in return, is obliged to purchase the currency for the exporter at the agreed-upon rate regardless of the rate that prevails on the day when the foreign currency is actually delivered by the exporter. Forward contracts are popular with customers and firms who want to avoid fluctuations in foreign exchange rates, particularly when buyers and sellers are not sure when the need for foreign currency will arise or when they will receive it. Intel Corporation, for example, reported in 1990 more than $405 million in forward contracts. Forward contracts are also particularly useful for protection against currency fluctuations. They give international traders the exact amounts of receipts in terms of foreign currencies.

Foreign exchange futures or currency futures are agreements to buy or sell at a fixed amount of foreign currency for delivery at a fixed future date and at a fixed dollar price (or other price). Buyers and sellers enter into foreign exchange futures through a contract clearing corporation rather than with each other. Future contracts are limited to only a very few currencies: Canadian dollars, German marks, French francs, Swiss francs, British pounds, Japanese yen, the ECU and Australian dollars.

Unlike currency futures, under foreign currency options buyers have the opportunity and also the right to buy and sell the foreign currency at a pre-agreed exchange rate in the future if this is to their advantage, but without any obligation to do so. Buyers could let their options expire without exchanging currencies if it is better for them to use the spot exchange rate. The maturity date for forward options is also left open, contrary to forward contracts where the exchange rate is irrevocably fixed for a certain date when the contract is signed (Buckley, 1990; Biger and Hull, 1983, pp. 24–9; Giddy, 1983, pp. 143–166).

Forward, futures and currency options markets are all used to avoid foreign exchange risks. There are other techniques used for managing exposure to foreign exchange rate fluctuations, but before detailing these methods of dealing with foreign exchange risk it is necessary to define what is meant by foreign exchange rates.

Foreign exchange rates are the prices at which different national currencies are traded for one another in the foreign exchange markets. These are determined largely by the interaction of demand and supply in the foreign exchange market. Many journals and newspapers report foreign exchange rates daily. Foreign exchange rates are partly determined by domestic factors that cause fluctuations, such as rates of inflation, interest rates or devaluation of the national currency. Spot and forward rates also fluctuate as a result of more international factors in the political environment, for example expected economic growth rate, economic stability, production and consumption rates. For example, if a war is expected in a particular country, the spot exchange rate may drop drastically due to the anticipated political unrest in that country.

Hedging is a way of managing foreign exchange risk. It usually takes place in the spot market or forward market, although more often in the latter. Hedging in the forward market eliminates the need to borrow funds or to tie up a certain amount of money for a period of time (Levi, 1990, pp. 225–52; Khoury and Hung Chan, 1988, pp. 40–52; Smithson, 1987, pp. 126–8).

Speculation is the opposite of hedging, but also operates in the spot or forward markets. Speculation in the spot market requires the speculators to purchase a foreign currency in either the spot or forward market using their own money or to borrow money with the intention of selling it at a later date at a higher future spot rate.

Currency swaps are an arrangement between two firms or a firm and a central bank or commercial bank, to exchange one currency for another at a certain time in the future, and at exactly the same amount of the original currency that was exchanged at the time of the swap. The advantage of a currency swap arrangement is that it does not expose the parent company to an exchange loss that might result from fluctuations in the foreign exchange market. Credit swaps are useful when an affiliate of a multinational firm needs local credit and cannot get it. The headquarters can deposit a certain amount of dollars in a central bank, which in turn gives a loan to the subsidiary in the local currency. Once the loan is repaid by the subsidiary, the original deposit is then returned to the multinational firm's headquarters, irrespective of the going exchange rate.

Arbitrage is when a currency is purchased in one market where it is cheaper, and sold in another market where it is more expensive in order to make profit from the differences in spot exchange and price quotations. This is also known as triangular arbitrage. Opportunities for arbitrage are becoming very rare in the 1990s due to modern information technology, which almost instantaneously eliminates the exchange rate differences before they are spotted by traders, and before the transfer itself can actually cause fluctuation.

Dramatic changes in exchange rate volatility have increased considerably in the last decade. Billions of dollars, yen, marks, pounds and francs are made and lost in a day as a result of these currency fluctuations (Levi, 1990, p. 11). This increased volatility of exchange rates makes it necessary for business managers to find more stable alternatives for raising capital and financing their international business operations.

International money markets

International money markets takes a number of different forms, and deal with many different money instruments. These include, for example, the Eurodollar market, the Eurocurrency market and the Eurobond market. The daily volume of transactions on these markets is estimated at about $500 billion (Vernon and Wells, 1991, p. 62).

The Eurodollar market

The development of the Eurodollar market started in the 1950s, after the Second World War and at a time when the USA was still occupying a clearly dominant position in international trade and in the world economy. Initially, the Eurodollar market started outside the USA, in money market dealing with the US dollars in Europe. Today, however, the Eurodollar market is not limited geographically to Europe but has a very large presence also in Tokyo, Hong Kong and Bahrain.

There are a number of reasons for the rise and growth of the Eurodollar market. One of the major reasons for the original creation of Eurodollar accounts deposited in banks outside the USA was Regulation Q of the United State Federal Reserve System, which limited US banks and other deposit-taking institutions to the maximum interest rate they could offer on deposits. To avoid the US interest ceiling on deposits, US investors started to deposit their dollars outside the USA, in London and other centres, where they would not be subjected to such interest limitations. As a result, many US banks opened branches overseas to receive these funds.

Another factor behind the growth of the Eurodollar market is the Federal Reserve Regulation M, which required the keeping of reserves against deposits. Various other regulations by the Federal Reserve System, such as the need to pay for deposit insurance on deposits held in the USA, or the tax deductions levied at source by the US tax authorities on some foreign deposits in interest-earning accounts held in the USA (Vernon and Wells, 1991, p. 70), also contributed to the growth of the Eurodollar market. The US Interest Equalization Tax, introduced in 1963, is another US regulation that has affected foreign demand for Eurodollar loans. This is a tax on US residents' earnings on foreign securities (Levi, 1990, p. 266). With deposits going abroad to escape Regulation Q, banks going abroad to escape Regulation M and the US Federal Reserve, and borrowing going abroad to escape the interest equalization tax and credit and direct investment controls, the Eurodollar market expanded very rapidly, and became an important sign of increased global financial integration within the overall process of globalization (Gunter and Giddy, 1978; Levi, 1990, p. 263).

The Eurocurrency market

The Eurocurrency market is an international monetary market in which funds are deposited and borrowed from commercial banks. The Eurocurrency market deals with major world currencies, including the US dollar, Japanese yen, French franc, Swiss franc, German mark and British pound.

The term Eurocurrency itself simply means currencies deposited outside the country of their origin. Eurocurrencies are also often referred to as 'stateless money' (*Business Week*, 21 August

1978, pp. 76–8) and can be deposited in any non-European financial markets such as Hong Kong, Singapore and Tokyo.

The Eurocurrency market performs two major functions. The first function consists of lending money deposited by the original owners to financial institutions which then lend the money on to end users. The second function relates specifically to international transactions, which the international financial institutions lend to each other (McKinnon, 1977, pp. 8–9).

The size of the Eurocurrency market grew from $400 billion in 1975 to $3 trillion in 1990 (Matsuura, 1991, p. 281). Several factors have contributed to this rapid growth. Originally the former Soviet Union was very much interested in investing in the Eurocurrency markets, because although it wanted to maintain currency deposits in US dollars to be able to pay for purchases from the West, it was reluctant to deposit them directly in US banks because of the risk of having them confiscated or frozen by the US in case of international conflicts (Buckley, 1990, p. 5).

During the 1960s and 1970s, many countries, particularly the OPEC nations, deposited their US dollars in European banks. The absence of banking regulations in the Eurocurrency market, such as controlling interest rates on loans, exchange controls, deposit controls and other banking regulations imposed in many countries, made it attractive to many multinational firms to deposit their funds. Additionally, there are few restrictions on entry. Any country's bank can set up in the Eurocurrency market easily, without any restrictions on bank transactions or government scrutiny. Moreover, since large volumes of transactions are conducted in the Eurocurrency market with deposits and loans made in millions of US dollars, the Eurocurrency market can keep average transaction costs low and provide the lowest possible interest loans, and thus offer a good return to depositors.

Business firms too, can earn substantial returns on temporary surplus funds while keeping their liquid assets available (Weekly and Aggarwal, 1987, pp. 234–6). The Eurocurrency market provides them with the possibility of borrowing against their Eurocurrency deposits if they need cash quickly. Loans available to multinational firms in the Eurocurrency market range from a short time period, such as overnight, to several months, in amounts from a few hundreds to billions of dollars.

The Eurocurrency market furthermore provides better security, due to the large amount of transactions conducted with deposits and loans made in millions of dollars.

Finally, the Eurocurrency market provides Certificate of Deposit (CD) facilities. Investors who buy CDs are assured a fixed interest rate until their CDs mature, with an option to resell their CDs for cash at any time if they wish to do so (Weekly and Aggarwal, 1987, pp. 235–6).

Eurocurrency centres today exist in Western Europe in London, Zurich, Paris and the Channel Islands; in the Caribbean in Central America, the Cayman Islands and the Bahamas; in the Middle East in Bahrain; in Asia in Singapore, Hong Kong and Tokyo; and in the USA.

The Eurobond market

The Eurobond market developed in the mid-1960s as an extension of the Eurocurrency market (McKinnon, 1977, p. 10). The Eurobond market is a bond capital market through which funds are raised on a long-term basis via the marketing of debt securities (Weekly and Aggarwal, 1987, p. 237). Bonds are issued as long-term securities. Eurobonds are issued in one or more countries, in currencies other than the local ones, and are payable in currencies other than that of the country of the issuer of the bond. Eurobonds are also marketed outside the country in which the issuer is located. The major borrowers in the Eurobond markets are governments, international financial institutions and private multinational firms.

The rapid rate of growth and development of the Eurobond market was mainly due to the financial needs of large corporations and governments. In 1989, the Eurobond market was estimated to be more than $90 billion, as compared with $8.6 billion in 1975 and $24 billion in 1980 (Morgan Guarantee Trust, 1986–89).

The Eurobond market developed for the same reasons as the Eurocurrency market, but with some additional advantages. Eurobonds offer a way for investors to avoid paying local taxes. In the Eurobond market there is no withholding tax deducted at sources, since all bonds are issued offshore. Eurobond purchasers are also not required to be identified or registered. Investors can therefore maintain their anonymity, and avoid declaring interest payments on their investment income. The international character of the Eurobond has also contributed largely to its rapid growth. Eurobonds can be marketed in several countries simultaneously. They can also be made payable in any one currency or even in a number of different national currencies.

Eurobond markets can be categorized into two groups: foreign bonds and Eurobonds.

Foreign bonds are bonds issued by foreign borrowers in a nation's domestic capital market, and are denominated in the nation's domestic currency: Yankee Bonds in the USA, Samurai Bonds in Japan, Rembrandt Bonds in the Netherlands and Bulldog Bonds in London.

Eurobonds are denominated in a particular currency and are usually issued simultaneously in the capital markets of several nations. They differ from foreign bonds in that most nations do not have registration or disclosure requirements, nor restrictions on the timing or amount of issues. The predominant currencies in Eurobonds are the US dollar, the German mark, ECU, the Canadian dollar and the Dutch guilder.

Because of the wide diversity of investors involved in the process, the placement of Eurobonds requires the involvement of a number of financial institutions.

1. The borrower normally asks a major international bank to arrange for the issue of the bond.
2. The international bank then arranges a large syndicate, with a worldwide group of underwriters, to approve the issuance of the bond.
3. Once the underwriters approve the issuance of the bond, a firm offer is made by the international bank to the borrower.

Information technology and the Euromarkets

The development and operations of the Eurodollar, Eurocurrency and Eurobond markets and their increased significance in the international financial system would not have been possible without the development of new communications and information technologies (Watchel, 1986, p. 18).

International transactions in the Euromarkets are arranged by bankers' dealers over the telephone, or by telex, telematics (which are the merger of telecommunications technology with data processing technology), satellite communications and computerized systems linking banks throughout the world and allowing 24 hour global banking. All of these modern telecommunications facilities have overcome time, distance and territorial boundaries (United Nations, 1985, p. 86).

On-line access to information through telecommunication networks is a development in information technology which has greatly benefited banks in their interbank transactions. There are various types of on-line database available.

The Securities Database covers information on stocks and on bonds. It contains historical and instantaneous price quotations for stocks and bonds in London, New York and Toronto.

The Financial Database contains detailed financial information about the world economy and/or the economies of individual countries.

The FX Share Database covers securities from over 30 world capital markets. The data for each security includes historical and current pricing, dividend and capitalization information, redemption date and stock exchange related items.

The Economists' Statistics provides daily, weekly and monthly time series of international interest rates, currency exchange rates, and major stock market indicators from London, New York, Toronto, Hong Kong, Singapore, Sydney, Paris and Tokyo.

International Financial Statistics contains information about financial markets and developments for over 70 countries. It has data on exchange rates, international liquidity, interest rates, prices and production, commodities, national accounts, government spending and international transactions.

SWIFT was set up in 1973. SWIFT is not strictly speaking part of an international funds transfer network, but it does provide a means by which messages can be exchanged between banks internationally. The system allows finance houses to buy and sell in a single worldwide market, and to make loans anywhere and at any time (Hamelink, 1983, pp. 62–5).

EUREX is another computer-based telecommunications network set up in 1973 by a group of 60 banks from 14 European countries. EUREX consists of a network of international leased lines connecting most of the European financial centres, with the key processing unit based in Luxembourg. Its purpose is to cover the whole range of information trading and back office services for the Eurobond market (Hamelink, 1983, p. 62).

REVIEW QUESTIONS

1. Why was the International Monetary Fund set up? Assess its role in the international monetary system.
2. 'The World Bank may take an interest in development but it can never become a development agency'. Discuss.
3. Why is the financing of operations abroad more difficult than the financing of domestic operations?
4. Currencies constantly change in value. Those fluctuations pose risks and opportunities for multinational firms. What can multinationals do to minimize their exposure to exchange rate losses? Describe the various methods that can be used, and list the advantages and disadvantages of each method.
5. Eurodollars are frequently referred to as 'stateless money'. Explain what this means.
6. How are interbank transactions completed in the Eurocurrency market and what methods are used during these operations?
7. What factors have contributed to the development of the Eurodollar market?
8. How have new international communication and information technologies contributed to the development and expansion of international money markets?

EXERCISE 5.1: Operating in the international money markets

Aim The aim of this exercise is to assist students to understand how the foreign exchange market and the international money markets may be used in order to pay for international transactions or to protect the company's financial assets.

Assignment Suppose you are the manager of a multinational that plans to import product X from country Y. The currency of country X is expected to change in value soon. What should you do to anticipate any loss, if the currency does eventually drop?

Format Students are asked to choose a particular country and investigate its foreign exchange fluctuations in relation to the question above. A brief presentation to the class should follow explaining how they plan to use the FX market to pay for the goods in that particular country.

FURTHER READING

Ayres, R. L., *Banking on the Poor: The World Bank and World Poverty*, MIT Press, Cambridge MA, 1983.

Chapman, C., *How the Stock Market Works. A Guide to the International Markets*, Hutchinson, London, 1991.

Jacques, L. C., Management of Foreign Exchange Risk. A Review Aricle, *Journal of International Business Studies*, Spring/Summer 1981, pp. 81–103.

MacBean, A. I. and Snowden, P. N., *International Institutions in Finance and Trade*, Allen & Unwin, London, 1981.

Mason, E. and Asher, R., *The World Bank since Bretton Woods*, Brookings Institute, Washington, 1973.

Redhead, K., *Introduction to International Money Markets*, Woodhead Faulkner, Cambridge, 1992

Weisweiller, R., *Introduction to Foreign Exchange*, Woodhead Faulkner, Cambridge, 1983.

THE INTERNATIONALIZATION OF BUSINESS

In addition to understanding the specific international environment of business, it is essential for business managers to be fully aware of the changes in the global political economy more generally and how these might affect their international business operations. Structural changes in the global political economy in recent history have altered the relationship between governments and firms, particularly in the context of international trade. While free trade, managed internationally through such institutions as Bretton Woods and GATT, flourished after the end of the Second World War, the era of the 1960s and 1970s witnessed increased national and inter-governmental intervention in regulating international trade. The early 1980s, on the other hand, seemed to call for the total retreat of the state. Privatization and deregulation of trade and finance led to the globalization of markets in the late 1980s and early 1990s, causing increased global competition, and fierce rivalry between governments and firms in their efforts to survive in global markets. Levels of increasingly differentiated development and possibilities for trade between advanced economies (USA, Japan, UK, France and Germany) and less developed countries became starker and the subject of increasing conflict and debate between the so-called northern and southern hemispheres.

The purpose of Part Two is to assist business managers in understanding the directions of contemporary world trade, and to provide them with an analytical framework upon which to base their future strategic plans for international business operations.

Chapter Six provides a comprehensive overview of classical theories of international trade in an attempt to explain why international trade originally took place and to assess its practical relevance in today's global production, distribution and market sites.

Chapter Seven examines the recent trends towards modern strategic theories of international trade, focusing more on the development of the firm and its role in international trade and in the process of globalization.

Chapter Eight examines changing conceptions of the role of government intervention in international trade, in order to provide a better understanding of the increasingly blurred relationship between states (public sector) and firms (private sector) of the 1990s, which seems likely to develop further along these lines into the 21st century.

The central aim of this part of the book is to alert students and practitioners of international business to the increasingly globalized nature of the international political economy. This is so that they might better appreciate that it is no longer sufficient to see the world in terms of separate national political economies or states, existing as relatively discrete units, with simply different domestic levels of economic infrastructure and development, education, capabilities, resources, culture and political organization, and in a context where the 'international dimension' is constructed as a separate, wholly different environment, external to them all. Part of what the historical process of globalization means, particularly since the end of the Second World War, is that these very same 'domestic', or national, conditions are now, to a very large extent, structurally determined or conditioned by the location of a particular country or state within a highly organized, managed and governed global political economy.

THE INTERNATIONALIZATION OF TRADE

The aim of this chapter is to explain why many countries trade even when they might be capable of producing all of the products they need more cheaply than their trading partners.

LEARNING OBJECTIVES

- To explain why international trade takes place
- To examine the historical development in international trade since the Second World War
- To provide a comprehensive overview of classical theories of international trade and to assess their relevance to contemporary international business

THE IMPORTANCE OF INTERNATIONAL TRADE

There are various reasons offered why international trade developed and why many countries trade even when they can produce many products more cheaply than their trading partners.

One of the major incentives claimed to lead to international trade is that of economic advantage. A recent textbook on international management describes international trade as follows: 'International trade creates value. It increases the efficiency of resource allocation worldwide, reduces production costs through economies of scale, lowers input costs and, through the international division of labour, lowers prices paid by consumers and increases product variety and availability' (Beamish *et al.*, 1991, p. 17).

The prospect of mutual benefit is another crucial dynamic behind international trade. Business firms and governments are unlikely to engage voluntarily in international trade if they do not expect either to improve their economic situation or to achieve any material gain in return (Weekly and Aggarwal, 1987, Ch. 5). It might, for example, be cheaper for them to acquire certain agricultural products from abroad than locally due to physical conditions, such as differences in soil, climate or natural resources. Some countries might have a large supply of certain products that other countries do not have, and are able to sell it more cheaply to them than a comparable domestically based producer, such as, for example, the case of coal production and consumption in the UK today and the recent plans to close down much of British Coal by the government.

Variations in the costs of production constitute another incentive for international trade to occur. Many countries find it more advantageous to specialize in the production of certain goods in which they have a greater efficiency in utilizing their resources, which provides them with a superior advantage over their competitors. International trade might also provide them with the benefits of large-scale production, which would be impossible if they had to concentrate on their domestic markets only.

Despite its claimed advantages, international trade has often caused serious international conflict, trade wars and even military hostilities between states. To understand better the effects of international trade on international business today and to determine the extent to which it could bring gains and losses to governments and firms, it is necessary for business managers to be aware of changes in the global political economy and how these might affect their international business operations.

THE DEVELOPMENT OF INTERNATIONAL TRADE SINCE THE END OF THE SECOND WORLD WAR

International trade has increased dramatically during the post-Second World War period. Total world trade, valued in US dollars, increased steadily from $50 billion in 1948 to nearly $2 trillion in 1980 (Weekly and Aggarwal, 1987, p. 48), surpassing $4.5 trillion in 1989 (Matsuura, 1991, p. 21). Various economic, political, technological and demographic factors have contributed to this dramatic expansion, mainly due to the international efforts launched at the end of the Second World War by the USA and its allies as part of a broad programme of European recovery and an economic reconstruction and development plan. The USA suffered minimal destruction during the war. In 1945 its industrial might, agricultural plenty, technological leadership and relatively great economic strength were preserved. Its influence over world commercial policies during that period surpassed that of any other country. The USA was therefore in a strong position to push actively for the liberalization of trade among Western European countries (Spero, 1990, p. 72). Two major international organizations were created during that period to regulate the international economy and to avoid a retreat into protectionism. These were the International Monetary Fund (IMF), to ensure the stabilization of the exchange rate and the world economy, and the World Bank (WB), to provide loans for reconstruction and economic development (together known as the Bretton Woods system). The General Agreement on Tariffs and Trade (GATT), to regulate international trade, was established in 1948 as a major multilateral treaty between states in the first instance and prior to de-colonization by the major advanced economies.

With the liberalization of trade and the reduction of tariff and non-tariff barriers, international trade flourished between the 1950s and 1970s (Spero, 1990, p. 75). This overall economic growth improved living standards, raised the level of income, and generated a growing demand for a wider variety of consumer goods and products that are only available through trade with foreign countries (Weekly and Aggarwal, 1987, p. 75). Furthermore, new developments in communications technology contributed to spreading even wider consumers' awareness and knowledge of different products throughout the world by making it easier for firms to communicate with customers and subsidiaries globally. Technological innovations also improved transport facilities, which made it easier and cheaper for goods to be transported across borders, and for production itself to be located in foreign countries.

These favourable conditions, however, were seriously altered in the late 1970s and early 1980s. The years between 1980 and 1982 witnessed the lowest average growth (0.37 per cent per year) in the world, with unemployment rising to a record 8.5 per cent in the OECD countries. The volume of world trade growth slowed down to 1.2 per cent in 1980, 0.8 per cent in 1981 and fell by 2.2 per cent in 1981 (Spero, 1990, p. 75).

Several factors led to the deep world economic recession in the early 1980s. First, as the result of the oil crisis in the 1970s the developed countries' real GDP growth dropped by 2.7 per cent between 1974 and 1979. Inflation exploded, reaching 13.4 per cent in 1974. Unemployment in the OECD countries increased to an average of 4.9 per cent between 1974 and 1979 (Spero, 1990, p. 76). Second, as a result of the breakdown of the Bretton Woods system and the system of fixed exchange rates, world trade grew by only 5 per cent between 1979 and 1980. This is mainly because under the fixed exchange rate mechanism negotiators were able to estimate the impact of agreements on their trade and payments, but under the new floating rates such calculations became much more difficult and complicated. Additionally, the creation of the Eurocurrency markets in the late 1950s (discussed in Chapter Five), not only grew to a huge proportion in the 1970s, reaching almost $1 trillion by 1978 (Spero, 1990, p. 72), but by offering large competitive interest rates, attracted huge sums of international capital flows. Many countries, such as the UK, France, Germany, Canada, Australia and Japan started to liberalize their financial regulations to make it easier for their currencies to be used in those international financial markets. This vastly increased the volume of financial transactions, which was furthermore facilitated by the revolution of telecommunications, information processing and new developments in computer technology, thus putting additional strain on the international monetary system.

A third factor contributing to the world recession in the early 1980s was growing interdependence, and the shift towards increased global competitiveness. As a result of the high level of foreign competition, domestic producers became increasingly unable to maintain prices, profits and employment, and started to shift their investment and production towards the newly industrialized countries, such as Taiwan, Korea and Brazil, which could offer cheaper resources and labour, and often higher productivity.

As a result of such enormous pressures on the international trading and financial system, calls for protectionist measures by national governments rose (Gill and Law, 1988, p. 244). By the mid-1980s, government protectionism, however, proved ineffective in dealing with the stagflation (economic stagnation combined with inflation) of the 1970s. Disenchantment and the dismal view against government interference in international trade is clearly illustrated in Eastern Europe at the close of the 1980s and in the recent global trends towards privatization and deregulation amid calls for the state to take a 'back seat in guiding the national economy' (Ohmae, 1990a, p. 212).

To prevent the economies of trading nations and the fortunes of individual firms from declining any further it is therefore crucial for governments and firms to respond constructively to the recent changes in the global political economy, such as the new trends towards the opening up of Japan as a leader in foreign technology, trade and foreign direct investment. Theories of international trade provide a useful analytical framework upon which to base government policies on international trade and to assist business managers in formulating their international business policies and operations.

CLASSICAL THEORIES OF INTERNATIONAL TRADE

It would be wrong to assume that the study of theories of international trade itself will provide complete answers to national governments' or multinational firms' problems in dealing with international trade, or that they can be used as a basis for prediction. International trade theories are valuable in explaining the rationale for the pursuit of different policies by different nations over time. They are also useful in assisting government authorities and business managers to assess the implications of a country's decisions regarding different international economic issues thus allowing them to formulate their international trade policies better and to make better judgements as to the direction of future world trade.

Classical trade theories were developed out of certain historical periods and events. Consequently, not all of them are applicable or relevant to the contemporary world. Many have had to be modified or improved as the world has changed, but nonetheless they have provided the basis for contemporary views about trade for the construction of assumed 'expert', impartial knowledge of trade within the discipline of economics, which is seen as fundamentally different from politics, over and above the state, and subject to natural, objective historical laws, and for the generally reductionist manner in which international business continues to be thought of, analysed and practised.

Mercantilism

Mercantilism coincided with the emergence of modern nation states and the trends towards colonialism during the 17th and 18th centuries (see Hecksher (1985) for a good description of the mercantilist era). According to the theory of mercantilism, an increase in national wealth increases national power and security. National wealth here was defined as the accumulation of silver and gold coins. The power and strength of a nation for the mercantilists could only be increased through an increase in national wealth. Exports, it was argued, increased a nation's accumulation of gold coins, and imports reduced its stock. A national government's duty consequently was to increase the national wealth by encouraging exports, restricting imports and by acquiring colonies (Daniels and Radebaugh, 1992, p. 130). It is clear that on this view, the currency is seen as serving the interests of (and is thus subordinated to) the needs of political organization, and maintaining a secure state.

Mercantilism can be criticized on two major grounds. First, it is mistaken to assume that the accumulation of wealth is equal to the accumulation of gold. Gold has no value in itself unless it is used or traded for other consumption or production of goods (Rugman *et al*, 1985, p. 27). Second, the underlying assumption of a zero-sum game in international trade (that one country's gain is only achieved by another's country's loss), as implied in mercantilism is unsustainable. Increased national wealth is not limited to the accumulation of gold coins and silver. Substantial gains could, for example, be acquired from production efficiency and increased specialization in using the nation's resources in the most efficient and productive manner. Mercantilist theories are also self-defeating. According to David Hume, as a nation increases its exports it accumulates more gold and silver coins, thus increasing the money supply in the national economy. This increase in domestic money supply then creates inflation and causes a rise in domestic prices. Domestic products as a result become more expensive for foreigners to buy and cause a decrease in exports. Foreign products then become relatively cheaper than domestic products, thus causing imports to increase (Hume, 1912, p. 319).

Theories of absolute advantage

Adam Smith, in his *Wealth of Nations*, rejected the idea that wealth is synonymous with gold and argued that a nation's wealth is based on its available goods and services rather than on gold, and that some countries possess an absolute advantage in producing certain products or goods. This 'absolute advantage', according to Smith, may either be the result of a natural advantage or an acquired advantage. A natural advantage refers simply to climatic, natural and mineral resources, and geographical features. An acquired advantage, on the other hand, refers to special skills and technology or scientific innovations developed in the manufacturing of certain goods. According to the theory of absolute advantage, since countries have different natural or acquired advantages they should concentrate on the production of those goods in which their country has an absolute advantage and acquire or purchase from abroad those goods which it cannot produce domestically as cheaply or efficiently. In doing so, it is claimed countries trading with each other would mutually benefit from international trade, so far as the development of their national economies and national wealth was concerned.

The limitation of such an assumption is in its failure to recognize the important role of country size in determining how much and what type of product will be traded. Large countries are not only generally more self-sufficient than smaller ones, due to the variety of their climate and natural resources; they also have higher transport costs and tend to rely more on their domestic output and consumption and import much less (Daniels and Radebaugh, 1992, p. 135). Additionally, innovations and new technological advantages last only for a short period of time while other industrialized countries catch up rather quickly (Matsuura, 1991, p. 23). Finally, the theory of absolute advantage does not consider the case where a country might be able to produce all its goods with an absolute advantage. Whether there would still be incentives to international trade remains an important question.

Theory of comparative advantage

According to David Ricardo, trading countries can benefit from trade even when one of the nations has an absolute advantage in the production of both commodities. As long as the gains from trade exceed the cost of doing business internationally, Ricardo's theory of comparative advantage argues that if one country could produce each of the goods more efficiently than another, it should specialize in and export that commodity in which it is comparatively more efficient. Ricardo explained his principle of comparative advantage and its application to the trading of any goods by providing an illustration of England and Portugal and the trade of wine and cloth between the two countries. According to this theory, if England produces cloth at a third of the cost of Portugal and its cost of producing wine was half that of Portugal, then England should specialize in the production of cloth, where it has a relative advantage. Portugal, on the other hand, despite the fact that it is inferior in the production of both wine and cloth, should specialize in the production of wine and import cloth from England, since it has a lower comparative disadvantage in producing wine than cloth (Ricardo, 1971).

The logic of this argument could be similarly applied to a company manager who has to use this information as the basis for choosing countries for production and export of goods and countries for import sales. Based on the theory of comparative advantage, if, for example, the manager finds it cheaper to produce in a foreign country, then the company should manufacture the product in that country and then import it back to its own country.

The theory of comparative advantage also claims that no country will lose under free trade. Countries jointly benefit from international trade as they specialize in exporting the goods in which they have a comparative advantage and import the goods in which they have a comparative disadvantage. The weakness of such a proposition is that it assumes an equal distribution of gains and losses between the two trading countries, while in practice gains from trade could accrue to one country, or benefit only one group of that country (Rugman *et al.*, 1985, p. 30).

The theory of comparative advantage also assumes full employment of the labour force in both countries, and ignores the fact that some countries' goals may not be limited to efficiency. They might want to restrict imports to employ idle resources, even though they are not employed efficiently (Daniels and Radebaugh, 1992, p. 138), as was the case in many Eastern and Central European countries prior to the recent breakdown of Communism.

Finally, both theories of comparative and absolute advantage focus on the production of commodities and manufactured goods, while an increasing proportion of today's world trade is in the services sector. Both theories also assume full mobility of labour and production facilities and do not take into account other factors such as existing national barriers, restrictions on migration of labour, tariff barriers, transportation costs or even the use of land and capital involved in the production of goods (Khambata and Ajami, 1992, p. 62).

Factor endowment theory

Developed by Eli Hecksher and Bertil Ohlin, the theory of factor endowment focuses more particularly on labour and capital. Factor endowment refers to the relative advantage of factors of production in one country. A country that has more capital relative to its labour force, for example, is called capital-intensive, while a country with more labour relative to capital is called labour-intensive. According to the factor endowment theory, a country should specialize in the production and export of goods which uses its productive factors more abundantly. In other words, countries with an abundance of labour should export commodities which are labour-intensive because of the availability of cheaper labour, while capital-intensive countries should concentrate on the production of goods which require capital-intensive technology (Asheghian and Ebrahimi, 1990, pp. 33–4).

Despite its apparent logic, the universal application of the factor endowment theory to international trade is questionable. Both Hecksher and Ohlin, by focusing too narrowly in their analysis on the causal observation of manufacturing in relation to labour–land proportions, failed to consider the qualitative variations that can exist within a particular resource, such as in labour resources for example, and the variations in labour skills, training and education of workers, which differs greatly within and among various countries. Factor endowment theory also fails to explain export production that arises from taste differences rather than factor differentials (Khambata and Ajami, 1992, p. 63). Another aspect of the narrowness of factor endowment theory is that it assumes that production factors are all identical in quality in every country of the world and that the production of a given commodity is similar across the world, thus totally ignoring the role of technology and innovation in the production process (Weekly and Aggarwal, 1987, pp. 120–1).

Leontief paradox

Wassiley Leontief examined empirically the labour to capital relationship, as proposed by Hecksher and Ohlin, within US industry and found that, contrary to the predictions of the factor endowment theory, US exports were less capital-intensive than US imports. A similar study was conducted in Japan in 1959 by Tatemoto and Ichimura, which also found that Japan's exports were capital-intensive and its imports were relatively labour-intensive, despite the fact that at that time Japan was believed to be more labour abundant (Asheghian and Ebrahimi, 1990, p. 34).

Product life cycle theory

Dissatisfied with the partial explanations presented by classical trade theories for the exchange of goods and services between nations, particularly in the role of technology and innovation, scholars in the 1960s started to look outside the theories about trade developed within economics in an attempt to establish the reasons why trade between nations occurs, and most particularly why business firms enter into international trade.

R. Vernon, of Harvard Business School, developed a theory of international trade in 1966, commonly known as the 'product life cycle', by focusing on market expansion and technological innovation, which have been neglected to some extent by classic theorists (Vernon, 1966, pp. 199–297).

The theory of product life cycles is based upon the assumption that certain products go through a life cycle composed of four stages, introduction, growth, maturity and decline, and that the location of production varies internationally, depending on the stage of the cycle.

The first stage, innovation, occurs when a new product is manufactured and introduced in the domestic market. Any international operation at this stage is achieved through export only and often to industrialized countries who can afford the price.

The second stage, growth, occurs when domestic and foreign sales increase as well as international competition. At this stage the company starts standardizing its products and considering foreign production facilities both to satisfy increased demands abroad and to meet competition.

During the third stage, maturity, the local market starts to become saturated, and exports from the home country decrease as manufacturing facilities abroad become more established. It is at this stage that the company may decide to shift its production facilities into developing countries to take advantage of cheaper labour costs and minimize its costs of production, and to meet the increased competition by re-exporting the product to the home country and selling it at a cheaper price.

Decline is the final stage, and occurs when new competitors in the market reach the same standards as those of the original manufactured goods.

Product life cycle theory provides us with a useful explanation of the life cycle of products and the various stages of their development. The theory, however, is limited in its application to consumer durables, such as synthetic fabrics and electronic equipment (Giddy, 1978, pp. 90–7). It also fails to explain why, for example, many highly sophisticated or capital-intensive industries have never left the industrialized world, such as aerospace, advanced pharmaceuticals, optics, scientific instruments and medical equipment, which will never enter the third or fourth stages of the product life cycle (Matsuura, 1991, p. 33). This theory, furthermore, does not tell us how long each stage will last, or how and when a firm should choose between exporting or setting up a local plant abroad (Grosse and Kujawa, 1992, p. 79). Vernon himself realized the shortcomings of his early product life cycle theory, particularly as it applied to the 1980s (Vernon and Wells, 1991, p. 84). He recognized, for example, that, as a result of the increasing ease of international communications in the 1980s, some firms had 'short-circuited' some of the steps portrayed in his early approach and that many multinational firms have been known to introduce products simultaneously in several markets of the world and to set up production facilities simultaneously in various countries (Vernon and Wells, 1991, p. 86). Japanese firms, particularly in the electronics and car industries, with their strategy of establishing production units in several markets, are illustrative of this. Furthermore, multinational firms in the 1980s are increasingly producing abroad, not in order to use raw materials available in other locations or to satisfy customers' requests, but simply to take advantage of production economies (Daniels and Radebaugh, 1992, p. 146). Volkswagen, for example, produces its cars in Brazil, and more recently in eastern Germany, not to supply the Brazilian or eastern German markets but to sell them in other export markets.

By the end of the 1970s and early 1980s, classical trade theories were failing to explain the problems in the global political economy, such as the decrease in world trade growth, high unemployment, increased global competition and world recession. Economists, politicians, academics and business people started to search for explanations outside the realm of pure economics and in the fields of business organization, corporate strategy and international relations.

REVIEW QUESTIONS

1. Why do many countries trade even when they can produce the products imported more cheaply than their trading partners?.
2. To what extent do classical theories of international trade contribute to our understanding of the origins and causes of international trade?
3. Discuss the practical relevance today of the study of international trade theories to the study of international business.
4. Briefly explain the various stages of the theory of product life cycles and assess its value in contributing to our understanding of the internationalization process.

FURTHER READING

Gill, S. and Law, D., *The Global Political Economy. Perspectives, Problems and Policies*, Harvester Wheatsheaf, London, 1988.

Hecksher, E., *Mercantilism*, George Allen & Unwin, London, 1985.

Pomfret, R., *International Trade: An Introduction to Theory and Policy*, Basil Blackwell, Oxford, 1991.

Ricardo, D., *Principles of Political Economy of Taxation*, Penguin, Harmondsworth, 1971.

Spero, J. E., *The Politics of International Economic Relations*, 4th edn, Unwin Hyman, London, 1990.

Yoffie, D., *Beyond Free Trade. Firms, Government, and Global Competition*, Harvard Business School, HPS Press, New England, 1993.

MODERN THEORIES OF THE FIRM

We have shown in the previous chapter some of the limitations of classical theories of international trade in dealing with changes in the global political economy, and their implications for international business. Considerable efforts have been undertaken by economists, politicians, academics and business practitioners to develop new theories of international trade that would explain more fully the changing nature of international business. All these new ideas have produced the so-called 'strategic trade theories' or 'modern theories of the firm', clearly reflecting the shift in trade theory from pure economics to the strategic operations of multinationals on the one hand and international relations on the other. The overall focus has moved from international economics to international political economy, and more recently to global political economy.

LEARNING OBJECTIVES

- To understand the reasons for the recent shift from classical theories of international trade to modern theories of the firm, and to evaluate their ability to explain the rise and expansion of international trade
- To examine critically the various approaches offered for the analysis of the contemporary internationalization process and its future orientation
- To provide business managers with a useful theoretical and analytical background upon which they can base the strategic planning for their future international operations

THEORIES OF INTERNATIONAL PRODUCTION

There are four broad bodies of theories of international production: the first focuses on the costs of production as determining the location of the industry, the second is concerned with the market power of the firm, the third is based on an institutionalist view of the firm as a device for raising efficiency by replacing markets, and the fourth combines elements of all the other three.

Weber's location theory

According to Alfred Weber, the location of industry is determined first by transportation and labour costs and second by location factors. Multinational firms, in his opinion, expand abroad to take advantage of location costs, such as minimal transportation costs, less expensive labour, lower taxes and tariffs. The major weakness of location theory is that it does not take into consideration cultural factors and the problems of operating in foreign markets. Its relevance today is also severely limited due to technological changes in transportation and communications and the automation of production methods. See Dicken and Lloyd (1990) for a detailed account of location theories.

The 'market power' approach

While Weber focused on geographical locations and the firm's internal resources, Hymer concentrated on the dynamics of the internationalization process itself. According to Hymer, firms move abroad to exploit the monopoly they possess through factors such as unique product marketing expertise, control of technology, managerial skills and access to capital (Hymer, 1976). Market power here is 'simply understood as the ability of particular firms, acting singly or in collusion, to dominate their respective markets (and so earn higher profits) to be more secure, or even to be less efficient than in a situation with more effective competition' (Lall, 1991, p. 21).

The main reasons offered by this approach for the internationalization process of the firm are (Spero, 1990, p. 112):

1. To exploit new foreign markets.
2. To defend or block competitors' moves into new markets.
3. To prevent competitors from gaining a survival-threatening advantage.

Multinational firms are thus believed to invest in foreign operations to reduce competition and to increase barriers to entry in their industry and decrease the efficiency of foreign plants (Pitelis and Sudgen, 1992, p. 21).

Hymer's main objective was to investigate why national firms went abroad, but he confuses the reasons given by firms, which are already a consequence of internationalization, with the *explanation* of internationalization. By simply focusing on the traditional, colonial and exploit-ative nature of international business, his theory may be valuable in explaining the internationa-lization process of the 1960s and the 1970s, but fails to recognize the impact of global competition on firms' attitudes and strategies in seeking global alliances in order to survive in global markets.

The eclectic paradigm

An alternative approach to the study of the internationalization of business, in addition to geographical location factors, the firm's internal resources and the dynamics of the inter-nationalization process itself, is offered by Dunning. For the internationalization process to occur, Dunning argues, three interrelated conditions must be satisfied (Dunning, 1980, pp. 31–3; see also Dunning, 1988, p. 21):

1. Ownership-specific advantages. These are specific advantages that a firm possesses over its competitors.
2. Internationalization of ownership-specific advantages. These are the firm's internal resources.
3. Location-specific factors, or geographical position.

Dunning's approach has been labelled 'The Dunning eclectic paradigm' because it combines the principles derived from international trade theories, location theories and organization analysis theories. Dunning's eclectic paradigm is not, however, a theory in itself but rather an overall analytical framework for comparison between theories, clarifying the relationships between them and identifying common ground or points of contact between them (Pitelis and Sudgen, 1992, p. 26). The weakness of Dunning's paradigm, though, is that it only lists the factors that contribute to the internationalization process of the firm, without explaining the reasons behind the process itself.

Theory of the new international division of labour

This theory was developed initially by F. Frobel, J. Heinricks and O. Kreye (Frobel *et al.*, 1980). Instead of analysing the external environment of business, geographical factors and internal material resources of the firm in explaining the trends in the 1980s towards international relocation and development of 'offshore' processing facilities, the new international division of labour theorists concentrated on the human capital or productive capital only. Since firms can reduce their production costs locally by minimizing their labour costs, they argue; similarly, in their pursuit for global profit they would search for cheap, controllable labour at a global scale. This is achieved, in their view, by relocating industrial production into the Third World to minimize labour costs. Three conditions determine the creation of the new international division of labour according to this theory:

1. Developments in transport and communication technology.
2. Developments in production technology allowing fragmentation and standardization of specific tasks which could use unskilled labour.
3. The emergence of a worldwide reservoir of potential labour power.

The new international division of labour, despite its apparently reasonable explanation of the motives behind the internationalization process of business, underestimates the important role played by new information technology and innovation which are increasingly causing a 'global shift' in the modes of production from the developing world back into the industrialized world (Frobel *et al.*, 1980). They also ignore the political dimension of internationalization, and the role and influence played by governments in the process.

However, the advantage of their theory is that it alerts us to the ways in which the organization and structure of the global political economy can and does affect the decisions and strategies of individual firms.

All the theories covered so far provide us with a comprehensive list of factors which contribute to the internationalization of business. They do not, however, explain to us why this process itself occurs. They are also static, in the sense that they all tend to describe the growth of multinational firms at a certain period of time, and do not take into consideration recent dynamic changes in the global political economy. International business activities in the 1990s have become much more complex than these theories would imply. The 1980s and early 1990s witnessed a new orientation and approaches to international trade theory and practice.

STRATEGIC THEORIES OF INTERNATIONAL TRADE

Theory of competitive advantage of nations

A fundamental reason why business firms internationalize their operations, according to Michael Porter, is to enhance the firm's competitive position. In his influential book *The Competitive Advantage of Nations*, Porter criticizes the classical trade theory of absolute advantage, which claims, as discussed earlier, that some nations possess *inherently* an absolute advantage in producing certain goods and products – a natural advantage or acquired advantage – and that states should concentrate on developing those goods in which they have absolute advantage. He argues that very few factor endowments or natural attributes are truly inherited, but are instead the product of investment. Porter also rejected the proposition of abundance of factor endowment as the only source of advantage. A disadvantage of factor endowment, in his view, such as labour shortages, lack of domestic raw materials or harsh climate, could on the contrary contribute to the development of national industry by stimulating innovation, pushing firms to upgrade and specialize using the available local infrastructure, materials or types of labour (Porter, 1990, p. 82). Japanese firms, Porter argues, face severe shortages in factory space and extremely high land cost. To overcome these difficulties they created just-in-time production, or *Kan ban*, which dramatically reduced needed inventory. Another illustrative example of how a disadvantage in factor endowment could contribute to competitive advantage is the Dutch fresh-cut flower industry. Despite the cold and grey climate, the Dutch fresh-cut flower industry has been able to become the world leader, exporting $1 billion of cut flowers per year. The inhospitable climate led to the adoption of an approach more favourable to innovation, such as for example glass-growing techniques, new strains of flowers and various conservation techniques (Porter, 1990, p. 85), than to upgrading the traditional cultivation techniques.

Porter asserts further that successful firms not only respond to their environment, but are also capable of influencing it in their favour in three different ways:

1. By changing the industry structure. Japanese firms have become the leaders in television on the strength of a shift in their industry structure towards compact, portable sets and the replacement of vacuum tubes with semiconductor technology (Porter, 1990, p. 34).
2. By introducing innovations, including improvements in both technology and methods or ways of doing things, or new possibilities in the design of a product and the way it is marketed, produced or delivered (Porter, 1990, p. 45).
3. By positioning within industries. Positioning refers to the firm's overall approach to competition by choosing either lower cost or differentiation. Lower cost is the ability of a firm to design, produce and market a comparable product more efficiently than its competitors, while differentiation is the ability to provide a unique and superior value to the buyer in terms of product quality, special features or after-sale service (Porter, 1990, p. 37). The chocolate industry provides a good example. American firms, such as Hershey, M & M and Mars, compete by mass production and mass marketing in contrast to Swiss firms, such as Lindt and Tobler/Jacobs, which sell mainly premium products at higher prices in hundreds of separate items and employing top quality ingredients.

Porter's theory of competitive advantage also rejects the assumptions behind the product life cycle by showing how companies in the computer and car industries have remained competitive for decades, either by moving early into global competition such as IBM, Kodak and Honda did, or by establishing a reputation that has been sustained for many years despite declining economic conditions such as experienced by the tobacco and whisky industries in Britain, or finally by constantly introducing innovation to adapt to changing circumstances.

Instead of using the factor endowment theory or the absolute or acquired advantage theory to explain why some nations are more prosperous than others, Porter focused his attention on four broad national characteristics which constitute his national 'diamond' model and determine a firm's ability to become more competitive in global markets. These four factors are (Porter, 1990, p. 71):

1. Factor conditions: the nation's position in terms of factors of production.
2. Demand conditions: the nature of home demand for the industry's product or service.
3. Related support industries.
4. Firms' strategy, structures and rivalry: the conditions within the national environment governing how companies are created, organized and managed and the nature of domestic rivalry.

The role of the national government could also be added to this 'national diamond', but only in its capacity as an 'influencer' on the four determinants. Government, for Porter 'can hasten or raise the odds of gaining competitive advantage (and vice versa) but lacks the power to create advantage itself' (Porter, 1990, p. 128).

Porter's model does provide us with some useful insights into the reasons why some nations are more successful than others in international trade by focusing on the firm and its actions and reactions to environmental factors within the national, domestic environment and domestic competitive rivalry. His analysis is consequently limited in several ways. First, all his analysis of domestic rivalry does not explain why competitors in the same country, for example, often adopt quite different strategies. Second, by simply focusing his analysis at the level of the firm and its national environments and 'almost wholly ignore(ing) the changes in the world system outside the country' (Stopford et al., 1991, p. 8), Porter ignores the changes in the global political economy and their implications for international business. Third, in his analysis of the role of government as influencer, Porter also fails to consider the existence of various groups of parties and their different interests within it (Stopford et al., 1991, p. 8).

Global shift theory

Globalization as a process in the internationalization of business is more fully explained by the global shift theory developed by P. Dickens. Recognizing the shortcomings of his earlier conception of the internationalization of economic activity, Dickens, in the new edition of his book *Global Shift*, moves clearly in his analysis from the internationalization process to the globalization phenomenon so characteristic of the 1990s. The major theme of his new edition is that the world has changed, and that economic activities have become not just internationalized but also increasingly globalized (Dickens, 1992). Dickens' overall argument is that globalization of economic activity is primarily the manifestation of the internationalization of capital as organized through business enterprises, of which the most important is the transnational corporation (Dickens, 1992, p. 95).

Globalization, for Dickens, depends on three major factors:

1. The existence of appropriate technology to overcome geographical distances for standardization and the possibility of fragmenting the production process.
2. The role of states in regulating and controlling international business.
3. The pursuit of global profit.

Besides the existence of incentives, such as increasing market share or achieving a market leader position, the basic nature of dynamic behind the internationalization process in Dickens' view remains that of profit. Since firms in today's global markets are no longer competing with national rivals but with other firms from across the world, their pursuit, according to Dickens, is now for global profits (Dickens, 1992, pp. 120–1). The internationalization of business must therefore be explained and understood in terms of the internationalization of capital and capital accumulation (see Radice (1975) and Harvey (1982)). This process is also heavily influenced by politics and power. Although the balance of power has shifted towards multinational firms, Dickens asserts that the extent to which multinational firms can expand through political boundaries and impose their own corporate strategies and implement them globally is strongly influenced and dependent on national governments' support (Dickens, 1992, p. 95). Multinational firms consequently are not the only force involved in the internationalization process. Governments and international organizations also contribute to this process. They are interlocked within this complex process of globalization (Dickens, 1992, pp. 149–50). This 'interlinked' economy is further expanded upon by K. Ohmae.

The borderless world theory

In his book *The Borderless World* (Ohmae, 1990a), Ohmae introduces his new 'strategic diamond' model in an attempt to explain the relationship between governments and multinational firms in the global political economy. To his old strategic diamond, which consisted basically of the '3Cs', customers, competitors and company, Ohmae now adds two more Cs: country and currency.

The volatility of current exchange rates, explains Ohmae, can severely affect international business. A sudden fluctuation in trade policy of exchange rates could cause an 'irreparable haemorrhage of cash' (Ohmae, 1990a, p. 2). To neutralize the adverse effects of currency fluctuations many firms are now trying to achieve a 'currency-neutral' position by moving more deeply into foreign markets (Ohmae, 1990a, pp. 8–9). This requires a deeper knowledge of foreign countries, not simply in terms of political risk analysis and attractiveness in terms of market size, growth and local competition, as was the case in the 1960s and 1970s, but to serve the needs of their customers in global markets (Ohmae, 1990a, p. 9). The role of governments in the internationalization process is also changing. Contrary to the claims made by classical theories of international trade, the prosperity of countries nowadays does not depend simply on the abundance of resources. Shortage of supplies, for example may put greater pressure on finding or developing alternative supplies (Ohmae, 1990a, p. 11). Switzerland, Singapore, Taiwan, South Korea and Japan are all characterized by small land area and few natural resources. They have achieved economic development and prosperity not through husbanding resources and technologies but through developing a well-educated hard-working workforce (Ohmae, 1990a, p. 12).

Theory of triangular diplomacy

The most recent explanation of the internationalization process developed in the early 1990s is offered by Professors J. Stopford and S. Strange (Stopford *et al.*, 1991). According to the theory of 'triangular diplomacy', governments in the 1990s, as a result of the increasing global competition and globalization of business, no longer merely negotiate among themselves but are increasingly pushed to negotiate with foreign firms. Multinational firms, too, are increasingly having to act in a 'statesman-like' way in seeking corporate alliances to enhance their combined capacities to compete with others for world market shares (Stopford *et al.*, 1991, p. 2). These negotiations are nowadays carried out on a triangular basis.

This interaction between firms and states is conducted in three dimensions. National boundaries no longer define the rules. International negotiations and action are now carried on a triangular basis, where traditional players in the embassies and foreign ministries are increasingly being joined by members of other governments' ministries and by executives of firms, both local and multinational. This blurring of the classical and neo-classical division between politics and economics, state and firm, and public and private sectors, is also emerging within global and regional international institutions, for example the IMF, ITU, UNESO and the EC.

In order to substantiate their thesis, Stopford *et al.* show how global structural changes in finance, technology, knowledge and politics often impel governments to seek the help and cooperation of managers of multinational firms. Six general propositions are made (Stopford *et al.*, 1991, pp. 2–5):

1. States are now competing more for the means to create wealth within their territory than for power over more territory. They now compete more for wealth as a means to power rather than for power as a means to wealth.
2. The basis of competition is shifting to emphasize product quality, not just costs. Attractive sites for new investments are increasingly those supplying skilled workers and efficient infrastructures.
3. Small, poor countries are facing increased barriers to entry in industrial sectors most subject to global forces of competition.
4. No longer do states negotiate only among themselves. They now must negotiate with foreign firms. This has recently become the norm, whereas previously it was exceptional.
5. The increased number of possible policy options for governments and firms complicates further the problems for both of managing multiple agendas.
6. All of these shifts have increased the volatility of change and divergence of outcomes.

REVIEW QUESTIONS

1. Compare and contrast traditional classical theories of international trade and modern theories of the firm and assess their relevance for understanding today's international markets.
2. What are the various factors that contributed to changes in the nature and extent of international business in the late 1980s and early 1990s?
3. To what extent does Porter's competitive advantage theory provide us with useful insights into international business?
4. To what extent do modern theories of the firm capture the changes in international business today? (You may support your analysis with any theory you might think useful.)
5. Examine briefly the theory of 'triangular diplomacy' and explain the reasons for the changing relationship between states and firms. Illustrate your answer with examples taken from recent relevant events.

FURTHER READING

Dickens, P., *Global Shift. Industrial Change in a Turbulent World*, 2nd edn, Paul Chapman, London, 1992.

Ohmae, K., *The Borderless World. Power and Strategy in the Interlinked Economy*, Collins, London, 1990.

Porter, M., *The Competitive Advantage of Nations*, The MacMillan Press, Basingstoke, 1990.

Rosenau, J. N. and Czempiel, E. O. (eds.), *Governance Without Government: Order and Change in World Politics*, Cambridge University Press, Cambridge, 1992.

Stopford, J., Strange, S. and Henley, J. S., *Rival States, Rival Firms. Competition for World Market Shares*, Cambridge University Press, Cambridge, 1991.

EIGHT

THE CHANGING RELATIONSHIP BETWEEN GOVERNMENTS AND FIRMS

Classical theories of international trade have stressed the substantial benefits to be gained from the liberalization of international trade, both for state and for firms. National governments, however, throughout history, have had strong tendencies towards restricting international trade by setting up various barriers to foreign trade. Protectionist policies have been followed by both developed and underdeveloped countries. Modern theories have emphasized the rapid globalization of markets in the early 1990s and the increasing global competition, causing not just deep rivalry, but also deep cooperation. This implies that the state–firm relationship is not inherently a struggle for power, as Dickens argued, but that they sometimes conflict and sometimes cooperate – which further implies a larger structure of the global political economy that determines their relationships. The aim of this chapter is to explain this changing relationship between governments and firms, and the blurring of the relationship between public and private sectors.

LEARNING OBJECTIVES

- To introduce the various methods of control most commonly adopted by national governments in regulating international trade
- To provide an overview of the major arguments put forward for and against protectionism
- To explain the recent changing attitudes towards the role of government intervention in international trade
- To assess the role of international organizations and GATT in regulating the conduct of international business.

FORMS AND METHODS OF INTERNATIONAL TRADE CONTROL AND REGULATION

Despite the claimed benefits to be gained from free trade, protectionist policies are often practised in many countries of the world, now as in the past. Measures adopted to control, restrict or regulate international trade can be grouped into two major categories: tariffs and non-tariff barriers.

- *Tariffs*   These are taxes imposed by governments on imported and exported goods. Depending on the purpose for which they are imposed, these tariffs could serve either to protect domestic goods from foreign competition or to increase government revenues, or indeed both.

- *Non-tariff barriers*   There are many ways in which governments can restrict international trade, without the use of direct tariffs. It is impossible to describe each one in detail. The list could also include a wide variety from country to country. Nevertheless it is important for business managers to be familiar with at least some of those that have a direct effect on their international business operations, such as import and export quotas, embargoes, subsidies, foreign exchange restrictions, and various government health and safety regulations, marketing standards, and packaging and labelling restrictions.
  - *Quotas* are quantitative restrictions and limitations set by a government on either imported or exported goods. Any additional quantities over the fixed quotas are subject to higher rates of taxation.
  - *Embargoes* refers to complete restrictions of trade exports or imports from a particular country. A boycott is another form of embargo carried out on the agreement among several countries to either partially or totally prohibit trade with a particular country such as the trade embargo carried out in 1988 against South Africa by the majority of industrialized nations to pressure the South African government into changing its racial policy of apartheid.

    The validity of trade embargoes is questionable. Although embargoes are often carried out for political reasons, their effect is meant to be economic in nature. During the Gulf War, for example, the USA put an embargo on all products exported to Iraq (except medicines and food) as a punishment for its claimed aggressive act against Kuwait, and also to make it more difficult for President Saddam Hussein to get supplies into the country. Furthermore, to be successful, trade embargoes must be adhered to by all participants, otherwise the target country may simply find alternative sources of supply, develop a capability of their own or retaliate causing damages to the countries imposing them. The trade embargo carried out against Iraq after its invasion of Kuwait is quite illustrative. Although Iraq lost quite a substantial amount of its oil exports as a result of the sanctions imposed against it, oil prices in the world rose sharply and many foreign multinational firms doing business with Iraq suffered great losses as a result.
  - *Subsidies* are low cost loans or tax breaks granted by governments to domestic producers to assist them in competing against foreign goods.
  - *Foreign exchange controls* are used for various purposes. Some countries use them as a means to restrict imports by limiting the ability of importers to pay for their suppliers in foreign markets. Others use them to avoid the devaluation of their national currency. Governments in Third World countries tend to use foreign exchange controls to increase their national revenues by maintaining dual exchange rates for the purchase and sale of foreign currencies.

Other non-tariff barriers include a number of government regulations affecting international trade. Some of these are, for example, the establishment of minimum health and safety standards and standard specifications of labelling and testing. A good example here is the rigorous safety inspection and product testing carried out by the government of Japan, particularly on pharmaceutical and medical equipment, which often takes months or even years to complete, thus delaying the introduction of competitive products into the Japanese markets. Marketing and packaging standards are also used to limit the import of certain goods and protect local markets. The creation of the Single European Market provides a good illustration here, where the Single European Act called for the removal of all internal barriers to trade within the Community, but at the same time explicitly requested that all imported goods carry the EC registration mark before they were allowed free circulation within the Single European Market. (This will be discussed in greater detail in Part Four.)

MOTIVES OF GOVERNMENTS FOR REGULATING INTERNATIONAL TRADE

While there is no one single reason why governments control the free flow of goods across borders, most of the arguments so far presented for and against protectionism can be grouped into three main objectives: political, economic and social (Weekly and Aggarwal, 1987, p. 130).

Political motives

Many governments insist on restricting foreign trade to protect national security and preserve national sovereignty. The argument put forward is that, despite its economic benefits, international trade may increase the national dependency on the flow of foreign supplies and raw materials needed for industry. Governments, it is claimed, must impose tariffs on crucial goods that are mostly needed for war and defence in order to ensure their domestic production and continued availability (Asheghian and Ebrahimi, 1990, p. 87). Defence arguments are also used by governments to restrict exports to hostile countries, thus preventing them from obtaining products that might either enhance their military capabilities or assist them in their economic development. The recent international cessation of trade with Iraq after its invasion of Kuwait provides an illustrative example.

Social and economic motives

Domestic full employment is another reason given by national governments for restricting international trade. Many national governments restrict imported goods as a remedy for unemployment. By limiting imported goods, it is claimed, domestic demand for locally produced substitutes increases, thus creating more jobs at home and improving domestic employment (Weekly and Aggarwal, 1987, p. 135). Such a justification is not only limited to manufacturing industry alone (failing to recognize recent shifts to the service sector in employment), but also totally ignores the possibility of direct retaliation by foreign governments for the restrictions that have been imposed on their products (Ohmae, 1990a, p. 15). Additionally, it is wrong to assume that increased imports always cause unemployment. The opening up of the market, on the contrary, could create opportunities for job creation in areas other than manufacturing, such as in distribution, warehousing, financing or retail marketing (Ohmae, 1990a, p. 15).

Infant industries

This argument is frequently put forward by some governments, particularly in developing states, for the protection of local industry (Asheghian and Ebrahimi, 1990, p. 86). It justifies trade restrictions to protect 'new' and 'young' domestic industries from international competition until they reach a certain level of maturity that would enable them to compete. The major shortcoming in the application of such infant industry protectionism is that it is difficult to predict which industry will be more competitive in the future and which will have a greater growth potential. In the absence of such a guarantee, government protectionism might result in wasteful misallocation of national economic resources. Second, some new industries may already have such an effective internal management structure and organization or be able to borrow capital in their early stage, that they may be able to survive without the need for greater government protection. Third, it might be very difficult politically to remove protectionism from particular industries. Those industries that have been protected for many years might have developed a relaxed attitude and might not be capable of meeting outside competition.

Balance of payments

According to this argument, governments interfere in international trade to maintain a favourable balance of payments and stable exchange rates. This is achieved, it is argued, through the use of tariffs and quotas in regulating import and export movements. International business operations could be seriously affected by a government's decision in balancing international trade. Decisions such as expansion into foreign markets, extending credit to overseas customers, import of needed raw materials and essential components could be subject to government constraints and restrictions. It is consequently very important for business managers to be aware of the government's attitude and policy towards the balance of payments issue, either in their host state or in the foreign state in which they seek to do business.

Most of the arguments so far presented for and against government intervention in international trade (for a detailed analysis, see Asheghian and Ebrahimi (1990, pp. 85–91); Matsuura (1991, pp. 75–91); Weekly and Aggarwal (1987, pp. 130–40); Daniels and Radebaugh (1992, pp. 168–77)) have been based on the observable actions and reactions of governments to international trade activities. Such an approach does not fully explain to us why, for example, protectionism in the 1970s and early 1980s seemed so essential after it was successfully undermined in the post-Second World War period, or the shift again in the late 1980s and early 1990s towards free trade, privatization and deregulation.

THE CHANGING CONCEPTION OF THE ROLE OF GOVERNMENT IN INTERNATIONAL TRADE

At the end of the Second World War, free trade was promoted as the best remedy for global and European economic recovery and reconstruction. Tariff barriers to international trade were gradually abolished, allowing the free flow of goods to flourish in the 1950s and 1960s. International trade grew rapidly, achieving fast economic growth. During the 1970s and early 1980s, however, the situation changed drastically. With the rise of inflation, increased unemployment and world recession, high demands for government protectionism were made in industries for both agricultural and manufactured products (Strange, 1979). Government intervention in international trade and regulations in the form of quota restrictions and exchange controls, import rationing and export restraints increased considerably. By the mid-1980s, and as a result of extensive stagflation, there was a general disappointment and disillusion with government efficiency in regulating international trade, reinforced further by the events in Eastern and Central Europe at the close of the 1980s. New trends towards privatization and deregulation are at present calling for the retreat of the state from the market throughout the world and demanding that governments take a 'back seat' in guiding the national economy (Ohmae, 1990a, p. 212).

Privatization and the total retreat of the state

The subject of privatization is an extremely complex one. This section will restrict its analysis to a brief introduction to the concept and its development in the late 1980s. The term 'privatization' in itself is a comparatively new word. It made no significant appearance in the political economy literature until 1979. Despite its relative novelty, privatization rapidly became one of the most important processes of the 1980s. In Britain alone the record of asset sales rose from a modest start of £377 million in 1978 to 1980 to over £5 billion in 1980 to 1988 (Pirie, 1988).

Geographically, privatization is now taking place in most parts of the world. It is being actively pursued in Eastern and Central Europe since the events of 1989 to facilitate the process of, and the transition to, a free market economy. (This is further discussed in Part Four.) Interest in privatization is also spreading among developing countries, such as Mongolia, the Philippines, Mexico and Pakistan (for detailed descriptions of privatization from the mid-1980s in Latin America, the Caribbean, Africa and Eastern Europe, see Fraser and Wilson, 1988, pp. 160–80; and World Bank Technical Paper No. 90, 1988.) It is important to note, however, that the main factor leading to privatization in the Third World is the result of external pressures from international organizations, such as the International Monetary Fund and the World Bank, which are increasingly making privatization an explicit requirement of their financial assistance (Aylen, 1987, pp. 15–30; *Business Week*, 21 October 1991, pp. 49–56; *Asian Finance*, **17**(9), 15 September 1991, pp. 56–9). Perhaps most striking of all are the recent changes or attempts to change by the People's Republic of China, which is seeking to maintain a strict form of socialist/Communist political organization while shifting the basis of the economy towards the accepted and supposedly successful mechanisms of capitalist economic operation. This implies an increasingly global consensus on the value of privatization and deregulation for wealth creation and business enhancement.

Privatization has been generally defined as primarily an economic, technical and administrative problem-solving concept consisting of the rolling back of the activities of the state (public sector) and its replacement by the market (private sector) (Kamerman and Khan, 1989, pp. 16–47; Starr, 1989, pp. 121–50).

Privatization, in other words, consists of:

1. Any shift of activities or function from the state to the private sector.
2. Any shift from the public sector to the private sector of the production of goods and services.
3. The application of private sector management and budgetary techniques to public sector administration, both national and international.

Many countries whose public sectors expanded in the 1960s and 1970s, it is argued, are now finding themselves confronted by rising debt and strong resistance to high taxes. Privatization is offered as a remedy to cut social expenditure and boost revenue, and to improve the overall financial structure of the economy. Privatization, it is firmly asserted, increases the efficiency of the public sector (Pirie, 1988) by taking away its political nature or political influence and making it more responsive to market pressures (Pirie, 1988, p. 53).

Government as facilitator, signaller and prodder

Instead of the passive role of governments mostly favoured in the early 1980s, the early 1990s witnessed a change of attitude towards the role of governments in international trade.

In his influential book *Competitive Advantage of Nations*, Michael Porter, of the Harvard Business School, set out to study a wide range of countries (Denmark, Germany, Italy, Japan, Korea, Singapore, Sweden, Switzerland, UK, USA), and within each one of them to investigate the details of competition in many industries. The aim of his book was to explain the role played by a nation's economic environment, institutions and policies and the competitive success of its industries. One outcome of the research was the view that, although government's role in international trade was partial, it was nevertheless influential in improving the national environment and in pushing and challenging its industry to advance (Porter, 1990, Ch. 12). The government's main objective, suggested by the results of the study, should be to enhance national competitive advantage. Its role in international trade should be to create an environment in which firms can upgrade competitive advantages in established industries by introducing more sophisticated technology and methods and by penetrating more advanced segments of the market (Porter, 1990, p. 618). National government policies, according to Porter, should be initiated to improve competitiveness rather than to 'help' industry through protective measures. Protectionism, the research found out, does not work in the vast majority of circumstances (Zysman and Tyson, 1983): it is a risky policy and does not often succeed.

Industries need competition to succeed internationally and the national government's role is to open markets by dismantling trade barriers. Some of the most effective policies to be adopted to achieve national competitiveness are devaluation, deregulation, privatization, relaxation of product and environmental standards, promotion of inter-firm collaboration and cooperation of various types, encouragement of mergers, tax reforms, regional development, negotiation of voluntary restraint or orderly marketing arrangements, improving the general education system, expansion of government investment in research and government programmes to find new enterprises (Porter, 1990, p. 619). In other words, the role of the government is to become a 'facilitator, signaller and prodder' (Porter, 1990, p. 672).

Government as a 'back seat rider'

In the 1990s, due to the internationalization of information and communication, production and finance, the old view that the government's role is to preserve national sovereignty, protect and represent the national interests of its people against foreign domination and foreign competition is no longer the case. As a result of the increased globalization of the world, we are, according to K. Ohmae, moving towards a 'borderless world' where people have greater access to global information, and consumers have become more informed about the availability of goods and services from around the world (Ohmae, 1990a, pp. 11–12). Government intervention in this 'interlinked economy', as he calls it, becomes an obstacle. In the light of the ending of the Cold War between the superpowers and the liberalization of Eastern and Central Europe, national security is becoming more of a myth, and the government's role, he argues, should be to ensure that people have access to the best and cheapest goods and services from anywhere in the world, and not to protect certain industries or certain clusters of people (Ohmae, 1990a, p. 13). To do this, government's role today must now concentrate on providing a first-class infrastructure for business by improving national education, providing wider access to information and making the national environment a most attractive location for global companies to do business, invest and pay tax (Ohmae, 1990a, p. 195).

THE BLURRING RELATIONSHIP BETWEEN GOVERNMENTS AND BUSINESS

Stopford *et al.* explored further this concept of an increasingly 'interlinked' world economy, or the growing global interdependence of states and firms in the 1990s, by conducting field research into the experience of over 50 multinationals and more than 100 investment projects in three developing countries: Brazil, Malaysia and Kenya (Stopford *et al.*, 1991, p. 1). Their aim was to show how global changes in finance, technology, knowledge and politics often impel governments to seek the help and cooperation of managers of multinational firms.

The conclusion of their study was that the rivalry between states and firms to secure a place in world markets in the 1990s is becoming fiercer. Instead of competing for power as a means to wealth, they argue, states nowadays are competing more for wealth as means to power – power to maintain internal order and social cohesion rather than power to conduct foreign conquest or defend themselves against foreign attack (Stopford *et al.*, 1991, p. 1). States are also increasingly realizing their dependency on scarce resources controlled by business firms. So, instead of negotiating between themselves, states are now negotiating with foreign firms to acquire the basic means to create wealth within their territory. Global competition has affected the operations of firms. They are now facing increasing difficulties in seeking new sources of competition and in establishing themselves in world markets. Realizing their need for government support and help to maintain their capacity to compete in global markets and to obtain states' cooperation and alliances, they are now having to change their traditional exploitative and colonial attitudes towards ownership and control and act more like 'statesmen'.

It is this mutual interdependence between states and firms which explains the recent blurring of the distinction between the private and public sectors in the 1990s. In such an 'interdependent' or 'interlinked' global economy the role of international organizations, such as the Organization for Economic Cooperation and Development (OECD), the Law of the Sea Convention, the United Nations Conference on Trade and Development (UNCTAD), the International Labour Organization (ILO) and the General Agreement on Tariffs and Trade (GATT), and how they adjust to the new changes in the global political economy, becomes even more important. It is impossible to cover all these institutions adequately in this chapter. We will concentrate instead on the General Agreement on Tariffs and Trade (GATT), given its direct relationship to the issues of international trade and business operations.

THE GENERAL AGREEMENT ON TARIFFS AND TRADE (GATT)

GATT was created in 1945 under the leadership of the USA, which suffered minimal destruction during the Second World War and maintained its industrial might, agricultural plenty and technological leadership (Rangarajan, 1984, pp. 126–64). GATT's original purpose was to combat the worldwide restrictions and protectionism that contributed to the post-First World War economic depression.

GATT's basic provisions were as follows:

1. *The elimination of tariffs and quotas* Freer and fairer international trade, according to GATT, could only be achieved through a gradual reduction in existing import tariffs through periodic negotiations between member states, until all tariffs and quotas were eliminated. To achieve this, all GATT members agreed to bind their tariffs at a ceiling level. If a country wanted to raise the rate above the bound rate, it would then have to lower its rate on other products or allow other member states to restrict some of its imports into their markets.
2. *The application of the principle of non-discrimination* Under this principle, each member country is required to treat other members equally and in a non-discriminatory way with regard to trade restrictions, customs regulations and trade regulations. To belong to GATT, countries had to agree to impose the same tariff rates on all other member states. This is known as the 'most favored nation rate' (MFN). According to the MFN clause, any change in tariffs agreed between two GATT members must be equally extended to all member countries at the same time.

Four exceptions to the MFN were allowed (Rangarajan, 1984, p. 138):

(a) Trade relations of member countries with their former colonies, such as the British Commonwealth.

(b) Associations of economic integration and countries in the process of integrating their economies into large units. The EC provides a good example here by allowing it to provide free trade for all its members while imposing common tariffs against the rest of the world.

(c) Developing countries under the General System of Preferences (GSP). Introduced in 1966, this principle allows industrialized GATT members to give tariff preferentials to underdeveloped countries without requesting an equivalent concession from them or granting such preferential tariffs to all other members of GATT.

(d) Exceptions made to particular countries based on their existing laws at the time of signing the GATT agreement, such as the exclusion of Switzerland's agricultural trade policy, for example (Daniels and Radebaugh, 1992, p. 187). Exceptions are also allowed in times of war.

3. *International forum for trade negotiations and conflict resolutions* Before the creation of GATT, trade disputes between countries went on for years and often resulted in retaliation and trade wars. Organizing international bargaining sessions, setting forums for trade negotiations and sponsoring periodic conferences for such purposes have been some of the most important activities of GATT since its creation.

In resolving trade disputes between member countries GATT acts as an international court of law by assigning a committee of experts from different countries to investigate the problem and make recommendations to the parties in conflict. GATT's efficiency and impartiality, however have been heavily criticized on several grounds. First of all there is the lack of enforceability of GATT's rules and principles. This is partly due to the lack of clear regulations on how GATT should penalize its members for violating its rules and partly due to the fact that GATT's rulings and sanctions are not legally binding. It is left up to member states to either accept GATT's penalties and sanctions and offer to redress them or to reject them. These rulings additionally are limited to GATT's signatories only. Second, GATT cannot anticipate or regulate changes in the global political economy, such as inflation, recession or the unexpected shock of the oil crisis between 1973 and 1974. Third, the existence of several exception clauses to the principle of the MNF clause has led to several discriminations against developing countries. Many countries have erected quotas and special trade restrictions using MFN restrictions to protect their own national industry against imported products such as textiles, footwear or clothing produced in the Third World. Finally, despite GATT's recent awareness of the increased importance of the international trade in services, this sector of the industry remains heavily regulated in many countries through the use of heavy taxation, local content requirements and licensing requirements.

REVIEW QUESTIONS

1. What are the various methods used by governments to regulate international trade? What are the intended economic effects of each method? Are they always realized? Which is the most efficient and why?

2. Despite the economic efficiency arguments for free trade and their widespread acceptance, national governments continually erect and maintain extensive barriers to trade with other countries. Why do they do this?

3. Examine and assess the arguments frequently put forward by governments in support of international trade restrictions. Which one do you feel is the strongest and most applicable today?
4. In his recent book *The Borderless World*, K. Ohmae argues that in the inter-linked economy of today's world, governments should stand back and let the people vote with their pocket book. Do you agree with this statement?
5. Explain what has contributed to recent changes in the conception of the role of government in international business and why.
6. GATT has been often criticized by the developing world for promoting the interests of the advanced nations and for supporting trade policies that do not support the development aspirations of the poorer countries. Can their conclusion be sustained?

EXERCISE 8.1: International organizations and international business

Aim The aim of this exercise is to increase students' awareness of the role of international organizations in international business.

Assignment Students are assigned one of the international economic, political or social organizations and asked to research fully their objectives, international operations and assess their relevance to international business.

Format and skills acquired Students are expected to work in small groups in conducting their research, collecting information, analysing their data and presenting their findings to the class. A written report should also accompany this exercise.

FURTHER READING

Behrman, J. and Grosse, R., *International Business and Governments. Issues and Institutions*, University of South Carolina Press, South Carolina 1990.

Business Guide to the New General Agreement on Tariffs and Trade Round, International Chamber of Commerce, Paris 1987.

GATT: What it is, what it does, GATT, Geneva, 1985.

Ohmae, K., *The Borderless World. Power and Strategy in the Interlinked Economy*, Collins, London, 1990.

Oxley, A., *The Challenge of Free Trade*, Harvester Wheatsheaf, Hertfordshire, 1990.

Porter, M., *The Competitive Advantage of Nations*, The Macmillan Press, Basingstoke, 1990.

Spero, J. E., *The Politics of International Economic Relations*, 4th edn, Unwin Hyman, London, 1990.

Stopford, J., Strange, S. and Henley, J. S., *Rival States, Rival Firms. Competition for World Market Shares*, Cambridge University Press, Cambridge, 1991.

THE GLOBALIZATION OF BUSINESS OPERATIONS AND MANAGEMENT

It is not enough for business managers to understand why international business occurs. They also need to know how to operate in it. It is essential for them to acquire practical skills and techniques to allow them to conduct their international business operations more efficiently and to be able to deal with the increasing globalization of competition. Many would assert that 'business is business' and that whether you are operating in the UK, USA, Japan, Asia or the Middle East you are still performing the same basic business functions of finance, human resources management, marketing and strategic planning; and that if you are operating efficiently at the domestic level there is no reason why you should not be as successful at the international level, assuming you are still implementing the same basic business functions. International business is much more complex than conducting business locally and this part of the book will show some of the important qualitative differences between them. The success of any firm depends to a great extent on the people it employs.

Chapter Nine deals with the various problems faced when conducting business in foreign markets and how business managers need to adjust their human resources management functions to the international context.

Chapter Ten provides a comprehensive review of international marketing functions and shows how they, too, differ from domestic marketing principles, particularly in dealing with the globalization of markets.

Finally, Chapter Eleven analyses the recent trends towards the process of globalization, and examines the various global strategic planning initiatives developed by firms to survive global competition in the 1990s and beyond.

NINE

INTERNATIONAL HUMAN RESOURCE MANAGEMENT

As a business firm expands its activities into international markets, its organizational structure might need to be adjusted to accommodate its foreign operations needs. The firm may also face serious problems of staffing, recruitment, selection and training for overseas assignments.

LEARNING OBJECTIVES

- To examine the different forms of organization structures utilized by multinational firms and to provide practical guidelines for designing an appropriate internationally oriented organization structure
- To understand how and why human resources management functions become more difficult and complicated at the international level
- To identify the problems that can occur when managers are transferred into foreign markets, and to consider ways in which these might be overcome

INTERNATIONAL ORGANIZATIONAL STRUCTURES

As business expands its activities into international markets the organizational structure may need to be adjusted to accommodate its foreign operations in an effective manner. 'Organizational restructuring' has become a new buzz-word of the 1990s in international business, in both the public and private sectors. International intergovernmental organizations, such as the United Nations Specialized Agencies, have been criticized for their wasteful and inefficient bureaucracy and are now undergoing large changes in their organizational structures.

Recent trends towards privatization and deregulation, increasing global interdependence, developments in new information technology and international communications, and increased innovation are all putting considerable pressures on multinational firms to rethink their organizational structure design, in order to survive the increasing global competition in world markets.

Inappropriate structures can create high costs and even sink an entire organization (Stoner and Freeman, 1989, p. 281). It is therefore essential for business managers to choose the best type of organizational structure for their international business operations. However, this is not a straightforward matter.

An organizational structure is 'the arrangement and interrelationship of the components parts and positions of a company' (Stoner and Freeman, 1989, p. 264). It clearly shows the division of work activities and functions within the firm, and their relationships. It also indicates the level of specification for each function, the hierarchy and authority structure, and how decision-making takes place (Miles, 1980, p. 17).

An organizational structure is neither predetermined nor permanently fixed. It should follow and reflect the growth strategy of the firm (Chandler, 1962). Many factors influence the design of organizational structure, such as corporate goals and objectives, management styles and philosophy, staffing and capital needs, product and production line, as well as factors in the external environment. The latter include government constraints and regulations, the level of involvement in foreign markets and the company's international experience (Matsuura, 1991, p. 455). Organizational structures may differ from one firm to another and from one country to another, depending on the nature of the business activities, environmental requirements and the assets employed. Consequently, there is no 'best' or 'universally' valid organizational structure suitable for international business operations. Various organizational structures exist, and these are constantly modified by firms to suit their own needs, evolving company strategy, or changes in the external environment. Before discussing the various forms of international organizational structure, let us look at the idea of an organization chart.

THE ORGANIZATION CHART

To show the organizational structure, an 'organization chart' is usually drawn showing the various departments, functions and activities within the firm, and their relationships. These usually appear in small boxes which are connected to each other by solid lines that indicate the chain of command, and the official channels of communication – who reports to whom (Stoner and Freeman, 1989, p. 265). Each box is then labelled to describe either the task or area of responsibility or to identify the individual occupying that position. The task of designing an organizational structure is not simply that of drawing neat boxes that represent positions within a hierarchy. The challenge is to develop a structure that can be used as a foundation for efficient decision-making within the company (Drucker, 1974a, p. 47; Drucker, 1974b).

DESIGNING INTERNATIONAL ORGANIZATIONAL STRUCTURES

There is no best way, or best approach, to designing an international organizational structure. The organizational structural design is a continuous process, because environments, organizations and strategies inevitably change over time (Stoner and Freeman, 1989, p. 280).

To assist business managers in designing or modifying their organizational structure to take into consideration their international expansion and international activities, Figure 9.1 illustrates the steps needed in this process.

Choosing the correct international organizational structure is vital for successful implementation of the company's strategy. The decision whether to adopt an international division, functional, product, geographic, matrix or global international organizational structure depends on the nature of the business, the organization's goals and objectives, and the benefits and operational limitations of each structure.

Steps needed in designing an international organizational structure

Step 1: Activity analysis   Activity analysis identifies what work has to be done, which jobs could be performed jointly and the role of each activity within the organizational structure.

Step 2: Design analysis   Design analysis examines all the decision-making needed, verifies at what managerial levels they must be taken, and clarifies their location within the organization.

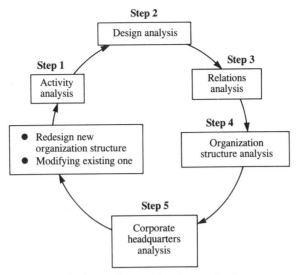

Figure 9.1   Designing an international organization structure

Step 3: Relation analysis   This analysis reviews each manager's role in the organization, and assesses his or her contribution to the overall corporate goals. (These first three steps draw heavily on Drucker (1974a).)

Step 4: Organizational structural analysis   There is no one standard model of international organizational structure. Multinational firms constantly change or modify their existing structures according to their needs, evolution and development. There are six international organizational structures developed so far for managers to choose from. These are (Figure 9.2).

- The international division structure.
- The international geographic/regional structure.
- The international product structure.
- The international functional structure.
- The mixed structure or matrix.
- The global structure.

The international division structure   An international division structure is mostly adopted by business firms in their early stage of internationalization, or when the firm has relatively small sales in foreign markets, by simply adding an 'international division' to the existing domestic structure responsible for handling all the international operations and activities. However, as international sales and production increase, and the number of foreign markets entered increases, the international division structure needs to be reorganized according to function, product or geographic area.

The international geographic or regional organization structure   In an international geographic structure, the company is divided into different geographical areas. Each geographic division has its own function departments.

International geographic structures are mostly adopted by large companies with a wide range of products to be marketed, such as consumer non-durable goods, food products, beverages and cosmetics.

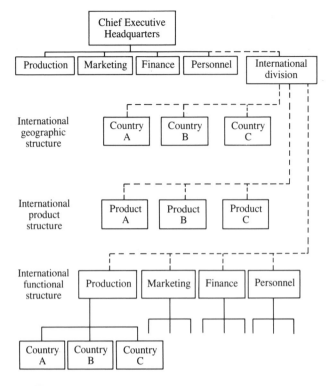

Figure 9.2 International organization structures

The international product structure In an international product structure, all similar products are grouped together and put in a one-product division. Each product division is then responsible for the production, sales and profits related to its own products.

An international product structure is mainly suitable for companies with several unrelated product lines, such as hotels and airlines companies, or companies that have expanded by mergers and acquisitions. Companies with a standardized market but which need to acquire more markets can also benefit from such a structure.

The international functional structure In an international functional structure, each department is responsible for its own international operations and profitabilities. International functional structures are limited to large firms having a high level of profits and low costs. Firms that adopt such structures are oil companies, steel producers, industrial product manufacturers and raw material extraction companies.

The matrix structure Matrix structures became very popular in the 1980s. They are also known as mixed structures, because they combine the functional, geographic and product structures, as illustrated in Figure 9.3. An example of a matrix structure is the project management structure, where a specific team is formed to meet a specific need or to work on a short-term project. After the project is completed, the project management team is dissolved and the members go back to their own previous position within the firm. Companies with substantial product and area diversification use the international matrix structure. High-technology multinational firms, turnkey firms and industrial construction firms utilize the matrix structure.

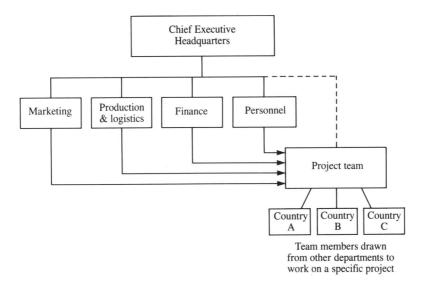

Figure 9.3 International matrix structure

Step 5: Corporate headquarters analysis   Finally, the success or failure of the implementation of any international organization structure depends largely upon the role and function of corporate headquarters. There are six roles that corporate headquarters can play in dealing with international business operations. These are:

1. Controller.
2. Coach.
3. Orchestrator.
4. Surgeon.
5. Architect.
6. Regional headquarters devolvement.

Corporate headquarters as controller   As a 'controller', headquarters gives considerable autonomy to subsidiaries, and intervenes only in exceptional circumstances, for example when performance does not match the set measurement of profit (Goold and Campbell, 1989).

Corporate headquarters as coach   In circumstances of decentralization of decision-making and greater authority and autonomy of subsidiaries, the role of headquarters in this respect is simply to provide support and advice. Intervention occurs only when necessary (Goold and Campbell, 1989).

Corporate headquarters as orchestrator   Headquarters, in this view, has central control over all the organizational operations. It is also responsible for all activities, such as manufacturing, research and development, and finance, and may intervene at any time (Goold and Campbell, 1989).

Corporate headquarters as a surgeon or architect   When major upheavals threaten the firm or industry, the company's organization may have to be restructured. Headquarters' role as a surgeon or architect at this stage involves the redesign of the organizational structure and functional and operational activities. It is an interventionary, invasive and restructuring role, one which is clearly a short-term and generally crisis-generated role (Terpestra and Sarathy, 1991, p. 662).

Regional headquarters devolvement   'If a company wants to operate globally, it has to think and act globally (Ohmae, 1990a, p. 105). Given the variety of conditions in each market, the degree of competition and changes in the global political economy 'decomposing the corporate center into several regional headquarters is becoming an essential part of almost every successful company's transition to global competitor status' (Ohmae, 1990a, p. 109). Nissan, Yamaha, Sony, Honda and Matsushita have all adopted such an approach to the role of their corporate headquarters. Even the location of their headquarters is no longer a matter of great importance (*Harvard Business Review*, March–April 1991). In global companies, headquarters are not necessarily located in the same country as the company's shareholders or majority of employees. Hewlett-Packard, for example, recently moved the headquarters of their personal computers business to Grenoble in France. Siemens AG, General Electric, are relocating their medical electronics division headquarters from Geneva to Chicago. GFT, the world's largest manufacturer of designer clothing, has its headquarters spread over three continents (Howard, 1991).

This recent movement away from the traditional hierarchical structure of multinational firms, dominant in the 1960s and the 1970s, towards the globalization of the firm, is best illustrated by the following case study of Asean Brown Boveri.

CASE STUDY 9.1: The theory and practice of building a global firm

Asean Brown Boveri (ABB) is a young company created in January 1988 as a result of a merger between two European companies: ASEA (Swedish) and Brown Boveri (Swiss). Soon after its creation, ABB started acquiring or taking minority positions in 60 other companies, representing an investment worth $3.6 billion, including two major acquisitions in North America: the Westinghouse transmission and distribution operation, worth $1 billion, and Combustion Engineering, worth $1.6 billion, both acquired in 1989.

ABB has grown largely through mergers and strategic investments. Today ABB is a huge enterprise, generating annual revenues of more than $25 billion and employing 240 000 people around the world. Although Europe accounts for more than 60 per cent of its total revenues, ABB's business activities are not limited only to the industrialized world. The company, for example, has 10 000 employees in India and 10 000 in South America, and is one of the most active Western investors in Eastern Europe.

ABB organizational structure

ABB is a global company with no geographic centre. It is a federation of national companies with a global coordination centre located in Zurich which employs only 100 professionals. ABB organizes its activities through a global matrix structure, which combines the functional, geographic and product international structures. At the top of the company sits the Chief

Executive Office (CEO) and twelve members of the Executive Committee drawn from different nationalities: Swedish, Swiss, German and American. The Executive Committee reports to the CEO and is responsible for ABB's global strategic performance. Each member of the Executive Committee is also responsible for a group of business areas (BAs) allocated to that person. There are 50 BAs located worldwide, into which the company's products and services are divided. Each BA is subdivided into eight business segments. BA leaders are responsible for optimizing the business on a global basis. They decide, for example, which factories are going to make what products, what export market each factory will serve, how the factories should pool their expertise, and research funds for the benefit of the business worldwide.

Alongside the BA structure is the country structure. These are separate companies, in different countries, organized as national enterprises with presidents, balance sheets, income statements and career ladders. ABB has over 1100 such local companies around the world. Their presidents report to two bosses: the BA leader, who is usually located outside the country, and the president of the national company of which the local company is a subsidiary. They also have two sets of responsibilities. They have a global boss, the BA manager, who creates the rules by which they run their business, and they have their country boss, to whom they report in the local setting.

Source
This case study draws heavily from Taylor, W., The logic of global business: An interview with ABB's Percy Barnevick, *Harvard Business Review*, March–April 1991, pp. 91–105.

MANAGING HUMAN RESOURCES

Designing appropriate international organization structures does not automatically guarantee success in international business. The success or failure of international business operations depends largely on the people employed. The basic personnel functions, such as staffing, recruitment, selection and training, promotion and compensation are much more complicated in international operations. International human resources management is much more complex, and faces greater difficulties than domestic human resources management. In a survey of expatriate assignments with 80 American nationals, R. Tung found that more than half of the companies had failure rates of 10–20 per cent. Her study also indicated that about 7 per cent of the companies had recalled home or dismissed 20–40 per cent of their overseas employees, due to their inability to function in a foreign environment (Tung, 1985, pp. 68–78).

Managerial failures abroad not only cost the firm vast amounts of money, but could also change its relationships with the host country, lose its market share abroad, or affect its employees' performance. It is therefore essential for business managers to be aware of the various problems of managing their human resources in foreign markets, and how to deal with them.

ADJUSTMENTS NEEDED FOR SUCCESS

Successful management of international human resources depends on the firm's ability to staff, recruit, select and train the right employees to fill jobs in a foreign subsidiary.

International staffing

Several factors should be taken into consideration when staffing overseas subsidiaries. Some of these are (see Brooke, (1990, pp. 147–52); Prasad and Shetty (1976)):

- The nature and characteristics of the firm, such as type of ownership of the foreign subsidiary, whether wholly owned, minority-owned or a joint venture.
- The time span or duration of the foreign operation of the firm: whether it is long-term, short-term or permanent.
- Method of establishing the overseas subsidiary: whether it is a take-over, merger or acquisition, or foreign direct investment.
- International organizational structure: whether the firm has a geographic, product, functional or matrix structure.
- The type of industry and product line: whether it is in the manufacturing or service industries.
- The market. If, for example, the product is manufactured locally and only for the local market, such as is the case with Bata shoes (recall Case Study 2.2), there will be less need for expatriates, in contrast with global brands, where global managers are needed to ensure the application of standardized global techniques in worldwide markets.
- The external environment of the host country, such as the host government's attitude towards foreign direct investment, the political system, the sociocultural environment, attitudes towards women, and geographical location. (These have been discussed in detail in Part One.)

International recruitment and selection

Recruitment is concerned with identifying and providing the firm with a sufficient number of candidates for a particular job, large enough to allow the firm to select the most suitable employees it needs. The recruitment process involves first of all the identification of a vacant position within the firm and writing up a job description or position description explaining the nature of the job and its function, accompanied by a job specification or hiring specification, which includes the minimum requirements or qualifications in terms of experience, background, skills and education necessary for the effective performance of the job described (Stoner and Freeman, 1989, pp. 332–9). Candidates are then located through newspaper and professional journal advertisements, employment agencies, word of mouth and visits to colleges and university campuses.

The selection process involves evaluating all the job applications received, conducting initial interviews, testing skills or ability to learn on the job, gathering references, checking the truthfulness of applicants' résumés, conducting physical examinations, and finally making the job offer, specifying the salary and benefit packages (French, 1982).

Recruitment and selection are much more complex at the international level. A candidate's technical expertise, education, local experience and past record of achievement are good indicators for his or her suitability and potential success in a domestic market, but do not automatically guarantee successful performance in foreign markets. In addition to having the appropriate technical expertise, potential candidates for a foreign assignment ideally must also have a good knowledge of the foreign environment to which they are to be assigned. This combination is not always possible. To assist personnel managers in making their choice in international recruitment and selections, or to put it another way, to choose between hiring expatriates (with technical expertise) or local employees (with local knowledge), or third country expatriates, the following eight factors must be carefully examined and assessed:

1. Location of the subsidiary.
2. Organizational coordination and control.
3. Company short-term, long-term or permanent objectives.
4. Company management orientation.

5. Company development policies.
6. Cost considerations.
7. Legal restrictions.
8. Gender and race.
9. Criteria for selecting and recruiting the ideal international manager.

1. *Location of the subsidiary*
   If there is great difference between the two operating environments, local people are more useful than expatriates because they are more knowledgeable about local conditions, cultures and business practices. When L. Weston was appointed to head Kentucky Chicken in Japan, he felt that a local manager would be more effective in dealing with local employees and clients. One of the first things he did was to hire a local deputy to advise him on various ways of adapting the American concept of fried chicken to local conditions, local business conditions and local culture (Stoner and Freeman, 1989, pp. 792–3).
   Local people are also a better choice if there is a strong or growing anti-foreign sentiment in the host country, and it is necessary to reduce the 'foreign' image and become more integrated within the local community. Employment law in Saudi Arabia, for example, makes it mandatory for any foreign firm to limit its foreign expatriate numbers to 60 per cent of the total workforce. The other 40 per cent must be recruited locally. There is also constant pressure from the government to provide full training for local staff so that they could occupy more senior positions within the firm. Employing local staff can also help to reduce the political risk involved in operating in countries where the local political and economic environment is not stable.

2. *Coordination and control*
   The transfer of expatriates from headquarters to subsidiaries helps to ensure that the foreign subsidiary is complying with the firm's overall objectives and policies, and to maintain worldwide standards. Expatriates are also a better choice if the subsidiary is highly technical, or a newly acquired subsidiary.

3. *Goals and objectives of the firm*
   The choice between locals and expatriates also depends on the objectives of the firm: whether these are long-term, short-term or permanent. If the firm's international operation is, for example, a short-term contract, such as a turnkey contract or a project team consultancy, hiring and training local nationals for a short-term contract would take too much time and money. Expatriates in such cases would be more suitable. They would already have the technical and managerial competence to carry out the project and they would also focus more on accomplishing their objectives within the limited time period assigned.
   If the foreign operations are for long-term objectives, or if they are permanent ones, employing local staff would be more suitable because they would be more committed to the long-term future success of the company. The costs of recruiting local people are also significantly lower. Local staff furthermore tend to stay longer in the position than expatriates, thus providing greater continuity in management.

4. *Management orientation policy*
   One of the major problems faced in international human resources management is the existence of mixed nationalities among the employees. These can be grouped into three major categories: home country nationals, host country nationals and third country nationals.
   Home country nationals are citizens of the country where the firm has its head office. These are also often referred to as 'expatriates'.

Host country nationals, or local staff, are citizens of the country where the firm has its own subsidiary.

Third country nationals are citizens of another country other than the parent or host country. These are also known as 'cosmopolitan expatriates'.

The nationality mix of an international operation depends on the general management orientation of the firm, whether it is ethnocentric, polycentric or geocentric (Perlmutter, 1969b).

An ethnocentric management orientation considers the home country's management practices as superior to those of other countries. In such firms, all key executives of the subsidiary are recruited from home country nationals.

A polycentric management orientation regards all countries as different and hard to understand. Key personnel in the subsidiary are recruited locally on the assumption that they are more familiar with the local culture and business ethics, and have better relations with the host country.

In contrast, in a geocentric management approach, nationality becomes much less important than the particular skills and experience of the employee. The American company Dow International provides an illustrative example, where its Italian Burroughs Corporation is run by a Frenchman, the Swiss company by a Dane, the German company by an Englishman, the French company by a Swiss, the Venezuelan company by an Argentinian and the Danish Company by a Dutchman (Cateora, 1990, p. 499).

5. *Management development*

Many multinationals transfer their nationals overseas in order to provide them with a general knowledge of overall corporate operations, to gain international expertise, or to train them in the international business operations of the firm. Citibank, for example, has a policy of rotating its senior executives every two or three years in each overseas subsidiary. Overseas assignments constitute a part of their professional development and training programme.

6. *Costs and repatriation problems*

Costs and repatriation problems can largely influence a company's choice in staffing its subsidiary. The cost of transferring expatriates to foreign subsidiaries can be very high. This often includes the costs of transporting the expatriate's family and their household belongings, and of providing suitable accommodation, health care and education for their children. It is estimated that an expatriate costs at least three times as much as a local (Grosse and Kujawa, 1992, p. 493).

7. *Local restrictions*

National regulations regarding the employment of expatriates can be complex and costly. Many countries have specific laws restricting the employment of foreigners. In the UK, for example, the Department of Employment will not approve the issuance of a work permit to any foreign national until it can be demonstrated that there is no qualified person available locally to fill the position advertised for. In Saudi Arabia, employees with certain religious affiliations or religious occupations are not allowed to work in the country. Employing priests, monks or nuns is prohibited. Work permits in the Bahamas are easier to get, but at a cost of a thousand dollars for each expatriate (Grosse and Kujawa, 1992, p. 27).

8. *Gender and racial bias and local acceptance*

Based on their race or gender, expatriates may meet local prejudices, such as employing a black manager in South Africa or a female executive in Saudi Arabia. A bias against employing women is mostly obvious in countries with a traditional patriarchical system, where a woman's place is considered to be at home (Adler, 1988; Nye, 1988, pp. 38–43; Williams, 1988, pp. 128–38; Symons, 1986, pp. 379–89; Rossman, 1986). In Saudi Arabia it is very rare to see women in top managerial positions, except in the nursing and teaching professions. Segregation in the workplace is also often practiced between male and female employees. In Japan, where seniority is mostly based on age and not on ability and achievement, a young expatriate occupying a senior managerial position would not be accepted by the local workforce.

9. *Criteria for selecting and creating the international manager*
   The following case study contains a list of the ideal characteristics of an international manager which personnel managers need to look for when recruiting and selecting for their international business operations.

CASE STUDY 9.2: Characteristics of the international manager

An international business manager ideally must have the following characteristics:

- A good understanding of local operations and conditions
- A high level of expertise in the job required and technical competence
- The ability to understand and implement headquarter's policies and procedures
- To be cross-culturally sensitive, and have a high level of adaptability and tolerance
- Proficiency in foreign languages, or the ability to learn foreign languages quickly
- Maturity and emotional stability
- Initiative and creativity
- Flexibility and adaptability to change
- Diplomatic skills
- High educational achievement
- Ability to communicate at all levels and with different cultures
- Family adaptability

To sum it all up:
'Ideally it seems he (or she) should have the stamina of an Olympic runner, the mental agility of an Einstein, the conversational skill of a professor of languages, the detachment of a judge, the tact of a diplomat, and the perseverance of an Egyptian pyramid builder . . . and if he is going to measure up to the demands of living and working in a foreign country he should also have a feeling for culture; his moral judgments should not be too rigid; he should be able to merge with the local environment with chameleon-like ease and he should show no signs of prejudice'.
Source
Heller, J.E., Criteria for selecting an international manager, *Personnel*, **57**, May–June 1980.

PRE-DEPARTURE TRAINING FOR MANAGERS

The training of expatriates in preparation for an overseas assignment is important and necessary before, during and after sending the expatriate abroad. These aspects are commonly known as pre-departure training, on-site orientation and repatriation programmes.

The training of employees can take place either within the firm or outside. External training programmes are offered at many universities and management centres, such as Canning International Management Development, which has clients from Aerospatiale, BASF, Colgate-Palmolive, Ericson, Hitachi Data Systems, ICI Pharmaceutical, Mitsubishi Bank and Pirelli (see

Reed (1991, p. 7); Guy and Mattock (1991); Rahim (1983); Murray and Murray (1986); Main (1989); Cawsgil *et al.* (1992)). Some programmes are tailor-made for the specific needs of an international assignment and are developed by the companies themselves, such as NEC, IBM, Lockheed and General Electric. Citibank, for example, has its own regional management training centre (MENA) in Athens.

Pre-departure training programmes include language studies, documentary and practical information, sensitivity training and field experience. Pre-departure training programmes usually have two phases: one for the executive and one for the executive's family (This section draws heavily on Phatak (1989, pp. 120–3).)

The pre-departure training programme for managers should include intensive language training. Mastering a foreign language can take years. The basic purpose here is to provide the employees with the basic words, idioms and phrases needed in their everyday activities. Many companies have introduced on-the-job language training as a normal and integral part of the employee's daily work.

Body language, diction and mannerisms of a foreign culture are also useful to include within the language training. Non-verbal communications specific to certain cultures includes appearance, orientation and posture. Each culture holds different expectations and norms (Ricks, 1983, p. 14; Hall, 1960, pp. 87–96). (Some of these were covered in Chapter Four.)

Documentary information about the subsidiary and its operations in the country is also essential to clarify the relationship between the role of the subsidiary and head office. It is important for expatriates to understand clearly the extent to which the subsidiary's operation relates to the overall company's goals and objectives. This is achieved either by bureaucratic control or by cultural control. Bureaucratic control means imposing explicit rules and regulations and operational procedures for foreign operations. IBM has a special booklet on the culture of IBM given to all new recruits during their induction session, explaining the company's overall culture and policy towards clients, including even a dress code. Cultural control, on the other hand, is best achieved by Japanese firms, where the expatriate is intensively familiarized with the company's culture before departure.

Documentary information should also include details of the company's relationship with the host country, and the government's policies in terms of job creation, localization, industrial relations, labour structure, labour laws and so on.

Sensitivity training and cross-cultural awareness

Cultural sensitivity training is crucial to the success of expatriates in handling foreign assignments effectively, and in acquiring the ability to interact with people who may have different lifestyles, habits and viewpoints. There are many cross-cultural training programmes conducted by professionals who understand cross-cultural education and challenges (Jaeger, 1983, p. 101).

There are three stages in cultural sensivity training:

- *Stage 1: Cultural awareness and self-awareness*
  At this stage, the trainee is exposed to a critical analysis of the role of culture in everyday life. Understanding oneself is critical to understanding others. Emphasis is on making individuals aware of their own cultural habits and objectives, and thereby of cultural difference (Guy and Mattock, 1991).
- *Stage 2: Simulation exercises and role playing*
  The purpose here is to expose candidates to various situations they are likely to face in a foreign culture, such as different management styles and practices in the country assigned,

labour productivity and motivation, and to teach them how to function within it. In these sessions, participants are asked to act out the situations, with instructors reacting as local employees would.

- *Stage 3: Field trips to the country of assignment*
This involves sending candidates to the country of assignment to meet the people they will be working with, and to have a first contact with the foreign environment to reduce the initial cultural shock.

PRE-DEPARTURE TRAINING FOR MANAGERS' FAMILIES

An expatriate's spouse and immediate family are important factors in the success or failure of an expatriate's overseas assignment (Black and Gregersen, 1991, pp. 467–77; Harris and Moran, 1989). A spouse's cross-cultural adjustment and ability to cope with the foreign environment is crucial. Spouses may not be as excited as their partners about an overseas assignment. It is important to prepare them for such a move. Pre-departure training programmes aim at preparing families for their cross-cultural adjustment. Language training for families will be limited to phrases commonly used and necessary in everyday life. The goal here is to provide elementary knowledge of the basic vocabulary so that they will be able to communicate with others on arrival in the host country: simple things, such as ordering a meal in a restaurant, asking for directions, reading street signs (Lanier, 1979, pp. 162–3). The basis of cross-cultural training for spouses and families is to reduce uncertainty by learning which behaviours are acceptable in the new environment and which are not, and to avoid the possibility of culture shock upon arrival.

During these sessions, candidates and their families should be provided with documentary and practical information to increase their knowledge about the foreign country. Booklets with factual information should be prepared for this specific purpose. They should contain documentary material on the history, religion, politics, geography and economics of the country, together with everyday business and social etiquette. Lockheed International AG, for example, has developed videos of life in Saudi Arabia to show its expatriates, including the accommodation expected and the compound facilities, and also explaining what to do and what not to do, when not to do it and so on. Gender and religious aspects are of central importance in the context of business in Saudi Arabia.

Orientation on arrival in the foreign country

The orientation programme should include documentary material on day-to-day living, tips from other foreign nationals, information on such things as where to buy a Christmas tree, where to eat, when the local holidays are, customs and traditions, which social clubs to apply for, where to go for aerobic classes, dance lessons, and school and college requirements. Citibank has a special booklet written by overseas families and published in the company's internal journal which is distributed to new arrivals with guidance and tips.

For the employees a one week induction is essential. A guided tour of the facilities, and a month or two coaching from the manager whom the expatriate will replace are essential. Lockheed, for example, allocates four weeks for such a 'hand-over' period.

Finally, repatriation programmes should also be developed by the company to solve the considerable problems expatriates might face upon returning home. Some of these problems are:

- *Financial*   Many benefits will be taken away upon return home. For example, some overseas benefits which allowed expatriates to live at a higher standard than at home, such as having a driver, a cleaner, a cook and so on, will be withdrawn when relocating, and the family will have to readjust.

● *Work-related* Employees might find that their peers have been promoted while they were away, and would need to adjust to the corporate changes.

Often expatriates return home to a mundane job that does not reflect their overseas experience.

● *Family-related* Adjustment to new schools, lifestyles and perhaps a new location.

INTERNATIONAL COMPENSATION

People performing relatively similar jobs in different countries may receive different amounts and forms of compensation. Designing an adequate compensation package for expatriates is crucial to attract and retain managers in overseas assignments. However, developing an equitable plan is quite difficult. This is especially true when a company operates in more than one country. Generally speaking, salaries paid to expatriates assigned to different foreign countries vary significantly according to local competitive conditions, cost of living, taxes, lifestyle, currency fluctuation, hardship factors, difference in cost of housing, education, recreation, food and so on.

An overseas compensation package should consist of the following:

1. A basic salary which is consistent with the firm's overall salary scale, regardless of overseas assignment.
2. Overseas allowances, depending on the country assigned to. Expatriates' salaries must be higher than those received by local staff to meet local competition and market conditions. In addition, the cost of living difference between the home and host countries should be seriously considered to enable expatriates to maintain the same standard of living that they are used to at home. This is usually done by a 'shopping basket' conducted in the foreign country. Foreign currency exchange fluctuations need also to be included in the final calculation of expatriate salary.

To overcome this problem, many multinationals have adopted a dual system of payment to their expatriates: one in the local currency to cover the local costs of living abroad, and one in the home currency which covers the basic salary.

Additional allowances are then added according to the location of the foreign assignment. Some of these are, for example:

● *Hardship allowance* A multinational will offer a greater hardship allowance for an employee going to work in Saudi Arabia, where the consumption of alcohol is forbidden and there are no local cinemas or public theatres as opposed to expatriates assigned to Paris.
● *'Rest and relaxation' allowance* Also known as 'bachelor's leave'. This is particularly offered by multinational firms for expatriates working in the Gulf on an unaccompanied or bachelor status.
● *Return flight ticket* to home country once or twice a year.
● *Allowance for domestic services*, e.g. a driver for the family.
● *Club membership* for tennis, swimming or health clubs.
● *Medical insurance*.
● *Educational allowance* and schooling for children

- *Housing allowance*   Some companies simply pay the difference between normal housing costs at home and the cost of housing in foreign country, or ask employees to pay a percentage of their salary for housing and the company is responsible for the difference. Or a company may provide its own accommodation, usually within a compound specifically built for the multi-national's expatriate community.

INTERNATIONAL HUMAN RESOURCES MANAGEMENT AND RECENT TRENDS TOWARDS GLOBALIZATION

International human resources management (HRM) today is undergoing a fundamental change from what it used to be in the 1960s and 1970s, when subsidiaries were viewed as appendages to company headquarters. The colonial attitude in sending home nationals to manage the subsidiary is no longer practised by the global firms of the 1990s. As a result of the increasing internationalization of business, new technology, improved communications, telecommunications and transport, and the globalization of business, multinational firms are abandoning the traditional colonial attitudes of sending overseas expatriates. Views about organizational structure are also changing in favour of either the global or the transnational structure. This transition to global structure is influencing traditional HRM practices. Expatriates, for example, are now often sent only on short assignments, and there is an increased movement towards building a global management team (Ohmae, 1990a, p. 90). The new trend adopted by global corporations today differs from the colonial style of the multinational firms of the 1960s and 1970s. Global staffing is achieved today regardless of nationality of candidates. Words like 'overseas', 'subsidiary' and 'affiliates', used previously to distinguish home operations from the rest of the world, no longer apply within the global firm, particularly in the light of the recent increase in joint ventures and strategic alliances (Ohmae, 1990a, p. 17). Honda, for example, has manufacturing divisions in Japan, North America and Europe. Its managers do not think or act as though the company is divided into overseas operations. In fact, the very world overseas has no place today in Honda's vocabulary (Ohmae, 1990a, p. 18).

REVIEW QUESTIONS

1. What are the problems and advantages associated with establishing an international division?
2. What are the various forms of international organizational structure available to multinational firms? How can each structure be utilized and in what circumstances?
3. Why do business firms need to change their organizational structure when operating at the international level?
4. Explain what is meant by 'the fading significance of world headquarters'. Illustrate your answer with examples.
5. How can expatriates be prepared to deal with overseas assignments? List the potential problems they might face with their families, and make a list of what can be done to prepare expatriates for the new foreign assignment.
6. What factors should you consider when deciding between recruiting a local or expatriate manager?
7. The most complex aspect of international staffing is designing an international executive compensation package. What approach would you adopt and why?

EXERCISE 9.1: Designing an international organizational structure

Aim   This project aims at improving students' skills in designing and drawing international organizational structures.

Assignment   The class is divided into small groups. Each group is given a particular international organizational structure and asked to find a multinational firm adopting such a structure, and to report their findings to the class.

One group may consider drawing the matrix organization structure of ABB based on the illustrative case provided in the text, and present their chart to the class, analysing its advantages and disadvantages.

Format   This exercise requires researching the annual reports published by various companies, and drawing an organizational chart for class presentation and discussion.

EXERCISE 9.2: International human resource management

Aim   This exercise aims at developing students' skills in international human resource management in different countries and cultures and in designing a booklet to assist expatriates in their overseas assignments.

Assignment   Students are asked to choose a country of particular interest, and to prepare a leaflet providing necessary information on living and working conditions in that particular country. This should include advice on how to overcome cultural differences, and how to adjust to the foreign environment. Students may use the country profile developed earlier in the course as a base for their research.

Format   This exercise requires an amount of creativity in designing, illustrating and editing the company leaflet, which might be called 'Living and working in Country X'.

FURTHER READING

Brewster, C. and Tyson, S., *International Comparison. Human Resource Management*, Pitman, London, 1991.

Dowling, P. J. and Schuller, R. S., *International Dimensions of Human Resource Management*, PWS Kent, Boston, 1990.

Guy, V. and Mattock, J. *The New International Manager: An Action Guide to Cross-Cultural Business*, Kogan Page, London, 1991.

Hodgetts, R. and Luthans, F. *International Management*, McGraw-Hill, New York, 1991.

INTERNATIONAL MARKETING

Marketing principles are universally applicable to all types of commodities, from consumer packaged goods, consumer durables and industrial goods, to professional services, such as insurance and medical services, legal consultancy and accountancy. Even non-profit organizations, such as museums, hospitals, police, colleges and leisure centres are now turning to marketing for the delivery of their services.

Marketing principles have been recently internationalized due to the growth of multinational firms operating throughout the world. Eastern and Central European countries, realizing the value of marketing to business, are increasingly expressing their interest in adopting marketing principles and techniques in their transitional efforts to move from centrally planned economies to free markets.

Although the basic marketing principles are universally applicable, entering a new market in a foreign country might often mean dealing with a different environment, different consumer tastes, different production processes and marketing approaches.

LEARNING OBJECTIVES

- To explain why international marketing is more complex and difficult than domestic marketing
- To introduce the international marketing mix concept
- To provide guidance on how to formulate a global marketing strategy

MARKETING: DEFINITION AND HISTORICAL DEVELOPMENT

Marketing principles were first adopted in Japan around 1650 by the first member of the Mitsui family when he opened his first department store in Tokyo based on policies such as 'to be a buyer for his customers, to design the right products for them, and to develop sources for their production; the principle of your money back and no question asked; and the idea of offering a large assortment of products to his customers rather than focusing on a craft, a product category, or a process' (Drucker, 1974b, p. 62).

In the West, marketing appeared in the middle of the 19th century, when Cyrus H. McCormick first made the distinction between marketing as hard selling and advertising, and marketing as 'the unique and central function of the business enterprise', and invented the basic tools of modern marketing, including market research and market analysis, pricing policies, parts and service supply to the customer, and instalment credit (Drucker, 1974b, p. 62).

Marketing as a discipline was further developed in 1905 when W. E. Kreusi taught the first course, 'The Marketing of Products', at the University of Pennsylvania, and in 1910 when R. Butler offered a course in 'Marketing Methods' at the University of Wisconsin. Marketing departments did not appear within firms until the early 20th century. Marketing did not crystallize as a business philosophy until the mid-1950s (Kotler, 1984, p. 20).

E. Jerome McCarthy was the first to develop the four factor classification, which has come to be known as the famour Four Ps of the marketing mix: Product, Price, Place and Promotion (Kotler, 1984, p. 70; McCarthy, 1981, p. 42).

- *Product* This includes a study of the product features, packaging, branding and servicing policies, and style.
- *Price* This refers to the money that customers have to pay for the product, such as a wholesale price or retail price, allowances and credit terms.
- *Place* This stands for various activities the firm undertakes to make the product accessible and available to consumers. This includes, for example, choosing retailers, wholesalers, physical distribution firms and intermediaries.
- *Promotion* This is simply the effort of the firm to persuade customers to buy the product, and includes activities such as advertising, sales promotions and publicity.

Theodore Levitt also made a clear distinction between selling and the marketing concept (Levitt, 1960, pp. 45–56). While selling, according to Levitt, focuses on the seller, marketing focuses on the needs of the buyer. 'Selling is preoccupied with the seller's need to convert his product into cash; marketing with the idea of satisfying the needs of the customer by means of the product and the whole cluster of things associated with creating, delivery and finally consuming it' (Levitt, 1960, pp. 45–56). Although selling starts with the firm's existing products, and calls for hard and aggressive selling and promotion to achieve profits, marketing, on the other hand, starts with the firm's target customers and their needs and wants and attempts to achieve profits through customer satisfaction (Kotler, 1984, pp. 22–3).

Consequently 'selling is only the tip of the marketing iceberg', as Kotler put it (Kotler, 1984, p. 20). Marketing aims at knowing and understanding customers so well that the product fits them and sells itself. All that should be needed then is to make the product or service available (Drucker, 1974b, pp. 64–5).

Domestic marketing vs. international marketing

Marketing principles are not fundamentally different in the international environment, but entering a new market in a foreign country can often mean dealing with a different environment, consumer tastes, marketing methods, production processes and promotion strategies. Each country has its own economic, political, cultural and social characteristics. Each country's readiness for different products and services, and its attractiveness, may vary considerably. There are hundreds of examples of companies who failed to succeed in the foreign environment (see Ricks, 1983).

The Marks & Spencer case study below points out many of the problems a firm may face in international markets. Although the firm did substantial research before it began expanding in foreign environments, it still faced unexpected problems that seriously inhibited its initial success.

CASE STUDY 10.1: Experiencing international markets—Marks & Spencer

Marks & Spencer's domestic operations

Marks & Spencer is the largest retailer in the UK today. The Marble Arch shop is listed in the *Guinness Book of Records* as the store that takes in more revenue per square foot than any other business in the world. Originally, clothes and household textiles accounted for about two-thirds of the sales. Recently, Marks & Spencer has added food lines to its stores, and has become a large and profitable food retailer in Britain.

Since its creation in 1884, Marks & Spencer has managed to develop an image that is as British as 'bed and breakfast' or 'fish and chips'. In the late 1970s, however, the company experienced a drop in its unit sales for the first time. It is at this stage that the company decided that since the domestic markets in the UK were nearing saturation, growth must be overseas.

Marks & Spencer in France

Marks & Spencer believed that since they were so well known in Britain, and since so many foreign tourists visited their London stores, their reputation had preceded them. Paris was seen as an ideal location for its stores outside the UK.

Marks & Spencer's first European venture in Paris faced many problems. The company soon realized, for example, that only 3 per cent of French consumers had heard of it and its St Michael brand name. The location of the store was also on the wrong side of Boulevard Haussman, opposite Galeries LaFayette, a major French retailer, similar to Harrods. Marks & Spencer also undervalued its French customers by simply trying to sell its Oxford Street collection in France, without any adaptation to French taste. The French cultural tradition was also severely overlooked. When potential customers went into the new stores they were unaccustomed to the starkness and lack of service. Inside the store, they were even more offended. Parisians like to try the clothing they are buying. When Marks & Spencer opened its first store in Paris, twelve years ago, there were no changing rooms and Parisian shoppers simply undressed in the middle of the store.

Marks & Spencer in Spain

In Spain, determined not to make the same mistakes as in its early operations in France, for the first time in its history Marks & Spencer installed 48 fitting rooms in its Madrid store. Since most of its customers were wealthy and dressed well, the company minimized its polyester lines and maximized its silk, linen and lingerie lines.

Marks & Spencer in Canada

In entering the Canadian Market, Marks & Spencer assumed that the 'Englishness' of its products would be of a greater advantage there than in the European continent. A Canadian supplier remarked that British management in Canada did things 'because that is the way they did it in England'. This policy included, for example, the placement of bigger sleeves on clothing, and the avoidance of lively colours in both clothing and advertising. As a result, the Canadians found the merchandise dull, the stores 'cold and clinical', and they did not like finding food next to clothing. Most stores were also placed in town-centre locations, as is the custom in the UK, while the Canadians were increasingly turning to suburban shopping centres. In response to Canadian tastes, Marks & Spencer had to add fitting rooms, introduce wood panelling, mirrors, partitions between departments, and wall-to-wall carpets.

Marks & Spencer in the USA

In 1987, Marks & Spencer appointed a top-level team to conduct an in-depth study of the US market place in order to set up stores under the Marks & Spencer name. It acquired Brookes Brothers in 1988, a company which had a dignified image, a high level of personal service and expensive clothing. Soon after the acquisition, the company sought to increase its sales by introducing some changes to the Brookes sales approach, in an attempt to bring less affluent customers into the store. The number of personnel was reduced, and glass display cases were gradually replaced with open displays. The company ran a six-week sale, instead of the customary one week, and decreased the number of sizes of casual coats by offering them simply as small, medium, large and extra large. During the first two years the results of the changes were disastrous, as sales and profits declined.

Marks & Spencer also went further and bought Kings, a 16 outlet food chain in New Jersey. This acquisition had seemed compatible, since Kings and Marks & Spencer shared an operating philosophy of emphasizing perishables and upmarket prepared food. Marks & Spencer began introducing its St Michael chilled prepared food lines in the stores, only to find out that the UK concept of overnight delivery from central kitchens was not practical for the US. Most of the food items had to be prepared locally in King's stores, which created additional problems of cost and quality control.

Sources

Marks & Spencer: From Paris to Madrid, Business Studies, BBC TV Programme, 18 January 1991.
Daniels, J. D. and Radebaugh, L. H., *International Business*, 6th edn, Addison-Wesley, Reading MA, 1992, pp. 655–9.

As the above case shows, international marketing is much more complex and complicated than domestic marketing. It can be defined as the process of 'finding out what customers want around the world, and then satisfying these wants better than other competitors both domestic and international' (Terpestra and Sarathy, 1991, p. 5).

THE INTERNATIONAL MARKETING MIX

The international marketing mix, illustrated in Figure 10.1, is useful in assisting a firm in making decisions about its international marketing strategy, and in successfully targeting appropriate international markets.

Product policy for international markets

There are two general classes of products marketed domestically and internationally (Khambata and Ajami, 1992, p. 379). These are industrial products and consumer goods. Industrial products are goods sold to manufacturing firms, businesses and governments. Industrial products include durable goods, such as steel, hardware, machinery and electronic components. Consumer products are goods sold to the public, who may have different needs and tastes. Consumer goods include items such as clothing, luxury goods, food products, appliances and automobiles.

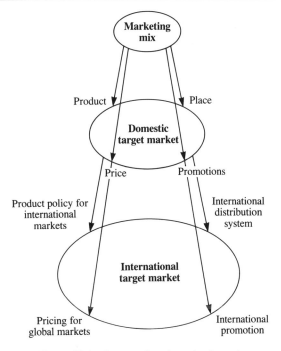

Figure 10.1   International marketing mix

In considering which products to market overseas, a firm must decide whether it wants to sell the same product, as it is, worldwide, or whether it should adapt the product to suit local culture and appeal to local tastes and social trends.

There are four main strategies from which to choose for targeting foreign markets:

1. Global extension.
2. Global standardization.
3. Product differentiation or adaptation.
4. New product development.

Global extension   This occurs when a firm decides simply to sell exactly the same product in foreign markets as in domestic markets. The underlying assumption here is that the domestic and international market needs for the product are the same, and that the product would fulfil the same needs or serve the same function abroad as it does at home. Such a strategy is applicable to scientific and medical instruments, laboratory equipment and heavy machinery.

Global standardization   This occurs when a company decides to produce one product and sell it in the same way everywhere in the world with the same specification and characteristics. Consumer products adopting such a strategy include, for example, Polaroid cameras, Cartier watches, Mont Blanc pens, Chanel perfumes and Estée Lauder cosmetics. The basic argument for adopting a global strategy is the claim that national and regional differences are steadily declining due to new technology, improved communications and transport, and that customers' needs and interests as a result are becoming increasingly homogeneous worldwide. Customers around the world, it is argued, have now one thing in common: 'an overwhelming desire for dependable, worldwide modernity in all things, at aggressively low prices which can only be achieved through product standardization' (Levitt, 1983, pp. 92–102).

It is also claimed that standardization of production can be economically efficient, because when a product has only one production source, standardizing it will gain the economies of scale of long production runs (Terpestra and Sarathy, 1991, p. 253). Research and development expenses normally needed to accommodate and adapt the product to each foreign market can also be redirected towards improving the product itself and towards innovation. A standardized production policy can also maintain stronger control over design, technology and quality, thus achieving a worldwide reputation and maintaining the global image of the product (Ohmae, 1990a, p. 25).

Global branding occurs when a company decides to establish a world brand identification for its products, even when it cannot standardize them. Three of the most powerful brand names recognized worldwide are Coca Cola, IBM and Sony (Rosen *et al.*, 1989, pp. 7–19). The main advantage of global branding is that production and quality can be better controlled because of standardized production methods and product design. There is also a greater possibility of standardizing promotion and advertising.

Despite the many advantages of product standardization, there are also a number of constraints which severely restrict a firm's ability to standardize its products and to adopt a global brand (Douglas and Yoram, 1987, pp. 19–29). Some of these restrictions arise from government and trade restrictions, such as tariffs, trade barriers, product pricing or promotional regulation, and quotas on imported goods, or local content requirements, which require that products contain a certain proportion of components manufactured locally. Government legislation and regulations may also affect the standardization of products and put certain restriction on whether an already standardized product can be sold without adaptation to national legislation. Some countries may even forbid the import of certain goods all together. Saudi Arabia, for example, prohibits the import of alcoholic drinks and pork meat and products. Government regulations on product packaging and labelling can also be a serious constraint on product standardization and might require product variation, especially where foods and drugs are concerned. An example is the new EC legislation on anti-pollution standards for small car engines. These new standards have had a heavy impact on manufacturers such as Peugeot and Renault, but have benefited German manufacturers, who already have stricter national German anti-pollution standards (Terpestra and Sarathy, 1991, p. 273).

Advertising regulations in certain countries can also severely restrict the use of media campaigns, for example, the recent EC legislation on harmonizing advertising. As part of these rules, it has proposed that cigarette print and poster advertisements be restricted to presentation of the cigarette packaging, and information about tar and nicotine content, with health warnings, must take up between 10 and 20 per cent of the advertisement space. Such restrictions can prevent companies from using their familiar company images, such as the Marlboro man, and the Virginia Slims woman (Terpestra and Sarathy, 1991, p. 268). Another government restriction can involve labelling laws, which may vary between countries.

Other constraints on product standardization may be internal to the company itself, and include for example the relationship between subsidiary and headquarters, corporate orientation and delegation of authority (Subhash, 1990, p. 342). A conflict might arise because of different points of view, depending on the company's orientation (Perlmutter, 1969a, pp. 9–18). The attitudes of local management may also impose a constraint upon the standardization of production. They might feel that a policy has been imposed by headquarters, even though it might not be appropriate to local market needs and conditions.

Product differentiation   Product differentiation is when a company realizes the need to introduce some modifications to its product in various foreign markets due to different lifestyles, tastes, religion, habits, language or other cultural elements, legal requirements, physical differences and different infrastructures.

The use of a product and its functional needs may vary considerably. For example, when US toothbrushes were first introduced in South Vietnam in the late 1960s, the company experienced a major jump in sales. It was not until later that the company found out that the Vietcong had bought the toothbrushes, not to ensure white teeth, but for weapon cleaning (Ricks, 1983, p. 3).

Differences in climate could influence consumer products, especially with respect to packaging and conservation. In spite of their reputation for quality and comfort, Clarks' shoes are not suitable to the hot weather in Saudi Arabia with their crêpe rubber soles and thick leather uppers, which cause feet to sweat (Yugur and Tuncalp, 1984, p. 44).

Clothing and dressing-up also vary in different cultures. Christian Dior in Saudi Arabia introduced recently a new line of designer 'Abbaya', similar to the traditional all-black 'shador', but more colourful, with gold sequin embroidery, which are sold successfully in the Gulf.

Adaptation is not only restricted to consumer products. The computer program Lotus 1–2–3 underwent major revision to serve the needs of the Japanese market. First, it had to translate all the text included in the menus, help screens and so on into Japanese. Second, it had to incorporate the latest techniques for entering the 7000-plus Japanese characters for a normal-size keyboard. Third, new functions, especially those used by Japanese business and analysts in quality control, had to be added to the program. Lotus, in other words, had to practically rebuild the product (Terpestra and Sarathy, 1991, p. 257; Lotus Development Corporation News Release, 10 September 1986 and 24 February 1987).

Advantages and disadvantages of product adaptation and differentiation   The main advantage of a product adaptation policy is that it increases profits by being capable of quickly responding to changes in consumers trends, tastes and unexpected environmental changes and needs. By modifying the product to meet local needs, climate, safety requirements and government regulations, product differentiation strategy also increases the efficiency of the product.

The main disadvantage of product differentiation is the cost involved in producing various products for various markets, such as the expense involved in research and development. Headquarters, moreover, could also lose control over quality if production is undertaken in different countries. The home national image too might be lost as a result of constantly introducing product variations to suit local market's needs and tastes, with the risk of ending up with a completely new line of product.

New product development: global product, global brand   The standardization vs. product differentiation debate first emerged in the 1960s. Traditionally, the discussion has been polarized around whether a product should be standardized worldwide, or customized on a market-by-market basis. In early interpretations of global markets, the issue was narrowly focused on the standardization or differentiation of products. The notion of global markets, global advertising and global marketing was simply linked to the existence of global markets for the products. Global marketing then simply meant product extension in overseas markets.

In the last decade, however, the resurgence of interest in the debate between standardization and differentiation is mostly due to the globalization of world markets and of most business activities, such as finance, technology, research, capital and production facilities, during the 1980s.

Theodore Levitt (1983), in his powerful essay 'The globalization of markets' explains how well-managed companies have moved from an emphasis on customized items to offering globally standardized products that are advanced, functional, reliable and low priced. National differences in product preference, he argues, have been steadily declining as markets become global. Consumer needs, interests and desires are also becoming increasingly homogeneous. Different cultural preferences, national tastes and standards, Levitt asserts further, are 'vestiges of the past'. Consumers all over the world are now more willing to sacrifice preference in product features, functions, design and the like for high quality at low prices.

This global preference for low price and high quality, however, does not automatically mean that markets everywhere are becoming the same. Globalization does not mean that all tastes are becoming identical, or that operating globally removes the obligation or need to localize products (Ohmae, 1990a, p. 24). The kind of globalization of marketing that Levitt argues for is applicable only to some types of products, such as battery-operated goods, cameras, watches, pocket calculators, cosmetics and perfumes. What globalization simply means is that as the boundary lines on maps fade, the underlying clusters of value and preference become increasingly more visible (Ohmae, 1990a, p. 185), thus making it easier for global firms to design their products accordingly. With the assistance of new technology, firms are now more capable of adapting their products to specific local needs and tastes quickly and cheaply.

Pricing for global markets

Until the late 1980s, pricing had been a major part of the marketing mix and was seen as crucial to the success of any marketing programme, whether domestic or overseas. Due to increased competition for world market shares, improved and cheaper transport and communications, and new information technology, even domestic markets which were once protected from distant competitors are now feeling the pressure of their presence. Beating competitors in their own markets has become nowadays the central concern.

Pricing for global markets is much more difficult and complicated than pricing for domestic markets, even though it may be based on the same basic principles and processes. This process, briefly stated, includes six steps (Kotler, 1984, pp. 505–36):

1. Selecting the pricing objectives, which can be any of survival, current profit maximization, market share leadership or product quality leadership.
2. Determining demand.
3. Estimating costs.
4. Analysing competitor's prices and offers.
5. Selecting a pricing method.
6. Selecting a final price.

Factors influencing international pricing can be grouped into three categories: company-specific factors, market factors and environmental factors (Matsuura, 1991, p. 342).

- *Company-specific or internal factors*
  International pricing is usually done at corporate headquarters and varies from one country to another. Company pricing objectives, depending on whether it is a growth market or stagnant market, are either to maximize profit and market share, or simply to survive.
- *External market factors*
  These include market structure and consumers' purchasing power, income, cultural habits

and attitudes towards certain products. These factors have an influence on market demand. As a result, a firm must charge different prices in different markets. For example, when Estée Lauder opened its first shop in Hungary, it had to sell its products at much lower prices than in other European countries. Avon products in Hungary were also very low priced, based upon the consumers' ability to buy and the company's long-term objectives in seeking to expand its market share rather than gaining immediate profit.

- *Environmental factors*

These are external to the company, such as inflation rates and currency fluctuation. Governments can influence a firm's pricing in several ways by imposing tariffs and taxes, such as on pharmaceutical products, housing, food, health and education. Inflation, particularly in developing countries, can cause serious problems in pricing and poses a constant threat. Exchange rate fluctuation can also have an adverse effect on pricing.

Considerable controversy has arisen in recent years concerning the most appropriate pricing policy for global markets. On the one hand, it has been strongly argued that new information technology, internationalization of production and finance, and fierce competition in the markets mean that the only way to succeed is in the use of aggressive pricing tools. Aggressive low pricing is the secret of success of Japanese companies. By forcing their costs and prices down, and then increasing quality and reliability, Japanese companies have been able to expand into global markets.

In contrast, K. Ohmae in his book *The Borderless World* argues that the concept of pricing in the 20th century has become obsolete, and has shifted from costs to value. In a borderless world, Ohmae writes, profit is no longer the major criterion, and does not mean 'building pyramids of cash flow by focusing on the discovery of new places to invest. Nor does it mean tracking down your competitors and preemptively undercutting them in their own home country ... instead it means delivering value to customers' (Ohmae, 1990a, p. 31).

Nintendo provides a good example of how a company can achieve great profits without beating its competitors and without cutting prices. Nintendo began marketing its first game-playing computer, 'the Family Computer' in Japan in 1983, and first tested its product in New York in 1984. By 1988, it achieved greater penetration of the market than any other computer or personal PC. Its sales in the USA rose from $800 million in 1987 to $1.7 billion in 1988, while still keeping the games at a relatively high price of $40 per cartridge. Nintendo pricing policy, rather than beating competitors, is to work with them. In Japan, for example, Nintendo created a network to help it succeed. It formed a joint venture with Fidelity Investments to develop and sell a home-based trading system for financial services. In the USA it also intends to cooperate with AT&T as the key to obtaining a US-wide communications ability (Cateora, 1990, p. 460).

International distribution systems

International distribution is more complicated than domestic distribution, and involves two stages. First, the international marketer must transport goods from the domestic production site to the foreign market, and then establish methods of distribution within the foreign country.

In international transportation, a choice must be made between ocean and air shipping, depending on the nature of the cargo (whether it is a perishable good, such as meat or vegetables, for example), the transit time, the relative costs and the specific needs of the customer, or urgency. In distribution in foreign markets, a choice must be made between various types of intermediaries and the nature of outlets. Various countries have their own distribution systems, which they have developed. It is very difficult for a firm to decide to standardize these distribution systems or to decide to have a uniform distribution pattern in a foreign market. Distribution structures also vary from one country to another. The challenge here is not in choosing one standardized form of distribution which could be more profitable, but in adopting the right approach in different countries.

International promotion/advertising

There are three basic steps involved in the development of an international promotion and advertising strategy.

Step 1: Standardization, differentiation or global advertising   Debate about the advantages and disadvantages of standardized vs. modified advertising is not new. The benefits of standardized advertising are first that economies may be gained from using the same advertising programme worldwide, and second, that by using standardized advertising, the firm has more control over maintaining a consistent image of the product so as not to confuse the consumer: Kodak and its yellow box is a classic example. Third, standardized advertising ensures global recognition. Executives who travel abroad, for example, like to recognize brands they are used to in their home markets. Finally, a fourth advantage of standardized advertising is in the costs of production. A standardized advertising campaign can often have a larger production budget, thus making it possible for a more sophisticated initiative, using media stars such as Michael Jackson and Tina Turner in Pepsi-Cola advertisements and Elton John in Coca Cola advertisements.

Despite these advantages, standardized advertising also has limitations. Many firms are increasingly realizing that customers all over the world react differently. They belong to different ethnic groups, religions and cultures. Just as products have to be adapted to suit local customers' tastes, advertising needs in some cases to be modified to suit various lifestyles, cultures, attitudes and beliefs. Companies advertising global products, such as Coca Cola, Nestlé and Levi, have increasingly been aware of the need to adapt and modify their advertisements according to local cultures, while at the same time keeping their logo intact.

CASE STUDY 10.2: Advertising for global products

Levi Strauss Jeans

Levi's jeans are sold in more than 70 countries. Although the product itself is identical in all markets, the image projected in the advertisements is not identical, but adapted to local culture and tastes. In Europe, for example, TV adverts for Levi's jeans have a super sexy appeal, particularly in France. In the UK, where young consumers are increasingly attracted by American brands, the advertisement figures American heroes in Wild West settings. In contrast, in Brazil, where the market is strongly influenced by trends emanating from the European continent rather than America, advertisements for Brazilian markets are all filmed in Paris.

Coca Cola

Although Coca Cola adopted a global theme 'Can't beat the feeling' in all its advertisements worldwide, featuring a variety of young and old people dancing, the commercials are altered for certain markets. One version, called 'Dance', will be shown in the Caribbean, South Africa and the South Pacific with the tune played in reggae style and with more black people appearing.

Playtex

Instead of having 43 different versions of ads running worldwide, as in the past, Playtex recently developed a global campaign for TV that would work in every market. Although the 'cross-your-heart' message remained the same everywhere, substantial differences were introduced to suit local cultures. For example, in France the advertisement shows lacy bras while in Germany and America the emphasis is on the plainer types. Even names of the bras had to be changed because 'WOW' (without wires) could not be translated literally. Dream wires – Traumbügel – was used in German markets, Wings was chosen for Spain and Armagique in France, a contraction of the words for structure and magic.

Sources
Ball, D. A. and McMulloch, W. H., *International Business: Introduction and Essentials*, 5th edn, Irwin, Homewood IL, 1993, p. 535.
Exporting a legend, *International Advertiser*, Nov/Dec 1981, pp. 2–3.
McCarthy, M., *Wall Street Journal*, 12 December 1988.

Step 2: Choice of appropriate message Apart from cultural diversity, other limitations upon standardized advertising are language and translation. Although English is becoming the international language of business, as it is already of commerce, it does not yet permit global use in advertising. Various examples illustrate the limitations of using the English language, as was the case with Playtex (mentioned above). Many humorous examples of advertising translation errors are recounted frequently. For example, the Ford Fierra Truck, when translated into Spanish means 'ugly old woman', while in Puerto Rico the word meant 'killer' (Ricks, 1983, p. 84). Libby solved this problem by simply introducing a clown in its standardized advertising features, pantomiming enjoyment in eating Libby products (Cateora, 1990, p. 465).

Standardized advertising may also face considerable legal constraints. What is allowed in one country may be banned in another. An advertisement's theme can be prohibited on moral and ethical grounds. Japan, for example, advertises products such as tampons, laxatives and haemorrhoid treatments, which are banned from being advertised in the USA (Darlin, 1980). The 'Silhouette' female tampons with 'wings' caused a great shock when it was first shown on British television. Benetton's recent advert of a white nun kissing a black priest has been banned in many countries. In Saudi Arabia, TV commercials were not allowed at all until 1985. Even then, commercials were restricted to industrial products only, showing products and product specifications, and women are banned from appearing in commercials. In the Single European Market, cigarettes and liquor advertisements will not be allowed on television after 1993. The use of superlatives such as 'this product is the best', or 'cheapest' are also banned. In Germany, it is illegal to claim that one brand is better than another, while this is still quite acceptable in UK and the USA. Pepsi and Coca Cola are classical examples here. Radion versus Ariel is also illustrative of this. In Italy, even words such as deodorant or perspiration are banned (Boddewyn, 1981, pp. 5–13; Williams and Ryans, 1982; Boddewyn, 1989).

Other constraints, not particularly restricted to cultural behaviour, consumer reaction or language, refer to different national broadcasting regulations. In the Netherlands, for example, Kellogg's commercials must delete any references to iron and vitamins. In Austria, children as actors must be removed, in France children are not allowed to endorse products on TV, and finally in Germany Kellogg had to change its message that Kellogg makes the best cornflakes because of German rules against making competitive claims.

Step 3: Media selection   Having decided on the message or the theme of advertising, the third stage in global advertising strategy is to select the appropriate media. International media selection is complicated by international differences in media. A TV campaign might be suitable in developed countries, where many own TV sets, but not in developing countries. The use of printed media for adverts is also relative to levels of literacy. In highly developed countries, such as Japan, the UK or Germany, the use of national dailies, magazines, radio and direct mail might be appropriate, while advertising on billboards is more useful in countries with high illiteracy rates. In hot countries, however, these billboards would not be tolerant of local weather conditions, and would not last more than two weeks.

Despite these limitations, some companies have been successful in standardizing their advertisements worldwide, e.g. BMW or Mercedes, by identifying a global target market that runs across national boundaries, with similar needs and wants that can be satisfied with a standardized product. There are some segments in most countries with similar demands for the same product. Young people, for instance have similar tastes in sport and cultural activities; trend-setters appreciate exclusive products and reject consumer stereotypes; and business people who travel abroad regularly have a taste for luxury goods (see Levitt, 1983). Some companies have been successful in marketing their products in overseas markets even without the need for advertising, as illustrated in the case of the Body Shop.

CASE STUDY 10.3: Does business need advertising?—The Body Shop

The Body Shop, a cosmetics manufacturer and retailer is already a legend in the UK. This $16 billion, now global, cosmetic empire was started in 1976 by Anita Roddick with a bank loan of only £4000. Today Body Shop has over 736 outlets in 41 countries around the world. Retail sales from franchised and company stores in 1990 reached $391 million, and earnings based on wholesale revenues of $197 million were $21 million. By the end of August 1991, Body Shop earned $41 million on sales of $231 million. In ten years, sales and profits grew on average by 50 per cent a year. Body Shop's operating profits are predicted to grow at an annual rate of 35 per cent to 40 per cent over the next five years, despite the recession in retailing.

While for most cosmetic manufacturers selling their products without media advertising would be unthinkable, Body Shop has succeeded so far with no marketing department or advertising campaigns.

The secret of Body Shop's success lies in the company's philosophy of selling 'well-being' instead of selling 'fantasy' or appealing to vanity. The company established its credibility with its customers and gained their loyalty by educating them. For example, Body Shop tells customers where its products come from, what is in them, how they are tested, and what uses they have. Cards on every counter tell customers about the ingredients and history of some of the lotions, and leaflets offering tips about skin and hair care are available.

The Body Shop is also very well known for its passionate environmentalism, and symbolizes the new ecological consciousness in business. Pamphlets throughout the store detail Body Shop's recycling efforts by using biodegradable plastic bags, encouraging customers to return their empty bottles and have them refilled for a discount, and supporting many environmentalist organizations such as Greenpeace, Friends of the Earth, Environmental Transport Association and Wastewatch. They promote themes such as 're-use, refill, recycle' and 'ozone or no zone', and are campaigning against the dumping of hazardous waste in the North Sea and against the causes of acid rain.

The company's literature in all stores also assures its customers that their products have not been tested on animals, and explains the company's opposition to animal testing for cosmetics.

Thus one of the most important things that makes Body Shop stand out from its competitors is its high profile stance on social issues. T-shirts worn by staff and window product displays often support important social causes and campaigns, such as fighting for human rights. The company delivery trucks are also used as mobile billboards. Each truck has a different quotation of the campaign issues painted in enormous white letters on its side.

'Trade not Aid' is the Body Shop's trading policy in overseas markets, particularly in the less developed countries. Staff working at Body Shop are not expected to act just as sales people. Each franchise is required to create its own community service programme. Instead of contributing a percentage of the profits to charity, the Body Shop reinvests some of its profits in the local development of the community.

Sources
Rahul, J., What selling will be like in the '90s, *Fortune*, **124**(1), 13 January 1992, pp. 63–4.
Zinn, L., Whales, human rights, rain forests – and the heady smell of profits', *Business Week*, Industrial/ Technology Edition, Issue 32, 15 July 1991, pp. 114–15.
Burlington, B., Body Shop bares its soul, *Business*, UK, Dec. 1990, pp. 82–5.
Seward, H., Establishing a social conscience at work, *New England Business*, **12**(11), Nov. 1990, pp. 97–8.
Burlington, B., This woman has changed business forever, *Inc.*, **12**(6), June 1990, pp. 34–47.
Wallace, C., Lessons in marketing – from a maverick, *Working Woman*, **15**, Oct. 1990, pp. 81–4.

THE INTERNATIONAL MARKETING PLAN

There are six major stages in constructing an international marketing plan. These are illustrated in Figure 10.2.

Figure 10.2   International marketing plan

Stage 1: Country profile   The first stage in developing an international marketing plan is to conduct a preliminary environmental analysis. Information on various countries needs to be collected to construct country profiles. (Refer to Chapter One for more details on how to construct a country profile.)

Stage 2: Company profile   At this stage, business managers are advised to analyse the company internal factors and conduct a SWOT analysis highlighting strengths, weaknesses, opportunities and threats facing the firm's international expansion strategic plan.

Stage 3: Product profile   To construct a product profile, business managers should conduct market research to collect the necessary information related to the market for the product. The product profile should include a detailed analysis of the four international Ps, i.e. international product, international pricing, international markets and international promotion.

Stage 4: Market profile – national/international/global competition   A competitive market analysis is essential to provide estimated market potential, and an evaluation of the marketing strategy to be adopted. A choice should be made between a standardization, differentiation or globalization strategy. The analysis here should include detailed information on the foreign competitors' products, characteristics and market share.

Stage 5: International marketing objectives product strategy   Based on the country, product and market profiles, a firm's global marketing objectives can then be defined in the light of prospects identified in the analyses. The main issue to be addressed here is what the company should do to increase its sales in foreign target markets. Marketing objectives must first be clearly determined in terms of expected sales, expected profit, level of market penetration and coverage. Then a product strategy must be agreed upon: should the product be standardized or be adapted to local market's needs? Consideration needs also to be given to political organization and to local regulations, culture and language.

Stage 6: International implementation   At this stage, decisions should be made regarding advertising and promotion policies. A choice should also be made as to what international business operations should be adopted: exporting, franchising, licensing, joint ventures, etc. (These operations and strategies will be discussed in detail in Chapter Eleven.)

REVIEW QUESTIONS

1. What problems does selling a standardized product in global markets generate?
2. In what ways might a product be adapted for global markets? Illustrate your answer with empirical examples.
3. What factors encourage the trend towards global standardization of a product?
4. What advantages are there for a firm to standardize its products and promote them worldwide as much as possible?
5. Identify one specific multinational firm known to you and follow its promotional strategy in the various countries it operates in. Are they all similar?
6. To what extent do the Four Ps of the marketing mix differ at the international level?
7. Assume you have decided to sell your product overseas. Outline the steps you would take to help you decide upon your international marketing plan.
8. What arguments are there for and against the proposition that we are moving towards a

homogenized market with homogenized customers? Are consumer tastes converging around the world?

9. In deciding what products a firm should sell overseas, the basic question is whether to standardize or to adapt the product to foreign markets. What factors encourage global standardization? What factors encourage global adaptation? Discuss and support your analysis with examples.

EXERCISE 10.1: The Body Shop

Aim   The aim of this exercise is to introduce first-year students to case study analysis and to develop their analytical skills and critical judgement.

Assignment   The case study to be considered in this exercise is the case of the Body Shop: 'Does business need advertising', given in the text.

1. Analyse and evaluate the Body Shop's international marketing strategy.
2. In what ways does the Body Shop's global marketing strategy differ from other traditional marketing strategies?
3. Most cosmetic industries rely heavily on advertising to sell their products. How did the Body Shop overcome the need for advertising? Do you think this is a good strategy? What general lessons can we learn from it?

EXERCISE 10.2: International marketing

Aim   This exercise is intended to develop students' skills in formulating an international marketing strategy, to help them consider some of the cultural and national issues that affect an international advertising campaign, and to develop their creative skills in using various media and designing their own advertisements and promotion.

Assignment   Choose a particular local product that appeals to you, and devise a marketing plan for entering a foreign market in a specific country, or a whole region.

Format   Students should work in small groups for this assignment. Each group should develop its own international marketing plan, including an advertisement and promotional campaign, to be presented to the class. Figure 10.1 may be useful as a basic guideline in preparing this project.

Students are strongly encouraged to include in their presentation any slogans, drawings, models, music or voice-overs, or even to get some experience in developing their own commercial on video, if possible.

FURTHER READING

Bradley, F., *International Marketing Strategy*, Prentice-Hall, New York, 1991.

Paliwoda, S. (ed.), *New perspectives on International Marketing*, Routledge, London, 1991.

Ricks, D., *Big Business Blunders*, Irwin Dow Jones, Homewood IL, 1983.

Terpestra, V. and Sarathy, R., *International Marketing*, 5th edn, Dryden, New York, 1991.

ELEVEN

GLOBAL STRATEGIC MANAGEMENT

Few companies are multinational from the start. They do not emerge as full global companies overnight or as if by accident. Global strategic management is very complex and requires a separate study of its own to be fully comprehensive. This chapter aims to provide an introductory understanding of the 'internationalization' and 'globalization' processes, essential to junior managers and first-year students who have a limited knowledge of strategic management.

LEARNING OBJECTIVES

- To explain how companies 'go international', to describe the various methods available for conducting international business, and to highlight the advantages and disadvantages of each method
- To clearly understand the difference between multinational firms and global firms and their implications for international business
- To provide guidance on how to construct a global strategic plan, and the various steps needed for effective implementation

THE INTERNATIONALIZATION PROCESS

There are various methods of international business operations available to firms to assist them in their internationalization process. Each method has its own strengths, weaknesses, benefits and limitations. The choice depends upon the nature of the business, company goals and objectives, environmental conditions, company products and competition abroad.

Although a firm might decide to choose one form of international expansion, it is increasingly becoming the case in the 1990s that a particular company will adopt several entry strategies simultaneously, in various countries. Pilkington, one of the world's leading glass makers, started operation in 1826 in St Helens, Lancashire and now has over 400 subsidiaries in almost 40 countries in the world. Pilkington adopted different ways to internationalize its business. In developed countries, such as Scandinavia, Germany, France, Holland, Australia and New Zealand, Pilkington has wholly owned subsidiaries. In contrast, in the less developed countries, such as Mexico, Brazil, India, Nigeria, Zimbabwe and Argentina, the company has a controlling share in partly owned subsidiaries. Joint ventures with host governments have been established in Poland and South Africa. The company has also expanded its operations in Eastern Europe through a series of acquisitions in the former East Germany and Poland.

Exporting

Exporting is the oldest form of entry into international markets, where a firm may decide to maintain its production facilities at home and export its products to foreign countries. There are two types of exporting: direct and indirect.

In direct exporting, export tasks are carried out directly by the company itself. Direct exporting functions include market research, study of potential international markets, international insurance, shipping and preparing export documentation, financing, pricing and accounting. All these tasks are initially handled by local employees as the orders come through. However, if the export business expands the company may then decide to set up a separate international division to handle the increased volume of export business.

Direct exporting requires relatively little capital, personnel and resources. Direct exporting also provides the company with the opportunity to test foreign markets for its product without committing much of its resources in doing so. It allows the company to sell its product overseas without transferring some of its capital into foreign markets, or exposing its personnel to the problems of operating in foreign environments. Direct exporting requires expertise in handling the technical aspects of export trading, in preparing export documents, in dealing with customs, and in safety and security codes, as well as in local import restrictions.

Indirect exporting is when the firm is not engaged in international business operations in a full sense, but delegates this function to outsiders. These can be either agents or export firms.

Export agents can either be independent intermediaries or export merchants, who may buy the product outright with the intention of reselling in foreign markets, or sell the company's products on a commission basis. The use of agents in exporting goes back at least a few hundred years, when both buyers and sellers would appoint representatives residing in each other's countries to carry out business on their behalf (Dudley, 1990, pp. 171–2).

Agents are useful in dealing with government contracts in particularly sensitive areas, such as the Middle East, the Gulf or South America. They can also be useful for their knowledge of the local market, culture and business ethics. Agents may also have established relationships with major customers in the foreign market or the host government, otherwise unavailable to a new exporter.

Using an agent carries some risks too. Most agents are concerned with earning commission, and may adopt selling methods that do not reflect the company's image. Additionally, few agents act solely for one firm. They usually have other products to sell, and cannot devote all their time to a particular company's products. Therefore, and in most cases, they favour acquiring established and profitable brands, and are often reluctant to spend their time on new and untried products.

Using exporting firms is another alternative to using foreign agents. Exporting firms can be foreign freight forwarders, export management companies or international trading companies.

A foreign freight forwarder company specializes in the export and import of goods across national borders. Once a foreign sale has been made, the freight forwarder acts on behalf of the exporter in recommending the best routing and means of transportation based on space availability, speed and cost. The forwarder also secures such space and storage, reviews the Letter of Credit, obtains export licences and prepares the necessary shipping documents. The main advantage of using foreign forwarders is that they can provide advice on packaging and labelling, purchasing of transport insurance and repacking shipments damaged *en route*, and are usually up to date with the latest shipping regulations (Daniels and Radebaugh, 1992, p. 529).

Export management companies act to some extent as the export departments of many manufacturers. They provide advice on overseas markets and help in marketing the company's product more efficiently, effectively and at lower cost. Export management companies operate on a contractual basis, usually for two to five years, and provide exclusive representation overseas. They are particularly suitable for small companies contemplating exporting their products, because they can provide instant knowledge of the foreign market. They are also cheaper to use because their costs are spread over the sales of several manufacturers' lines, which provides for economies of scale in shipping and marketing to foreign markets (Brash, 1978, pp. 59–72).

International trading companies have purchasing offices in many countries. These firms are usually the major suppliers of foreign goods in their home markets. The largest of these are the Japanese Sogo Shosha, such as Mitsubishi, Mitsui and Sony (Marubeni Corp., 1979; Tsurmi, 1980). Their range of products varies from advanced technology, electronics, computer software and telecommunications to complex financial services, fashion, retailing, food processing and consumer products. Mitsubishi Trading Corporation and Sumitomo Corporation are also deeply involved in biotechnology, and Mitsui in international telecommunications and satellite communication technology. Mitsubishi is the world's largest trading company, with a worldwide chain of subsidiaries. Its activities today include oil refineries, energy, mining, metals, chemicals, banking, insurance, electronics, computers, aircraft, automobiles, shipbuilding and electrical appliances (Matsuura, 1991, p. 194).

Gray MacKenzie and Company is a British firm which illustrates the operation of an International Trading Company in the Middle East. The company covers all the Middle Eastern countries, and deals in consumer products ranging from toiletries to Mercury outboard motors and scotch whisky (Cateora, 1990, p. 599).

Piggyback exporting is when a manufacturer in one country distributes its products in another country through a network already established by another manufacturer.

Foreign production or direct investment

This simply means 100 per cent ownership by the firm of its overseas operations. There are various ways in which a company may establish its production facilities in another country while retaining total ownership. This can be achieved by acquiring foreign production facilities or by establishing a complete manufacturing system or assembly plants through direct investment by the firm in a host country.

The advantage of wholly owned subsidiaries to the parent company is that the parent company will have total control of operations, decision-making and control of profits, management and production decisions. Wholly owned subsidiaries also help the firm to maintain greater security over its technological assets and know-how.

The major constraints of having wholly owned foreign subsidiaries are the capital requirements and the shortage of management personnel with necessary international experience. The host government and its nationals may have some degree of anti-foreign sentiment, or might be resentful about foreign domination of its economy. The company might therefore risk expropriation, although many states in the modern world, especially less developed countries, are anxious themselves to attract foreign direct investment, and compete openly for it.

International licensing

International licensing is the process in which one firm – the licensor – provides certain resources, for example technology, brand-name use, the right to use certain patents, copyrights or trade marks, to another firm – the licensee – in exchange for a fee or a royalty or any other form of payment according to a schedule agreed upon by the two parties. International licensing can be negotiated for intellectual properties such as patents, know-how, trade marks, copyrights, brand names and technical production.

There are a number of internal and external circumstances where international licensing seems appropriate. Some of these are, for example:

1. When the cost of entry into a foreign market is too expensive, due to high rates of duty, import quotas, prohibitions or technical barriers, and the firm lacks the capital, managerial resources or knowledge of foreign markets but wants to earn additional profits with minimal commitment.
2. When a firm needs to test its product in a foreign market before deciding on foreign direct investment.
3. When the host country is politically unstable and the risk of nationalization or expropriation is high. International licensing provides some protection against political risk. It also protects the firm's intellectual property in some countries where they ignore trade marks and patent rights, at the risk of patent litigation.
4. When the licensor wishes to exploit a secondary market for its technology, but where the smaller market does not justify large investments.

International licensing is often used as a first step for entering a new market and to gain knowledge of the foreign environment before the firm establishes foreign plant and service facilities. It also provides a relatively quick, low-cost, low-risk means of penetrating new markets. It allows new firms to test foreign markets for their product, and to become associated with locally established firms. International licensing provides the firm with additional revenues in the form of fees or royalties in return for information or assistance that the company can provide at very little cost to itself. Finally, international licensing does not require heavy investment in the production and marketing facilities required in the foreign environment.

Although international licensing may seem the easiest, cheapest and quickest way to enter a foreign market, there are several disadvantages and risks involved in international licensing agreements.

First, the licensor's profit is limited to receiving royalties, and it cannot share in the licensee's profits. Second, the licensor might create its own competitor in the foreign market. Since the licence is usually limited to a certain period of time, and may not be renewed, after the expiry date of the licence foreign manufacturers may still be able to produce the product using the licensor's technology acquired over the previous years. Third, the international licence is usually drawn under the local laws of the host nation, and thus comes under its local jurisdiction. The licensor may also lose control over the quality of its products, due to the possible difficulties of controlling and ensuring the maintenance of quality and service standards for foreign licensees. The use or misuse of the international licence might damage the corporate reputation and corporate image. Fourth, the licensor may face difficulties in receiving the royalties under the agreement, especially in countries where there are strict foreign exchange controls or other restrictions on royalty payments, such as withholding tax on royalty payments to non-resident licensors (Beamish et al., 1991, pp. 61–5; Stitt and Baker, 1985).

Techniques for minimizing the pitfalls of international licensing and increasing its potential advantages taken from Stitt und Baker, 1985

● Capability, reliability and trust are absolutely crucial in the selection of the licensee.
● A draft agreement with the licensee must be carefully put together. The licence agreement should make explicit reference to the product, a description of the two parties to the agreements, their reasons for entering into the agreement, and their respective roles.

- The duration of the agreement, and any necessary provision for its automatic extension or review, should be clearly specified.
- Details regarding the royalties, methods of payments and the percentage rate of the royalty must be explicitly defined.
- Control and monitoring. Minimum performance requirements must be specified. Penalties for lack of diligence, rights of inspection, and number of visits permitted per year, together with inspection of the licensee's accounts, should be determined.
- Agreement on arbitration methods, in case of infringement of the licence agreement and the type of appeals permitted, with details of specific reasons for termination by licensor or licensee must be determined.
- Requirements for the training of technical personnel must be set out.

International franchising

International franchising has become the fastest growing form of international licensing in recent years. In an international franchising agreement, the franchisor provides the franchisee with its trade mark and the necessary material to run the business. This may include equipment, products, product ingredients, managerial advice and often a standardized operating procedure (Opack, 1977, pp. 102–5; Hayashi, 1989, pp. 22–5; Harrigan, 1983). Franchised operations usually have a specific set of procedures and methods and a set of quality guidelines set up by the franchisor, as well as the layout of physical facilities that the franchisee must use to produce and market the product. The franchisee is also expected to provide the capital needed to run the franchise. Examples of international franchises vary from service industries and restaurants, fast food, soft drinks, home and auto maintenance companies, automotive services, motels and hotels to car rentals. Examples of successful international franchises include the Holiday Inn, Baskin Robbins, Kentucky Fried Chicken, McDonald's, Hertz and Avis. Not all franchises are American. Some European franchises have also acquired an international reputation, such as Pronuptia, the French bridal wear company, Benetton, the Italian retailer, and Body Shop, the famous British cosmetics retailer.

The advantages of international franchising are similar to those of international licensing. In addition, it provides for the expansion of brand name recognition and requires low capital investment.

The major disadvantages of franchising are the restrictions in marketing, and at the start, slight adjustments or adaptation to the standardized product or service.

Difficulty is often faced when changes to ingredients need to be introduced to suit local tastes and preferences, or operating adjustments are made to suit local culture. But this is not an impossible task to overcome. Many successful international franchises have shown more flexibility in adapting their product to local needs and tastes than expected. McDonalds provides a good illustrative example of how an international franchise can adapt to changes in the environment and still be successful.

CASE STUDY 11.1: Franchising the World—McDonald's

McDonald's is a leader in the fast food industry in the world. It has more than 600 000 employees at over 11 000 restaurants in 52 countries and $17 billion in annual sales in 1990. The secret of 'Big Mac's success lies in its flexible approach to the international franchising concept.

Big Mac in Moscow

To service a potential market of 290 million consumers, and to ensure the quality of its products, McDonald's built a 100 000 m^2 goods distribution centre that includes a meat plant, a bakery, a potato plant, a dairy and quality assurance laboratories. It brought in seed potatoes and pickling cucumber seeds from the Netherlands to grow on Russian collective farms. The company also brought in bull semen to improve the quality of the cattle there. To accommodate such a crowded population, McDonald's modified its traditional store layout and changed it to suit local tastes. For example, it introduced samples of its food products made out of wax and silicon and displayed them in front of every store in response to the Russians' desire to see what they order.

Big Mac in Japan

To boost its sales in Japan, McDonald's latest adaptation policy to local tastes is reflected in its decision to sell Mac Chao, a kind of lunch box with fried rice.

Big Mac in Paris

In response to consumers' attitudes towards healthy food, involving a move away from red meat and fried foods, Big Mac introduced a new line of salads, chicken and decaffeinated coffee in its Parisian franchises. It is now also planning to add four varieties of pizza to its menu, for which it has already tested the market in its American restaurants.

Big Mac in Canada

In Canada, Big Mac now serves cheese curds and hot gravy for French fries to create a Canadian dish called 'poutine'.

Finally, McDonald's in Hong Kong did not hesitate to change its name to mean 'at your service' in Chinese.

Sources

Deveny, K., Pluenneke, J., Yang, D. J., Maremont, M. and Back, R., McWorld, *Business Week* No. 2968, 13 October 1986, pp. 78–86.

Goad, P., In the US they'll probably try renaming it McGlop or Big Muck, *Wall Street Journal*, 8 March 1990.

International joint ventures

International joint ventures are business partnerships jointly owned by two or more firms from different countries, foreign multinational firms and local governments, or foreign multinational firms and local business people. In an international joint venture each party contributes capital, assets or equality ownership, but not necessarily on a 50/50 basis. Some countries limit the amount of ownership allowed to foreign firms to 40 per cent.

Peter Killing identifies four basic purposes for establishing international joint ventures. The first is to strengthen the firm's existing business, the second is to take existing products into new markets, the third is to obtain new products which can be sold in the firm's existing markets, and the fourth is to diversify into a new business (Killing, 1982, pp. 72–89).

Establishing international joint ventures can have many advantages. These include, for example, the opportunity for a firm to share its risks, to learn about a partner's skills and proprietary processes, and to gain access to new distribution channels (Lei and Slocum, 1991, pp. 44–62). Joint ventures are also less exposed to the danger of expropriation. Club Med, for example, has a policy of minority ownership in its foreign operations or 'villages', but big enough to make sure that if Club Med is thrown out, local interests will suffer first.

Unlike wholly owned foreign subsidiaries, international joint ventures also enable the firm to utilize the specialized skills of local partners, together with their knowledge of local markets, culture and government contacts. They provide wider access to the local partner's distribution system, particularly when the company lacks the capital and personnel capabilities itself to expand overseas (Habib and Burnett, 1989, pp. 7–20). A further advantage of using international joint ventures is that they are less expensive. One party may provide the technology and management skills needed, and the other might raise the capital (Beamish *et al.*, 1991, pp. 74–89; Hamel *et al.*, 1989; Killing, 1982, pp. 120–7).

Firms considering entering a joint venture should make sure that this is the best option available to them. International joint ventures are difficult to maintain. A company should determine clearly its objectives and its partners' objectives before forming the venture. What type of partnership, in terms of management role – dominant role, degree of independence of operations, or share management – needs to be established (Beamish *et al.*, 1991, pp. 66–71). International joint ventures carry risks and problems as well. Successful operations could become a target for nationalization or expropriation by the host government. The transfer of management skills to the other partner might create a local competitor in the foreign market by providing greater access to information and technological know-how. Different parties might also have different objectives for the joint venture. A local partner might be more interested in long-term profit. There could also be a wide difference in management styles, corporate cultures and missions between the two partners.

International management contract

An international management contract is an agreement by which a business firm provides managerial assistance to another firm by training its personnel to assume managerial positions in return for a fee for providing such assistance. These arrangements are usually for a short period of time. They are preferred by small firms that lack capital. International management contracts require less capital investment than any other international business operations. No political risk is involved either, since the company simply receives a fee for providing the expertise needed. International management contracts are often operated in combination with turnkey operations.

Turnkey operations

Under this type of agreement, a business firm agrees to construct an entire manufacturing plant or production facility, equip it and prepare it for operation in a foreign country, and then turns it over to the local owners when it is ready for operation. When a turnkey operation is used in combination with a management contract the multinational has to provide training and instruction for local personnel. Turnkey operations include the whole process of establishing an operation from design and construction through to operation. Examples of turnkey projects include road construction, factories, refineries, airports, dams and automobile plants. Turnkey projects are very popular in Eastern Europe, India, Iran, Turkey and the Gulf. Developing countries favour turnkey operations, because they provide a way of acquiring Western production methods without accepting a permanent Western presence on their territory.

Counter-trade

It is estimated that between 25 and 40 per cent of the world's total exports are generated via counter-trade. Counter-trade is a process which links imports with exports.

From the mid-1970s to the mid-1980s, counter-trade expanded rapidly. By the mid-1980s, the percentage of world trade accounted for by counter-trade was as high as 30 per cent (Welt, 1984). A recent study listed over 1300 such deals entered into by developing countries between 1980 and 1987, and concluded that most agreements were established due to the instability of the local financial system. For example, 10 per cent of Brazil's exports of both raw materials and manufactured goods is conducted under counter-trade agreements. Brazil exchanged $360 million-worth of locally made Volkswagen cars for Iraqi oil in 1984 (Stopford *et al.*, 1991, p. 117). Pepsi-Cola recently agreed with Russia to trade Pepsi liquid and bottling equipment in return for Stolichnaya vodka and caviar (Cateora, 1990, p. 563).

There are six aspects of a counter-trade agreement that international business managers must be aware of. These are (Lecraw, 1991, p. 51):

1. Timing of the flow of goods.
2. Duration of the contract.
3. Counter-trade percentage.
4. Counter-trade conditions whether voluntary or mandatory.
5. Penalties for non-compliance with counter-trade contract.
6. Product requirements.

One of the advantages of counter-trade is that it helps to ovecome foreign exchange shortages. The company can make purchases from abroad and pay for them out of future exports, or in exchange for other nationally produced products. Counter-trade also helps to overcome distortions caused by inappropriate exchange rates. It also serves as a forward sales agreement which may be valued both by exporters and importers, and provide greater access to closed markets and controlled economies.

The disadvantage of counter-trade is mainly that such an operation needs particular skills and should be left to counter-trade experts. For example, many products might not measure up to world standards.

Barter and counter-trade have been significant tools of trade throughout the 1980s, mostly because firms confronted by saturated traditional markets were propelled into searching for new markets, which were mostly debt-burdened (Huszagh and Huszagh, 1986, pp. 7–19).

There are three features that distinguish counter-trade from barter. First, barter is an exchange of goods and services without money, as opposed to counter-trade, which includes partial or full compensation in money. Second, a barter agreement normally requires only one contract, while counter-trade transactions require a minimum of two contracts – one representing the initial sales agreement between the supplier and foreign customer, and the other representing details of the suppliers' commitment to purchase goods from either the foreign customer or a designated industry. Third, barter in general has a short time-frame of one year, while counter-trade transactions may extend over several years.

Barter can take different forms:

1. *Classical barter*, or straight barter, is when two parties directly exchange goods or services without the use of money. Barter is particularly useful when the local currency is extremely volatile. It is also very simple, can be implemented in a short time and does not require large capital. 'Closed end' barter is when both parties exchange goods of equal value so that neither party has to acquire hard currency. It is the best method for overcoming foreign exchange controls and foreign currency shortages.

2. *Buy-back or compensation trading*   These are agreements to sell the technology, the construction of an entire project, or the licensing of patents or trade marks in return for agreeing to buy part of the output as payment. Many examples illustrate the magnitude of this type of international business transaction. Volkswagen, for example, recently constructed a plant in the former East Germany based on a buy-back agreement. Fiat, too, built its automobile factory in Russia in the context of this form of agreement. The most fascinating example, however, is NEC, which assembles televisions in Egypt in return for Japan exporting about 3000 tourists per year to Egypt on Egypt Air (Terpestra and Sarathy, 1991, p. 253).

3. *Counter-purchase, or parallel barter*, is more complicated than simple barter. It involves the exchange of products that are delivered now for goods to be delivered in the future from a list mutually agreed upon between the two parties. In counter-purchase, the products received could be unrelated to the suppliers' product lines, and therefore might pose some difficulties in marketing or distribution. Gillette in the UK, for example, counter-purchases anything from Eastern Europe, from rabbit skins to butter, from carpets to pyjamas, in exchange for razor blades (Terpestra and Sarathy, 1991, p. 523).

4. *Switch trading* involves at least three or more countries. In a switch trade, the products exchanged might not be of any use to the importer or cannot be converted for cash unless sold in another market or country. A trading house is often used for this form of trade.

5. *A clearing arrangement* is when two parties agree to exchange their products by signing a purchase and payment agreement specifying the goods to be traded, their monetary value and the date of settlement. This is also known as 'evidence account transaction'. The importing country's bank of foreign trade and a bank in the exporter's country simultaneously maintain an 'evidence account' in order to ensure that transactions balance (Kerzariu, 1985, p. 32).

Japanese *Keiretsus* and Korean *Chaebols*

While joint ventures and counter-trades expanded rapidly in the 1980s due to the saturation of established markets in the world and the need for expansion into new markets, which were unfortunately burdened with foreign debts, with the increasing global competition of the 1990s a need for new and more sophisticated forms of strategic alliance other than international licensing, joint ventures or even counter-trade is being experienced by many firms to meet the challenges of the 1990s and to survive global competition in world markets.

In the USA, such attempts to develop international consortia are being made by IBM and Motorola to overcome resource scarcity and to share research programs to improve product and process standards. In Europe, too, efforts are being made to develop this new type of strategic alliance, as shown with the formation of Airbus Industries. The EUREKA (a joint program bringing together scientists and engineers to engage in research projects) and ESPRIT (European Strategic Program for Research and Development in Information Technology) initiatives are also attempting to restore European competitiveness is semiconductors and micro-electronics. It is important for international business managers to be aware of these operations and to familiarize themselves with their functions. An examination of their Far Eastern equivalents, the Japanese *Keiretsu* and the Korean *Chaebol* might be useful (Lei and Slocum, 1991, p. 59).

The Japanese *Keiretsu* is a combination of 25 to 50 different industrial companies centred on a large trading company or bank. Examples of Japanese *Keiretsus* are Sumitomo, Mitsubishi and Mitsui. *Keiretsus* get their financing from group banks and are largely run by professional managers.

Similar to the Japanese *Keiretsus* are the South Korean *Chaebols*, in that they too represent a combination of large companies, centred on a bank or a holding company. The difference between the two, however, is that in the Korean *Chaebol*, the central holding company is usually dominated by founding families. They also rely much more on the government for capital, and are managed by family members. Examples of Korean *Chaebols* are Lucky Gold Star and Samsung. Korean *Chaebols* are formed by merchant and industrialist families. Blood relations dominate the management structure across the *Chaebol*.

The main benefits of *Keirutsu* and *Chaebol* organizational structures are the long-term focus on profit potential, economies of scale and technological cooperation. Resources are directed into growth industries with the potential to achieve further global competitiveness. Strong buyer–supplier relationships within the group also provide the necessary economies of scale for building world-class plants and enhancing quality. Extensive resource sharing of components and end products is encouraged. Since each company competes in its own particular industry, technological competencies gained from competing in different industries are then shared across the group of companies, thus reducing duplication of effort and increasing specialization (Lei and Slocum, 1991, p. 59).

Keiretsus and *Chaebols* also rely on government encouragement and financial support in providing preferential interest rates and capital allocation. Here, the increasing importance of the state in relation to competition for world market shares in international business can be clearly seen.

The adoption of *Keiretsus* or *Chaebols* and their successful operation in the West would involve a major change in human resource practices. Unlike their counterparts in the West, who are trained and rewarded for results and individual achievements, employees in *Keiretsus* and *Chaebols* are encouraged to develop managerial interactions and fraternal relationships, building mutual long-term trust, commitment and pride in membership, with a continuous job rotation to gain wider exposure to many different industries and processes (Ferguson, 1990; Steers *et al.*, 1989).

GLOBAL STRATEGIC MANAGEMENT

Corporate policies that proved successful a few decades ago are not necessarily appropriate for the 1990s and beyond. In the face of economic, political and technological changes in the global political economy during the last decade, and increasingly intense international competition, managing efficiently is no longer sufficient. Even small firms operating purely at the domestic level are being affected by globalization. International competitiveness does not in fact require a foreign presence abroad. In many countries, tough competition does not come any more from local firms but from multinational firms and global firms. The challenge for business managers is therefore to formulate a global strategy for their company to meet its objectives and to survive this increasing global competition.

Before expanding on global strategies and their implementation, it is essential to distinguish clearly the differences between multinational firms, transnational firms and global corporations.

Multinationals, transnationals and global corporations

There is a lack of consensus as to the exact definition of a multinational corporation. In the absence of a universally accepted definition, several descriptions of what a multinational is have been presented. For some, a multinational is a large corporation with operations and subsidiaries spread in more than one country, but controlled by a central headquarters (Stoner and Freeman, 1989, p. 771). Others insist that a multinational is a firm having investments in six or more foreign countries. The Ford Motor Company, for instance, has 48 per cent of its employees outside the USA; Philips, of The Netherlands, has 79 per cent of its employees outside the home country; Imperial Chemical Industries has 58 per cent outside Britain, and Matsushita Electric has 43 per cent outside Japan (Vernon and Wells, 1991, p. 2).

Many argue that a multinational is not simply a group of business units located in different countries whose operations are controlled by headquarters, but that a multinational should have global objectives, with its decisions made on the basis of maximizing global profits.

The characteristics of a multinational are consequently grouped into two categories: structural characteristics and operational characteristics (Weekly and Aggarwal, 1987, p. 311). Among the structural characteristics listed are the number of foreign subsidiaries, the number of overseas expatriates, overseas earnings, management styles and practices and corporate culture. Operational characteristics include types of ownership, such as wholly owned, joint venture, franchise and licensing, and company goals, such as expansion, market leadership, turnkey operations, management consultancy and, more recently, strategic alliances.

There are three main functional types of multinational: those in extraction, those in manufacturing and those in services (Gill and Law, 1988, p. 122).

While the definition of a multinational suggests operations in a substantial number of countries, a transnational corporation implies operations in at least two countries, including the firm's home country (Dickens, 1992, p. 47). A more widely accepted definition of a transnational corporation is that offered by the United Nations Economic and Social Affairs Committee as any enterprise which controls assets – factories, mines, sales offices and the like – in two or more countries (United Nations, 1973, p. 5).

Global firms are often immediately identified with the transnationals or multinationals of the 1960s and the 1970s, despite their fundamentally different structures and orientations. A multinational or transnational firm considers its subsidiaries as independent units, each serving their national market in which they are located. Consequently, a multinational might develop individual business strategies for each foreign market and have subsidiaries that are essentially autonomous. The global firm, in contrast, operates as a worldwide integrated system in which all its operations are interdependent in terms of operations and strategies (Holden, 1990, pp. 22–5). In a global firm, unlike the multinational, all subsidiaries must work together to form one integrated whole. For example, the global firm might buy its basic components from three different countries, ship them to be partially assembled in a fourth country where labour is inexpensive and then put the finishing touches in factories closer to its customers.

Another basic difference between global, multinational or transnational corporations is that a global corporation seeks to serve a basically identical market that appears in many countries around the world (Chidomere and Amyansi-Archinbong, 1989, pp. 34–7). Furthermore, it makes no distinction between domestic and international business (Terpestra and Sarathy, 1991, p. 654). This global outlook applies to all the corporation's activities, from investment policies to staffing and function operations.

CHARACTERISTICS OF A GLOBAL FIRM

Cosmopolitanism of the management team

Managers of global companies come from different nations. For example, the executive committee of Whirlpool, the US/Dutch joint venture is not only located in Italy, but its members come from six different countries: Sweden, Holland, Italy, the USA, Belgium and Germany. ABB (Asean Brown Boveri), too, has a similar cosmopolitan management. Its executive committee consists of Swedes, Swiss, Germans and Americans.

Common language: English as the official language

In such cosmopolitan organizations, communication could cause serious problems. English has therefore been adopted as the official language of many global firms, regardless of the location of the headquarters or the national origin of the corporation. For ABB, although a joint venture between a Swiss and a Swedish company, English is the official language. Even when correspondence is between two colleagues in Sweden itself, their correspondence is conducted in English (Taylor, 1991, p. 94). However, English as a global language is not enough for effective communication in a global firm. The corporate language, the unofficial culture of the organization, its common values, standards and expectations, must also be global (Ohmae, 1990a, p. 117).

Nationality-lessness of the global firm

The nationality of a truly global firm is blurred and vague and is becoming already out of date in the 1990s (Ohmae, 1990a, p. 23). An illustration of what nationality-lessness means to a global corporation is the example of Mazda's newest sports car: the MX-s Miata. The car is designed and financed in Tokyo and New York, its prototype was created in Worthing, England, assembled in Michigan and Mexico using advanced electronic components invented in New Jersey, and fabricated in Japan (Reich, 1991, p. 79). Is it a Japanese, American or European car?

Global web of alliances

Companies do not emerge as full global companies overnight or as if by accident. Globalization is often achieved through a gradual process of coalitions, strategic alliances and cross-border consortia. In the face of increasingly intensified global competition for world market shares, many multinational firms have put the formation of cross-border alliances firmly on their agendas for the 1990s and beyond (Bleeke and Ernest, 1991). There are many empirical examples of this tendency towards global alliances, recently adopted by multinationals. Corning Glass, for example, abandoned its national pyramid-like organization in favour of a global web, giving it the capability to make optical cables through its European partner, Siemens AG, and medical equipment with Ciba-Geigy. AT&T transformed itself from a bureaucratic monopoly into a multilateral global web, with Japan's NEC and the Dutch-owned Philips. France's Renault has recently teamed up with Sweden's Volvo. Fujitsu of Japan has acquired Britain's ICL, and

Italy's Olivetti is nowadays distributing mainframe computers for Hitachi (Morden, 1991, pp. 32–9). It is important to note that all these developments could not have occurred without the impulse of privatization and deregulation, involving explicit intervention by state governments in the conditions of markets, trade and business, and the establishment of free enterprise zones around the world.

Decentralized global structure

A global corporation aims to 'think globally and manage locally' (Reich, 1991, p. 80). In a global corporation, there is a greater preference for decentralized and divisionalized structures, autonomous production or geographical divisions. GFT provides a good illustration of the efforts of a global corporation to preserve its global strategy, while at the same time decentralizing its structure to allow the company to optimize its business globally, while becoming an 'insider' in each of its major markets. (For further details see the case study later in this chapter.)

'Faded' significance of headquarters

The location of headquarters for a global firm is not a matter of great importance. Headquarters' location is no longer necessarily in the country where most of the company's shareholders or employees are. In the case of ABB, for example, although the company employs 240 000 people worldwide, their work is organized in small units. There are only 100 people at ABB headquarters in Zurich, not in Sweden, where ASEA had its headquarters for 100 years. ABB operations are divided into 1200 companies, and these companies are divided into 4500 profit centres. In an interview, ABB's Percy Barnevick was asked what it means to have a headquarters in Zurich. Barnevick answered 'It is where my mail arrives before the important letters are faxed to wherever I happen to be. It's where Abacus (Management Information System) collects our performance data. Beyond that I'm not sure if it means much at all' (Taylor, 1991, p. 104).

This decomposition of corporate headquarters into several regional headquarters is becoming an essential part of the structure of global firms (Ohmae, 1990a, p. 88). Global companies have now developed a new approach to headquarters, whereas traditional multinational firms viewed headquarters as the central decision-making process from which spread out all the subsidiaries as locations for the implementation of corporate strategy. And these headquarters usually remained in the country of origin of the firm – the home country.

Today's global corporations share in and contribute towards the creation of a global value system which is a combination of price, quality, reliability and delivery factors for the products it produces (Chidomere and Amyansi-Archibong, 1989, pp. 34–7).

Truly global corporations now serve the interests of customers worldwide. While multinational firms of the 1960s and 1970s were mostly concerned about profits, corporate growth and increasing market share, at the risk of having conflicting interests between the host and parent countries, global corporations do not exploit local situations and then repatriate all the profits back to a home country. They invest, they train, they pay taxes, they build up the infrastructure and claim to provide good value to customers in all the countries where they do business (Ohmae, 1990a, p. 115).

GLOBAL STRATEGIC PLANNING

Without competition there would be no need for strategy. The sole purpose of strategic planning is to enable a firm to gain, as efficiently as possible, a sustainable edge over its competitors

(Ohmae, 1983, pp. 36–7). A good business strategy is one that assists a firm in gaining a competitive advantage over its competitors at an acceptable cost to itself.

Global strategic planning, however, is much more complex and complicated than domestic strategic planning, due to the diversity of the environment of international business and the wider variety of competitors and consumers. Global firms must compete not just against domestic firms in each country in which they operate, but also worldwide against other multinational and global firms (Wortzel and Wortzel, 1990, p. 59). Global strategy can be defined as 'the formulation of plans to place the multinational in a position where it can survive and prosper relative to its global competitors' (Rugman *et al.*, 1985, p. 321). Consequently, global strategic planning is concerned with the assessment of the international environment determining future worldwide opportunities and threats, and formulating global objectives and strategies (Phatak, 1989, p. 45).

There is no one single best global strategy. Many strategies have been developed and adapted by various multinational firms in their effort to survive global competition. It is up to business managers to choose which market to contest, and to decide which strategy to adopt for competing in that market. The following is a basic introduction to the various global strategies formulated by various schools of thought. Four major types of global strategy have been developed (Vernon and Wells, 1991, pp. 4–19):

1. Exploiting a technological lead.
2. Exploiting a strong name.
3. Exploiting advantages of scale.
4. Scanning capability and diversification.

To these, and because of the increasing globalization of business in the late 1980s and early 1990s, we can now add:

5. Becoming a 'Triad Power'.
6. Achieving a value chain.
7. Achieving global competitive advantage.
8. Achieving global flexibility and global mobility.

Exploiting a technological lead   Under this strategy, firms that exploit a technological lead abroad do not need to have manufacturing bases abroad. They can rely on exports rather than on foreign production facilities, as was the case with the Boeing 757 or the Airbus A-310.

Exploiting a strong trade name   Trade names can provide a firm with strong competitive advantages over national competitors in foreign markets. A strong name can lead to quick entry into foreign markets (Vernon and Wells, 1991, pp. 4–19).

Advantages of scale   For many global industries, for example, it is claimed that technological innovation or trade names are not enough to provide competitive advantage. Seeking advantages of scale can then be the primary motive of globalization.

Scanning competencies   This strategy provides a better opportunity for global firms to monitor their competitors closely, to monitor changes in the global environment, and to search the world for low-cost sourcing, new technologies and new marketing opportunities.

Becoming a 'Triad Power'   According to this strategy, firms desiring to compete globally must build a strong internal position in the Triad Market, that is Japan, Europe and the USA (Ohmae, 1990b, pp. 62–74). The traditional advantages of producing in low labour cost countries and then exporting to the Triad are gradually eroding. It is now becoming imperative for business firms to have an 'insider' presence in all the three Triad regions, which represent 600 million consumers. The advantages of becoming a Triad Power are numerous. First, by establishing a presence in the Triad, business firms avoid surprises from foreign competitors or from domestic competitors by forming alliances with foreign companies. In addition, by knowing the basic needs of Triad consumers the company can develop a universal product. Or, having developed a highly competitive basic product at home, the company can then tailor its features and look to local tastes. It can then market its product simultaneously to 600 million consumers. With a presence in the three regions, it is also believed, the company would be able to strike into a market in a relatively short time. If a local competitor develops a new product with high potential, Triad power can allow swift copying and pre-empt the local competitor's opportunity in the other two Triad markets (Ohmae, 1985).

Value chain analysis   In a value chain analysis, a firm's strategic planning must reconcile economic and political imperatives with the firm's strategic predisposition. This is achieved through balancing the economic imperatives of global integration with political imperatives imposed by host governments, while at the same time maintaining suitable control to ensure proper integration of the subsidiary's strategy with that of other subsidiaries (Chakravarthy and Perlmutter, 1985, pp. 3–10).

Three imperatives must therefore be reconciled in order to achieve a value chain strategy. These are: economic imperatives, political imperatives and the multinational firm's own strategic predisposition. Economic imperatives refer to the choice of strategy depending on the segments of the value chain that a firm competes in. Political imperatives refer to the bargaining power of the multinational firm and the bargaining power of the host country. The bargaining power of the multinational firm is based on three sources: proprietary technology, worldwide market shares and product differentiation. The bargaining power of the host government is derived from its desire and ability to control market access and the size and attractiveness of the national market that it controls. A host government, in addition to its role as regulator, can be a co-negotiator, a supplier, a competitor or even a distributor (Doz, 1980, pp. 27–46).

Regarding the strategic predisposition of the firm, there are four distinctive predispositions in a multinational firm where all strategic decisions are guided by values and interests of the parent company. These are ethnocentricism, polycentrism, regiocentrism and geocentrism (Heenan and Perlmutter, 1979).

- *Ethnocentricism* is when strategic decisions are guided by the values and interests of the parent company alone.
- *Polycentricism* is where strategic decisions are tailored to suit the cultures of the various countries in which the multinational firm competes.
- *Regiocentrism* is a strategy that tries to blend the interest of the parent company with that of the subsidiary, at least on a limited regional basis.
- *Geocentrism* is a predisposition that seeks to integrate diverse subsidiaries through a global systems approach to decision-making.

The challenge in global strategic planning is to reconcile these four forces described above. One way of dealing with this is for the multinational firm to position itself in a quadrant where the economic and political pressures are not so conflicting, or it could attempt to rectify the power imbalances with the host government by manipulating the resource dependencies of the subsidiary, or it may seek the cooperation of select competitors in order to resolve the tension between maximizing the firm's profit goals and emphasizing the needs of the host government in its human resource management by nurturing relevant attitudes in its managerial workforce.

Competitive advantage strategy   According to Michael Porter, multinational firms should focus more on their competitive advantage than seeking to balance their economic and political imperatives. There are four generic strategies found in global industries: the broad line global strategy, the global focus strategy, the national focus strategy and the protected niche strategy (Porter 1980, pp. 294–5).

The broad line global strategy is when a firm competes worldwide in the full product line of the industry.

The global focus strategy targets a particular segment of the industry for competing worldwide. It aims at creating differentiation or low-cost positioning.

The third strategy is the national focus strategy, which takes advantage of differences in national markets. In this strategy, a firm chooses one or two major markets out of many, and focuses its efforts upon them.

Finally, the fourth strategy is the protected niche strategy. This is when a company seeks countries where government restraints exclude global competition to a large extent, either through high tariff barriers, or by requiring a high proportion of local content in the product.

The worst strategic error, for Porter, is to be stuck in the middle or to try to pursue all strategies simultaneously, due to their inherent contradictions (Porter, 1990, pp. 40, 55–62).

Global flexibility and mobility   For Lawrence Wortzel, the choice between global strategies and global flexibility involves identifying and responding to the opportunities as well as the threats of both strategies (Wortzel, 1990, pp. 135–48). Some of the assumptions behind global standardization include cost advantage, lower price, cost savings from cost advantage, and added R&D and marketing activities. Global consumers are assumed here to have become similar enough in tastes and preferences that the same product will satisfy all of them.

Arguments in favour of greater flexibility and product differentiation include the view that standardization locks the firm into a particular competitive posture while other sources of competitive advantage continually change. The consumers, on this view, have different preferences in different countries and prefer a customized product. Standardization also faces political constraints, such as government regulations of product content, packaging and labelling and so on.

Standardization and customization can be viable strategies depending on the product. In setting a global strategy, two key product characteristics must be taken into consideration. One is the extent to which consumers will accept a standardized product and the second is the speed at which the product changes.

The global mobility concept simply refers to the means through which the management of local business can transfer their firms into positions of global leadership. According to this strategy, this is achieved through global vision and global capability.

Global vision is the ability to analyse the dynamic competitive environment and to develop superior strategies in a way that is relevant to the new global opportunities through a sophisticated process of data collection and analysis. Global vision here refers to rapid collection and analysis of information or key elements of strategy, such as markets, competition, resources, technologies and so on. A global analysis requires the rapid collection of up-to-date information, assessing all relevant sources of information regarding the legal, political and economic environments, markets, customers' needs, raw materials, human resources, technology and competitors in that region, and analysing them in relation to the firm's interests and capabilities.

Global capability, on the other hand, refers to the ability to use rapidly productive human resources, technological and financial resources at the right time and the right place. There are four major aspects to the global capability of a firm. These are organizational effectiveness, market bridgeheads and bases, deal capability and financing capability. Italy's GFT illustrates vividly the globalization process described in this chapter.

CASE STUDY 11.2: GFT, the new global corporation

GFT is the world's largest manufacturer of designer clothing, and is world famous for its well known European designer labels, such as Georgio Armani, Emanuel Ungaro and Valentino. The company today employs 10 000 people, and has 45 small companies and 18 manufacturing plants. It distributes its branded collections in 70 countries around the world.

Created after the Second World War, GFT was the first European company to introduce mass-production techniques. In the 1950s and 1960s the company established itself as a highly efficient producer of standardized men's clothing and acquired an international reputation. In the 1970s, however, as a result of massive labour unrest in Italy in the late 1960s, the introduction of new restrictive labour laws, and in response to the growing interest in more expensive and more stylish clothing, GFT decided to move up-market. To compete in these exclusive niches GFT started to forge alliances with top fashion designers in Italy and France. By the late 1980s it had acquired several licensing agreements with well-known fashion designers, such as Ungaro, Armani, Valentino and a further 10 European designers.

Initially, GFT manufactured global products and shipped them worldwide. The Armani jacket sold in Milan was identical to the one sold in New York or Tokyo. By the end of the 1980s, GFT realized that this formula was no longer working. For example, suits that were best sellers in Italy often did poorly in the USA. Sizes, fabrics and colours that worked in Germany and the UK did not seem right for Florida or California. The global product had to be adapted to meet the very different needs and expectations of different local markets.

Another factor that contributed to GFT's global strategic change was the realization that the designer label phenomenon of the 1970s was no longer valid in the 1990s. With the increased globalization of information technology and communications, consumers worldwide have become more educated and discerning. They now expect high quality at a lower price with a greater emphasis on 'value'. GFT was now faced with a situation where it had to compete on price, or customers would go elsewhere. While in the 1970s and 1980s the emphasis was on image and quality, and price was not a great issue, in the 1990s, in contrast, an increasing trade-off between quality and cost is being made by customers.

To achieve this, GFT realized that it needed to adapt its global strategy accordingly. It had to know better its local market, its local consumers and exactly what they wanted.

In order to get closer to its local market and become an 'insider' in each one of them, GFT changed its organizational structure and formed a financial holding company made up of six autonomous operating divisions. Two are now based in North America and the Far East, and the other four in Europe. The company's headquarters have also been dispersed into three cities. One is in Turin, in Italy, where GFT's original corporate centre and the source of the company's expertise was located. The second location is in New York, the home base of GFT USA, and the third is in New Bedford, Massachusetts, where the company has its Riverside Manufacturing

Company. Each subsidiary is allowed to develop its own strategy according to the local situation and local market. GFT also started to develop relationships and links with local fashion designers, to capture the customer wants of a particular region or country.

When asked about the real location of GFT, its Chairman Marco Rivetti answered: '. . . it is not so much at the centre or even on the periphery but in the minds of its global managers'.

Source
Howard, R., The designer organization: Italy's GFT goes global, *Harvard Business Review*, September–October 1991, pp. 28–44.

BUILDING AN INTEGRATED MODEL FOR A GLOBAL STRATEGIC PLAN

There are five major stages involved in global strategic planning, as illustrated in Figure 11.1. (Figure 14.1, which shows a strategic plan for the Single European Market, may also be very useful.)

Step 1: Global vision/global mission

The first step in formulating a global strategic plan is to determine the overall goal of the company. For example, this could be maximizing profit, control of a market, production of a

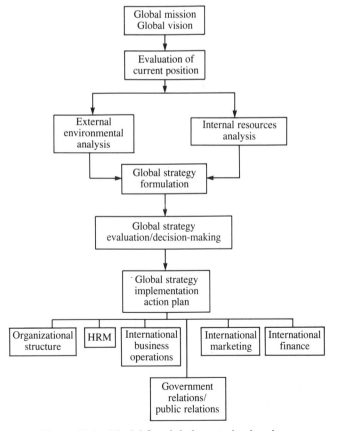

Figure 11.1 Model for global strategic planning

higher quality product, expansion of existing activities, entry into a new business, elimination of present activities, take-over of a rival firm or expansion into new geographical markets. This stage is also known as identifying the global vision of the company. In other words, deciding what the company hopes to achieve from its international operations and what its global objectives are in terms of profitability, marketing, production, finance, technology, personnel and host government relations.

Step 2: Evaluating the current position

This must be done in relation to the identified overall company objectives. It involves analysis of the external environment, particularly those factors over which the company has little or no control. This is achieved through:

- Initial global environmental scanning, that is an assessment of the economic, social, political and cultural factors and any changes in them (see Chapter One).
- A more specific country profile analysis.
- An analysis of global competition.

According to Ohmae, in the construction of any business strategy three main players must be taken into account. These are the corporation itself, the customer and the competition, which have come to be commonly known as the strategic Three Cs (Ohmae, 1983, pp. 91–162).

- *Corporate-based strategies* These are the functional aims to maximize the company's strengths relative to the competition. The role of functional strategy, according to Ohmae, is to design and deliver a cost-effective function, which is done in three ways. The first method is to reduce costs much more effectively than the competition. The second method is simply to exercise selectivity in terms of orders accepted, products offered or functions to be performed. The third method is to reduce functional cost and to share a certain key function among the corporation's other business or even with other companies.
- *Customer-based strategies* Since the corporation cannot reach out to all its customers with equal effectiveness, it will have to segment the market and identify one or more subsets of customers within the total market, concentrating its efforts upon meeting their needs. Segmentation can be done either by product objectives (different ways customers use the products), or by the corporation's own circumstances, such as the corporation's ability to sell and the constraints limiting its resources.
- *Competitor-based strategies* Some competitor-based strategies include the power of an image, exploiting functional strength, capitalizing on profit and cost structure differences.

Michael Porter, of the Harvard Business School, identifies five major forces in his competitive advantage analysis, each of which threatens an organization's ventures into a new market. According to Porter, it is the company strategist's job to analyse these forces and propose a programme for influencing or defending against them. These five forces are:

1. The threat of new entrants.
2. The threat of substitute products.
3. The bargaining power of suppliers.
4. The bargaining power of buyers.
5. Rivalry among existing competitors.

Analysis of these five factors can contribute to an evaluation of the company's strengths and weaknesses. The strengths of these five forces vary from industry to industry and determine the long-term industry profitability, because they shape the prices that firms can charge, the costs they have to bear, and the investment required to compete in the industry (Porter, 1990, pp. 34–5).

Internal resources analysis   This should include:
- Financial appraisal, for example profit contribution, return on investment, cash flow, budget, return on investment used to determine the relationship of profit to invested capital and cash flow.
- SWOT analysis, identifying strengths, weaknesses, opportunities and threats
- A review of the organization structure and human resource allocation and management (see Chapter 9).

Step 3: Global strategy formulation

Based on the above-mentioned internal and external analyses and in line with the company's objectives, it is at this stage that a global strategy needs to be formulated. This process involves the identification and development of possible global strategies available to the firm.

Step 4: Global strategy evaluation and decision-making

This includes the evaluation of each strategy proposed, assessing each one of them and selecting the most appropriate to the company.

Step 5: Strategy implementation or development of action plan

This stage consists of various activities:

1. Designing a suitable international organizational structure as well as deciding whether the company's international operations should be centralized or decentralized (see Chapter Nine).
2. Assessing the existing human resources capability of implementing the company's global strategy (these issues have been discussed in detail in Chapter Nine).
3. Reviewing the various international business operations available and choosing the most appropriate strategy for the firm's international operations (see Chapter Eleven).
4. Evaluating the various international marketing strategies and choosing the most suitable one to assist the firm in achieving its global objectives (refer to Chapter Ten for further details).
5. Financing of global operations. This includes decisions concerning which international financial institution to approach, why and how (for details refer to Chapter Eight).
6. Designing a public relations policy for the firm's international operations and establishing contacts and closer relations with national and host governments (discussed in Chapter 8).

REVIEW QUESTIONS

1. As a business graduate you have just given an address at the annual graduation ceremony. The title of your address was: 'The globalization of international business'. In your presentation you commented on the increased global competition and its implications for business.

You have been asked by a newspaper's reporter to explain what you meant by your statement. How would you explain it?

2. Compare and contrast the various methods of international business operations, highlighting the advantages and disadvantages of each. Illustrate your answer with examples taken from companies known.
3. Why are international joint ventures so popular? What problems do they present, and how can these be overcome?
4. Global firms are often immediately identified with multinationals or transnationals. Are they the same? Support your answer with illustrative examples.
5. Introduce briefly the various global strategies known to you, and discuss their implications for international business today.
6. What has contributed to the recent growing trend towards global alliances?
7. Why should business managers adopt a more global vision of their business? What are the various stages involved in formulating a global strategic plan?

EXERCISE 11.1: International business operations

Aim   The purpose of this exercise is to familiarize students and business managers with the multiple forms of international business operations.

Assignment   Global firms conduct their overseas operations in a variety of ways. The class is divided into small groups. Each group is asked to consider one method, conduct an in-depth analysis and be ready to introduce the results to the class.

Format   Students should consider the following points when preparing for their class presentation:

1. Definition of each method chosen, its function and operations.
2. An illustrative example of a firm that has adopted such a form of international business operations.
3. An evaluation of the advantages gained, and analysis of the difficulties experienced by that particular company as a result of implementing such a method.
4. Your personal evaluation of such an operation.

EXERCISE 11.2: Global strategic planning

Aim   The aim of this exercise is to develop students' skills in designing and formulating a global strategic plan, and to learn how to cooperate and coordinate their strengths and weaknesses within the group.

Assignment   As an international business consultant working for the Department of Trade and Industry (DTI), you have been approached for advice by a local company wishing to expand its operations overseas. The Board of Directors expects a brief presentation within three weeks, supported by a detailed global strategic plan.

Format   This major assignment integrates all the skills and knowledge covered in the book. Students are encouraged to work in groups, so they can identify and best utilize the strength of each member within the group (whether it is in finance, human resources management, international marketing or strategic operations) and coordinate their efforts in preparing for a class presentation.

To do this assignment, students may choose either a local company known to them, a local product or a well-known brand, and formulate their own global strategic plan using overheads, charts and visual aids as they see fit. Alternatively, students may wish to analyse the internationalization process *already* adopted by a business firm known to them, evaluate its international business operations, and provide advice and guidance on the possibility of globalization.

The model developed at the end of this chapter for global strategic planning (Figure 11.1) may be used as a guide in organizing and structuring this project.

FURTHER READING

Beamish, P., Killing, J. P., Lecraw, D. J. and Crookell, H., *International Management. Text and Cases*, Irwin, Homewood IL, 1991.

Harrigan, K., *Strategies for Joint Ventures*, Lexington Books, Lexington MA, 1983.

Ohmae, K., *The Mind of the Strategist*, Penguin, Harmondsworth, 1983.

Porter, M., *Competitive Strategy: Techniques for Analyzing Industries and Competitors*, The Free Press, New York, 1980.

Porter, M., *The Competitive Advantage of Nations*, The Macmillan Press, Basingstoke, 1990.

Stitt, H. J. and Baker, S., *The Licensing and Joint Venture Guide*, 3rd edn, Ministry of Industry, Trade and Technology, Toronto, 1985.

Wortzel, H. V. and Wortzel, L. H. (eds.), *Global Strategic Management: The Essentials*, 2nd edn, Wiley, New York, 1990.

FOUR

BUSINESS IN THE SINGLE EUROPEAN MARKET

Two people were walking through the Black Forest where it was rumoured a very dangerous lion lurked. They took a break and were sitting in the sun when one of them changed from his hiking boots to jogging shoes. The other one smiled and asked:

'You don't think you can run away from the lion with those jogging shoes?'

'No', he replied. 'I just need to be faster than you'.

Companies that wait will be those who lose. 'It is not necessary to be first, but what is needed is to be faster than the others'.   (Gianluigi, 1991)

The Single European Market (SEM) represents the third largest trading bloc in the world, after the USA and Japan. The European Community covers a vast geographical area, spread over 2 253 000 km^2 with a population in excess of 320 million. The creation of the Single Market will have an effect upon every business in the world. There will be winners and there will be losers. International business managers must be aware of the changes occurring in the Single European Market in order to take advantage of the business opportunities it now provides, and be ready at the same time to face the threats of increased competition within the European Community.

In addition to the provision of normative, prescriptive and empirical knowledge of the Single European Market, Part Four aims to contribute to a wider explanation of the economic, political, social and cultural challenges facing international business after 1992.

The Single European Market is not a new idea. It is an extension of the Treaty of Rome, a revival for a fuller more complete European economic integration. In order to understand why and how the recent interest and revival in completing the Single Market arose, Chapter Twelve begins by looking at the original political and economic motives behind the creation of the European Community in 1957, leading to the revival of interest in European economic integration in the 1980s and the call for closer political and monetary union in the 1990s. Business in the Single Market does not operate in a vacuum, but is heavily influenced by EC legislation and policies. This chapter will also provide an overview of the European Community institutions, and explain the decision-making processes involved. It will also provide practical advice on how to influence EC policy-makers and how to develop an active role in determining key policies affecting business in Europe.

Chapter Thirteen examines the Single European Act itself, its aims, objectives and the philosophy of 'Europe without frontiers' and considers what national and international implications it has for business. The Social Charter and the European Monetary Union are also examined, as well as the recent calls for closer political union made at Maastricht.

Chapter Fourteen focuses on the most immediate and practical issues relating to doing business in the Single European Market, such as human resources management for the Single Market, trading and marketing in the European Community, and formulating Single Market strategies.

Finally, no book embracing international and European business would be complete without considering the recent dramatic changes in Eastern and Central Europe. Chapter Fifteen examines these recent developments, and outlines their implications for international business.

TWELVE
THE CREATION OF THE SINGLE EUROPEAN MARKET

Knowledge about the European Community is generally limited, and while students should become better informed with recent events and changes in the European Community, it is not the purpose of this chapter to provide facts, dates and a mass of detailed descriptive and legislative material which would either become obsolete or would need updating regularly. The main aim in this chapter is to go beyond the descriptive level to a real understanding of the *issues* and *principles* which underlie the various sectors of European integration and doing business in the Single European Market.

The Single European Market is not a new idea. It is an extension of the Treaty of Rome, a revival in a fuller, more complete form of European integration.

To understand why and how this recent interest and revival in completing the Single Market in the 1990s arose, we need to look at the original political and economic motives behind the establishment of the Treaty of Rome in 1957.

LEARNING OBJECTIVES

- To understand what European integration means and to analyse the original political and economic motives behind the creation of the European Community
- To provide a brief overview of the Treaty of Rome: its aims, objectives and limitations
- To consider the issues arising for international business around the new interest in closer European economic and political integration particularly from the Single European Act and the Maastricht Treaty.

THE MOVEMENT TOWARDS A SINGLE MARKET IN EUROPE

Facts mean nothing without some idea of how they relate to each other. Integration theories can shed some light on the dynamics behind European integration, and the recent push towards greater economic and political union. A sharp distinction is often drawn between theory and practice, especially in the business and political world. Many business and political practitioners deny the existence of theory altogether. They often consider practice as the real and central consideration, while theory is only something fanciful, ideal and contrary to experience. Theory, in this view, is speculative thought and a set of statements on how things ought to be. In other words, theory is nothing but a guide to action. According to them, nothing in theory can substitute for experience, commonsense and intuition, upon which practice must ultimately rely.

It is self-delusion on the part of decision-makers or business people to believe that they can operate without theoretical propositions. All our actions are based on some kind of theory, or a set of preconceived assumptions. Theory in fact provides the basic principles of practice. Theory is a 'guide for action', a set of statements either about how things ought to be or about how they are. Theory can be used for several purposes: as a basis for legitimation, a guide for action, a framework for organizing facts, or a basis for the explanation of events and historical developments.

Theory as a guide for legitimation

Theory can be used for political purposes. Politicians and diplomats often rely on theoretical arguments in their briefs to legitimize their action and to gain public approval and consent. They will often refer to theory as a convenient and often convincing explanation of their actions by relating them to broader considerations which they feel are relevant, such as those pertaining to the domestic environment, or to the national interest, or involving suitable comparisons with other states.

Theoretical arguments play a crucial role in the context of the European Community, particularly in dealing, for example, with conflicts between different national interests, national sovereignty and national identity. It is, for example, much more powerful to explain the reasons why the UK opted out of the European Exchange Rate Mechanism and the Social Charter at the Maastricht Conference not only in terms of the issue itself but by relating it to the wider context of a country's power status, national sovereignty and identity, and other more general foreign policy interests.

Theory as a guide for action

By stating how things ought to be, linked to an analysis of how they have developed in the way they have, theory could be used as a guide for action that can provide us with a 'prescription for change': to make the world a better place to live in (Waltz, 1979) or to shift developments towards our own particular interests or to take better advantage of opportunities as they arise.

Theory as an analytical framework for organizing facts

Theory can help us to organize the storage of data, their classification and their retrieval. It enables us to proceed with clarity in the process of identifying relevant values and appropriate variables, and in determining the most rational course of action. Theory can therefore help us to separate and identify more clearly the relevant factors of an issue, thus allowing a more comprehensive understanding of its complexity and of different ways of analysing the issue.

INTEGRATION THEORIES

Before considering the various major approaches towards explaining European integration it is useful first to define what is meant by 'integration'.

Integration is generally defined as 'a process whereby a group of people organized initially in two or more independent nation-states, come to constitute a political whole which can be described as a Community' (Pentland, 1973, p. 29). Such a general definition is nevertheless limited, especially in respect of the concepts of 'globalization', the borderless world and global financial integration developed in previous chapters. First of all, it is essentially a political, state-centric one; second, it identifies integration as a consequence or an effect of governments, two or more intending to integrate, and third, it assumes integration as a future outcome.

There are various general approaches that have been developed in order to explain European integration (Harrop, 1989, Chs. 7–10). These are known as the Federalist, Functionalist, Pluralist, Neo-functionalist and Marxist theories.

The Federalist theory

The aim and means of integration for the Federalists is to create a political community based upon strong rule-bound central political institutions, superimposed upon autonomous nation states to keep order and control among them. Federalism was the main focus of the debates over the future of Europe at the Maastricht Conference, and caused major concern and worry about the idea of supranationality to both the UK and Danish governments.

The Functionalist theory

The Functionalists claim that there is a concrete distinction between activities that are political and those that are economic or technical. Technical/economic decisions are seen on this view as less controversial than political ones. By separating economics from politics, increased technological cooperation, for the Functionalist, will lead to political cooperation. The Functionalist theory of integration basically claims that only activities concerned with national security are political, while areas such as public health, transport and agriculture are non-political. Cooperation in these areas is therefore easier to organize and institutionalize, they argue, since it is beneficial to all.

The validity of such arguments is of course questionable, given recent events in international public organization and the claimed development of 'politicization' in many of the United Nations' agencies. Even the most apparently technical agencies are not immune to political influence.

Functionalism has contributed greatly to the recent development of and increase in mergers and acquisitions, joint ventures and strategic alliances in Europe, and it is important for students of business, and business managers, to understand the dynamics underlying them.

The Pluralist conception

According to the Pluralists, integration is seen as the formation of a 'Community of States', defined by a high and self-sustaining level of diplomatic, economic, social and cultural exchange between member states. This conception is popular among statesmen because the major concern of the pluralists is the problem of developing peaceful relations among states, while maintaining national sovereignty and state security. According to them, peaceful change can be achieved without the need for recourse to arms. Integration, they claim, will be enhanced not by the elimination of state borders, but by the development and improvement of the conduct of relations between them, by developing the capacities of states to handle information about their political environment and to adjust to each other's behaviour through increased social communications. To be fully integrated in a pluralist sense, states would have to form a 'Community of States'. This was the Gaullist vision of Europe – *L'Europe des Patries* – also known as political union.

The UK's view on European integration provides a classic example of a pluralist view of the creation of a single market, and encourages European political and economic cooperation only so long as they take the form of inter-governmental organization, without causing loss of national identity or national sovereignty.

The Neo-functionalist approach

Integration, for the Neo-functionalists, is 'the process whereby political actors in several distinct national settings, are persuaded to shift their loyalties, expectations and political activities towards a new centre, where institutions possess and demand jurisdiction over the pre-existing national state'.

The end result of political integration, in this view, is a new political community, superimposed on the pre-existing ones, leading to the development of a new supranational state.

Integration for the Neo-functionalist is therefore more concerned with why and how states cease to be wholly sovereign, how and why they voluntarily mingle, merge and mix with their neighbours so as to lose the factual attribute of sovereignty while acquiring new techniques for resolving conflicts between them. Theories developed about the working of the Community in Brussels, the decision-making processes, and the dialogue between the Commission, the Council and the Parliament, all provide good illustrations of a Neo-functionalist approach to integration. The Single European Act, the removal of physical, trade and monetary barriers, the ratification and debates before, during and after Maastricht, especially the French referendum – during which every household in France received a detailed copy of the European Union Treaty, including the proposed ratifications – is a triumph of and for Neo-functionalist thinking.

The Marxist theory

For the Marxist, in order to understand European integration one must seek to understand the present as history. Integration for the Marxists is a response to interdependence. European integration, in their view, emerged as a policy response to the necessary expansion of Capitalism. The way to achieve and sustain economic growth is by taking advantage of economies of scale. This explains, for example, why European nations came together to counterbalance US hegemony, and why mergers are increasingly encouraged in order to create firms large enough to compete against American and Japanese multinationals. The state, in this view, plays an important role in both economic and political integration. It must ensure the creation of a secure environment for industry and commerce, complete with legal systems protecting private property contracts and the provision of a cooperative labour force. It must also construct an ideological climate favourable to capitalism (Pentland, 1973, pp. 29–186; Cocks, 1980).

THE CREATION OF THE EUROPEAN COMMUNITY

Economic and political motives

To understand the recent European pressures demanding greater European integration, it is important to identify what the political and economic motives behind the creation of the EEC were, without which the recent Single Market cannot be fully understood.

The idea of creating a 'United Europe' to maintain peace and to create a common European culture dates back to the 14th century, when Pierre Dubois proposed a European Confederation to be governed by a European Council. But it was only in 1945, following the end of the Second World War, that concrete efforts were made to create a secure union of countries in Western Europe (Gibbs, 1990, p. 16).

The end of the Second World War did not automatically result in peace and improved economic and social conditions. Until the late 1940s, most of Europe was still in economic and political chaos. Many Western powers lost their colonies. Territorial realignment, and the reshaping of national boundaries, increased the number of separate customs unions and created massive problems by dislocating industrial links. Germany suffered substantial territorial losses, with massive reparations payments imposed on it, which exceeded its capacity to repay them. Massive borrowings were undertaken by the European states, far exceeding their capacity to repay, thus leading to the collapse of the international financial system.

There were also massive losses of labour and capital, which resulted in the collapse of industry and trade. A great depression set in all over Europe. The division of Europe into East and West as a result of the Cold War also resulted in the Soviet Union consolidating its position and control over Eastern European countries, which was seen as posing a security threat to the West.

In the face of this deep economic and political chaos, there was a strong desire in Europe to create a unified Europe to achieve peace and stimulate recovery.

Early attempts to achieve integration by military aggression had failed under Hitler and Napoleon. An attempt to establish a political community based upon integrated defence forces was also defeated in the French National Assembly. This idea of a political union was then transferred into the economic field. This is when Schuman, supported by Monnet, proposed the Schuman Plan in 1950, which resulted in the creation of the European Coal and Steel Community in 1954. This later led to the possibility of further integration, developed in the Spaak Report, and which led to the Treaty of Rome in 1957, thus creating the European Economic Community. The Spaak Report of 1955 was originally suggested at the Messina Conference, held in Sicily. The original report suggested the integration of atomic energy, the establishment of a common market, the creation of a European Fund and a European Investment Bank, and the harmonization of conditions of work and pay (Jensen, 1967, pp. 46–69).

The Treaty of Rome

The Treaty of Rome was signed in March 1957 by the six founding European states: Belgium, France, Germany, Italy, Luxembourg and The Netherlands. It took effect from January 1958, thereby creating the EEC. The general objectives of the creation of the EEC are summarized in Article 2 of the Treaty:

> The Community shall have as its task, by establishing a common market and progressively approximating the economic policies of member States, to promote throughout the Community a harmonious development of economic activities, a continuous and balanced expansion, an increase in stability, an accelerated saving in standard of living and a closer relation between the states belonging to it.

These objectives could be achieved through (a) the establishment of a Common Customs Tariff, (b) a common commercial policy towards Third World countries, (c) a common agricultural policy, (d) the free movement of people, goods, services and capital, and (e) the creation of a European Social Fund and a European Investment bank.

The European Community decision-making process

The Treaty of Rome did not set out precisely how the general aims of the EC would be achieved, but provided for the creation of various Community institutions where policies would be formulated and administered. All Single Market proposals have to go through the European Community before becoming directives to be implemented in the EC. Since most of these decisions affect all areas of business in the Community, it is important for business managers to understand how these decisions are taken, and how to influence the process in Brussels.

There are five main Community institutions: the Commission, the Council of Ministers, the European Parliament, the Court of Justice (Noel, 1988, 1991) and the Economic and Social Committee.

The Commission

The European Commission headquarters are in Brussels. It has offices in Luxembourg, information offices in each of the member states and delegations in many of the world's capitals.

The Commission is currently divided into 23 directorates general, generally responsible for the technical preparation of legislation and its implementation (Department of Trade and Industry, 1992a). The Commission is headed by 17 Commissioners, appointed by the Community governments, two from each of the larger member states and one from each of the smaller states. France, Germany, Italy and the UK have at present two each, while The Netherlands, Denmark, Portugal, Luxembourg, Ireland, Belgium and Greece have one each.

Commissioners are not appointed as national delegates, but are required to act in the interests of the Community as a whole. Each Commissioner takes an oath in which he or she pledges not to seek or accept instructions from national governments or political parties, but to serve the interests of the Community as a whole. When Commissioners travel abroad they do so as representatives of the Community as a whole and not of the member state to which they belong. Commissioners are appointed for a four-year term. They are chosen on the basis of their general competence in their own established careers, with lawyers, economists, ex-ministers and ex-diplomats dominating.

Functions and powers of the Commission   The Commission is responsible for the initial preliminary design of Community policies, proposals and legislation. It is also responsible for implementing decisions taken by the Council of Ministers. As the Community 'watchdog' (Budd and Jones, 1989, p. 35), the Commission sees that decisions of the EC institutions are properly implemented. It has a direct role in the supervision of the daily operation of major policies upon which agreement at 12 nations level has been reached.

The Commission is also the 'guardian' of the Treaties. It can initiate action against member states, institutions and firms which do not comply with EC rules, if necessary with the aid of the European Court of Justice. The Commission is thus in a position not only to effect EC policy, but to affect it too. It has, for example the power to fine firms which break certain operational rules. The Commission is also responsible for the administration of Community funds, such as the European Social Fund, the Regional Development Fund and the Agricultural Guarantee and Guidance Fund.

Finally, the Commission liaises closely with member states and firms in order to keep them up to date with the latest developments, such as new legislation and new policies associated with the Single European Act.

The Commission's decision-making process   The Commission is often accused of being slow and bureaucratic. The current programme of the Commission runs into thousands of words (Budd and Jones, 1989, p. 49). Apart from religion, it touches upon almost every aspect of human endeavour, requires the integration of the interests of the 12 member states, and has to work in nine different languages. A massive process of consultation and preparation takes place before a policy proposal reaches its first published draft. The Commission acts collectively. Cabinet staff have regular inter-cabinet committees, called Chefs de Cabinet, which are designed to identify those issues upon which Commissioners need to focus at their weekly meetings. The Commission Chefs de Cabinet, after studying a proposal in depth, present it to the Commissioners for their review. Each Commissioner has a 'cabinet' of six or more permanent administrators, together with secretarial support. The majority of the Cabinet staff are of the same nationality as their Commissioner. These are called the 'Services', and are staffed mainly be career officials recruited by competitive examination from the 12 member states. These are normally the first port of call to find out the basis of Commission thinking and to seek to influence it. Commissioners discuss these proposals and then decide on the nature of the final proposal collectively. They usually have one week to review, adopt or reject the proposal. Decisions are taken by a simple majority vote, which means at least nine out of the 17 Commissioners. If adopted, the proposal is then sent to the Council of Ministers.

The Council of Ministers

Until 1986, the European Council had no legal standing in terms of the Community's Treaties. It was set up by the heads of state themselves in 1974 (Budd and Jones, 1989, p. 41). Today the Council of Ministers is the most powerful institution in the Community. As Emile Noel, Secretary General of the Commission put it, 'Today the paramount importance of the Council is not only beyond doubt, it has sometimes seemed in danger of submerging the identity of the Community itself'.

The Council's headquarters and General Secretariat are in Brussels, but in April, June and October, meetings of the Council are held in Luxembourg. Originally, the Council of Ministers met four times a year to offer top-level guidance, and to review progress over the previous months. In addition to the normal Council meetings the 'European Council', often referred to as the 'European Summit', comprising heads of state and heads of government, now meets twice a year to discuss broad areas of policy. These European Council meetings are chaired by the member state holding the presidency for a six-month period on a rotating basis.

The Council of Ministers is made up of one representative from each member state. It is presided over by one of the members acting as President for six months by rotation. Each government delegates to the Council one of its members. Members of the Council are therefore representatives of their own states, and they act on the basis of instructions received from their own governments.

Functions and powers of the Council   The Council is the Community's central decision-making body. It acts at the request of the Commission by adopting or modifying proposals from the Commission. It may occasionally issue opinions and initiate proposals, but these are not binding. There are three methods for decision-making in the Council depending on the nature of a given proposal and the Treaty Article under which it is based. These are unanimity, simple majority voting requiring at least seven members in favour, and qualified majority. A veto on decision-making should in principle be used only when the vital national interest of a government is seen to be at stake. The relative weight of the votes held by member states under the qualified majority system mean that 54 votes out of 76 are needed for a measure to be adopted. The UK, Germany, France and Italy have ten votes each. Spain has eight, Belgium, Greece, The Netherlands and Portugal five, Denmark and Ireland three and Luxembourg two.

The European Parliament

The European Parliament is a directly elected body, with 518 members. The first direct election for the European Parliament was held in June 1979 with nine member states taking their place. Each state uses its own national electoral system. The European Parliament plenary meetings are held in committee meetings 12 times a year in Brussels (Department of Trade and Industry, 1992a, p. 8).

Anyone can stand for election. Members of the European Parliament are elected to serve for a five-year term of office. The largest countries in the Community, such as the UK, France, Germany and Italy each have 91 seats. European members of the Parliament, once elected, sit in political groupings regardless of nationality and not in national blocks of representatives of member states. They choose which of the various political groupings they wish to join. Virtually all members play an active part in one of the 18 committees, which cover political affairs; agriculture, fishery and food; budget, economic, monetary and industrial matters; energy, research and technology; external economic relations; legal affairs and citizen's rights; social matters and employment; regional policy and planning; transport; environmental, health and consumer affairs; youth culture and education; information and sport; overseas development; budgetary control; procedural matters; women's rights; institutional affairs; and members' credentials.

Functions and power of the European Parliament   The European Parliament (EP) does not make decisions, but debates European legislation. It receives reports from the Commission and recommendations from the Council which it then rejects, amends or passes by an absolute majority of its members.

Until 1987, the powers of the EP were limited, and consisted of budgetary, consultative and supervisory powers. The EP can reject the Council's draft budget with an absolute majority. This happened in 1985/1986, for example. The EP also has the right to propose amendments to non-compulsory expenditure in the budget, but it has no say over compulsory expenditure, which accounts for 70 per cent of total expenditure. The EP can also dismiss the Commission by a two-thirds majority vote, but only through '*en bloc* dismissal'. It has no say, however, over its reappointment, and in principle the same Commission could be reappointed by national governments. The EP has the right to issue an opinion on draft legislation, but these opinions, until 1987, were not binding on either the Commission or the Council. Finally, the EP has a delaying power. The Court of Justice ruled that any legislation adopted by the Council without receiving an EP opinion is invalid. The Single European Act gave the European Parliament additional powers in 1987, such as the assent procedure. Since 1987, the EP is required to give its assent to any new application for membership in the EC, giving the EP additional veto power over EC enlargement in the future. EP assent is also required for any new association agreements with Third World countries, including the renewal of existing agreements. For example, in December 1987 the EP postponed two draft agreements with Turkey because of concern over human rights in that region, and three protocols with Israel were also rejected. This assent procedure has proved to be a powerful weapon to pressurize Third World countries on their human rights records.

An additional competence given to the European Parliament recently is that known as the Cooperation Procedure. Until 1987, the EP gave only its opinions and proposed amendments to draft legislation. However, neither the Council nor the Commission were under any obligation to act upon EP recommendations. The Council could overturn the Parliament's amendments by unanimous vote. Article 149 of the Single European Act, introduced the 'Cooperation Procedure', according to which all legislation necessary for the Single European Market must return to the EP for a second reading. The EP has two or three months to either accept, amend or reject it. If rejected, the Council can only adopt such legislation after a second reading and by unanimous vote.

Decision-making within the Parliament   Much of the work of the Parliament is done by its specialist committees, divided by issue area. When the Parliament is consulted, it refers the proposal to one of these committees (Department of Trade and Industry, 1992a, p. 10). The Committee appoints a 'rapporteur' for the proposal; the particular MEP has to then prepare a report, and the Committee then discusses that report. Each report must include a draft opinion on the proposal, which is then put to the Parliament as a whole by the Specialist Committee. It is then adopted as the Parliament's opinion.

The European Court of Justice

The European Court of Justice rules on the interpretation and application of Community laws and sits in Luxembourg. It has 13 judges, including one from each Community country, and six Advocates General, whose task is to give detailed submissions on cases brought before the Court in order to help the judges make their decisions. A Court of First Instance has been established, where rulings on matters pertaining to the internal market can be made, and where issues relevant to business, including competition policy infringements, can be brought. However, this new court, specializing in the processing of commercial cases, does not take cases brought by member states or the Commission.

Functions and power of the Court of Justice   The European Court rules on the application and interpretation of Community Law. It gives final judgment on the interpretation of the Treaties. It also deals with infringement of the European Treaties by member states, and initiates preliminary rulings on questions referred to it by national courts. It also helps national courts in the process of interpreting EC legislation.

The European Court works in a similar way to the Appeal Courts of member states. The process of appealing to the Court on infractions of Community Law is often complicated and can be very lengthy. Private individuals, firms, local authorities or others can appeal to the Court when they consider they have been unjustly served by Community legislation. There are no court costs involved, but appellants must pay their own lawyers' fees. The easiest first step, however, is to complain to the Commission by initiating a letter to any of the Commission's office.

Judgments of the European Court are binding on member states. Even though there is no explicit provision in the Treaty which states that Community law ranks above national law, Community law has precedence over national law by implication, because it is a principle of the Treaty that the status of Community law cannot be called into question by member states.

The Economic and Social Committee

This is based in Brussels. It is an advisory body of 189 members consisting of representatives of employers, trade unions and consumers. It must be formally consulted by the Commission on proposals relating to economic and social matters. Members of the Economic and Social Committee are appointed for four years from lists supplied by member states, and are drawn from the three groups mentioned above. Members are independent of individual governments. The Committee meets eight times a year. Although only a consultative body, the Economic and

Social Committee can be very valuable for business people. It sees all important Commission proposals in draft form and delivers over 100 detailed opinions on these every year.

Influencing the decision-making process

Any firm, local authority, trade or professional association has the right to plead its case to the Community (Budd and Jones, 1989, pp. 60–1). To influence the decision-making process effectively, pressure must be exerted at the stage when drafts are being written, evidence gathered and opinions expressed.

Before legislation is proposed to the Council, the Commission will often discuss its ideas with national experts and professional and business organizations. It is during these first stages of the Community legislation process that it is important to ensure that business interests are properly represented. It is the Commission's absolute duty to canvass as many points of view as it can reasonably assimilate. Business managers need to be aware of this system and work with the Commission to ensure that '*fiches d'impact*' provide adequate assessments of the effect of new proposals on business (Department of Trade and Industry, 1992a, p. 12).

CASE STUDY 12.1: Influencing the European Commission

In order to ensure that firms contribute their views at the proper time, the Department of Trade and Industry in the UK recommends the following five key points for success in Brussels.

- *Get in early*
  Try to get your views in before the Commission has reached a decision and produced formal drafts for EC proposals. To do this, the first step is to obtain clear and up-to-date information on what is happening. The European Information Service is a bulletin published 10 times a year by the International Union of Local Authorities and is the best initial source of information about decision-making in the Community. You may also consult the Annual Reports and monthly Bulletins of the Community, Agence Europe and the European Report, which are both published in Brussels. Spearhead is a comprehensive database on current and prospective Single Market measures and is regularly updated. It is accessible via many personal computers, and through many Chambers of Commerce, Trade Associations and Public Libraries. MEPs also will be up to date on the work of their committees and can be consulted.
- *Work with others*
  A spread of opinion carries more weight than a lone voice. It is important to work with European Trade Associations. Keep in touch with your own trade or professional association. The staff of these organizations know exactly what legislation is planned and the stage it has reached, and can put you in contact with other members who might have the same concerns as you. Even firms that compete with one another should coordinate their efforts when trying to influence Brussels.
- *Think European*
  Your lobbying should reflect a clear understanding of the Single Market Programme and Community interests, so that specific or general business interests are presented as consistent with 'European' interests and developments
- *Be prepared*
  Collect as much information and evidence as you can in preparing your report to support your views.

● *Get involved*

It is very important to remain linked to the Brussels network so that you will be able to react quickly to events affecting your business as and when they arise. A single trip to Brussels is unlikely to do the trick. You need to establish long-term contacts in Brussels and keep in touch with European MPs there.

Source

Adapted from *Brussels Can You Hear Me*, DTI Publications, 1992.

REVIEW QUESTIONS

1. To what extent do theories of integration help us to understand the dynamics behind European economic and political integration?
2. What were the economic and political motives behind the creation of the EEC following the Second World War?
3. Is the decision-making process in the Community democratic?
4. As a business person wishing to expand your business in Europe how could you influence the decision-making process in the Community to your benefit?
5. Is the EC a structure for peace or an alliance for economic defence?
6. To what extent, if at all, is national sovereignty being eroded by Brussels?

FURTHER READING

Department of Trade and Industry, *Brussels Can You Hear Me?*, DTI Publications, 1992.

Harrop, J., *The Political Economy of Integration in the European Community*, Edward Elgar, Aldershot, 1989.

Nicoll, W. and Salmon, T., *Understanding the European Community*, Philip Allan, London, 1990.

Noel, E., *Working Together. The Institutions of the European Community*. Office for Official Publications of the EC, Luxembourg, 1991.

Pentland, C., *International Theory and European Integration*, Faber & Faber, London, 1973.

Reynolds, C., *Theory and Explanation in World Politics*, Robertson, London, 1973.

Taylor, P., *The Limits of European Integration*, Croom Helm, London, 1983.

Waltz, K., *Theory of World Politics*, Addison-Wesley, Reading MA, 1979.

THIRTEEN

FROM ECONOMIC TO POLITICAL UNION

The Single European Market will affect not only domestic markets within the European Community, but the whole world of international business. The aim of this chapter is to provide managers and students with a basic understanding of what the Single European Market means in terms of the changes that it will bring to their business environment, and to assist them in being able to identify the opportunities and threats it presents.

LEARNING OBJECTIVES

- To understand the pressures towards greater European integration in the 1980s and 1990s
- To explain the philosophy behind 'Europe without Frontiers'
- To introduce the Community Charter of Fundamental Rights and explain its aims and objectives, problems and barriers of implementation, and its implications for business
- To provide an overall view of the main issues related to European Monetary Union
- To explain the debates at Maastricht related to the call for closer political union in Europe

THE DYNAMICS BEHIND THE CREATION OF THE SINGLE EUROPEAN MARKET

The recent revival of interest in closer economic and political integration in the European Community is in part a reflection of large-scale economic and political problems in the global system as a whole (Palmer, 1988).

The oil recession in the 1970s made Europeans increasingly aware of their dependence upon the international monetary system. Many large firms became insolvent due to the rising price of oil. As a result, a recession gripped Europe, with high levels of unemployment and inflation rates rising very sharply. By the 1980s, there was a real fear in Europe of a breakdown of the international monetary system, due to large US deficits and the inability of the USA to continue financing them. There was a major concern that these deficits might lead to an increase in international interest rates by the end of the decade. As a result, it was feared that those Third World countries with the greatest levels of indebtedness to Western banks would be obliged to default on their debt payments, which would lead to a collapse of the international monetary system and to worldwide economic depression. The stock market crash of October 1987 in London, for example, seemed to confirm the worst apprehensions of Western European governments. Additionally, the economic recession in the early 1980s in Europe resulted in industrial decline and decay of social provision. Europe was increasingly unable to counter the growing commercial challenge from the USA, Japan and the Pacific Rim.

Another dynamic force behind the push towards closer economic integration in Europe in the 1980s was the worsening of transatlantic relations between Europe and the USA, which started to sour as early as 1973, due mainly to the deficit in the US trade balance under Presidents Ford, Carter and Reagan. Throughout the 1970s, both the USA and the EC had several conflicts over international trade protectionism, such as when the USA sought to protect its steel industry through triggering prices designed to ward off European and Japanese competition. OPEC prices were also cut to help American chemical and synthetic textile manufacturers to undercut foreign competition. Additionally, in 1985 the USA spent billions of dollars to develop its Strategic Defense Initiative. Europe complained that this would give an indirect boost to America's competitive edge in advanced information technology, and reinforce Europe's relative technological backwardness and dependence on the USA.

The challenge of an increasingly competitive external world also provided much of the incentive for increased European integration. The information technology revolution of the 1980s posed a threat to Europe. American and Japanese firms were evidently superior in this area of new technology, and EC competitiveness was at stake. Europe became unable to counter the growing commercial challenge from the USA and Japan and the developing Pacific Rim competition. European states and firms realized that a major cause of their lack of growth and competitiveness was due to the fragmentation of the EC into national markets. After the 1970s recession, although non-tariff barriers were removed, each nation imposed its own barriers to protect its industry against outside competition, whether from within the EC or outside.

Another factor which stimulated the need for the creation of a Single European Market was the increasing internationalization of capital, labour and production, which was made easier by new developments in information technology (IT). The past thirty years have seen an extraordinary expansion, not only in world trade, but also in the deployment of international finance and new forms of international production, due to developments in computer technology and international communications which facilitated the internationalization of production, distribution and consumption. Subcontracting and franchising grew rapidly. With the increased ease of international capital movements and production dispersal, multinational firms established factories in countries where labour was cheaper.

Finally, the rise of Japanese competition, through economic development and emergence as a leading world economic power, placed a serious strain on European performance. The European Community began to look for new ways of shielding their domestic industry from the new competitive threat.

'EUROPE WITHOUT FRONTIERS': THE PHILOSOPHY

Against this background, the Heads of States and Governments of all member states in 1985 asked the Commission to put forward concrete proposals for the completion of an internal Single European Market.

The Commission subsequently published a White Paper in June 1985, setting out proposals for a comprehensive programme, together with a timetable for what action was considered necessary to achieve a 'frontierless Europe'. The White Paper attempted to identify all the existing physical, technical and fiscal barriers which were claimed to justify the existence of frontier controls, and which prevented the free functioning of the market, and put forward 300 legislative proposals required for their removal (Commission of the EC, 1989).

The Commission believed that this Single European Market would work efficiently only if it were expanding and flexible, so that resources of people and materials and of capital and investment could flow to areas of greatest economic advantage (Commission of the EC, 1989, p. 20). The objectives, set out in the Commission's White Paper on completing the internal market and achieving a 'Europe without Frontiers', are based on the achievement of four freedoms of movement:

1. Free movement of goods.
2. Free movement of people.
3. Free movement of services.
4. Free movement of capital.

The White Paper argued that the achievement of these four freedoms required:

1. The removal of physical barriers.
2. The removal of technical barriers.
3. The removal of fiscal barriers.
4. The liberalization of internal competition through strict competition policies.

We will return to these issues later in this chapter.

The Single European Act was signed on February 1986 and entered into force on 18 July 1987. The adoption of the Single European Act reflected a renewed political will on the part of the Community to halt the economic fragmentation of the Community, and to complete within a given time-frame the aims of the original treaties. The importance of the Single European Act is that, once ratified by all member states, it would provide political impetus and a legal framework for achieving a truly unified market by 1992. The Single European Act defines the Single European Market as 'an area without internal frontiers in which free movement of goods, persons, services and capital can take place' (Department of Trade and Industry, 1992b, p. 2). The Single European Act contains a number of amendments to the original Treaty of Rome, covering a variety of subjects such as Economic and Social Cohesion, the Environment, Cooperation between Institutions, and Political Cooperation. A qualified majority procedure replaced the unanimity requirement provided for in the Treaty of Rome. The unanimity requirement has in the past made any decision a complex and lengthy process and meant that in practice the rate of progress was dictated by the most reluctant member states. Once ratified by all members the treaty becomes a legal framework (Department of Trade and Industry, 1992b).

The removal of physical barriers

The removal of physical barriers must be examined in its relationships with people and goods.

Free movement of people   To ensure the free movement of people the Commission proposed the removal of controls for travellers, except for spot checks for taxes due on goods. The Commission proposed that spot checking should only be carried out on exit from member states, and not at both exit and entry. External border checks will remain to protect the Community from illegal immigration, crime, drugs, terrorism and the carrying of firearms. It is agreed that common policies should be established for the movement of third country citizens between member states, and for better coordination of all rules of entry, of residence, of access to employment, of right of asylum, of refugee status and of visa policy. The European passport will also help in speeding up travel across frontiers by providing instant identification of community citizens at a glance, thus facilitating the free movement of people without the restrictions of work permits or residence permits.

Free movement of goods   Frontier controls have for a long time frustrated European business people, especially when transferring goods across borders involved considerable delays and excessive amounts of documentation, which raised the costs of moving products across borders. To ensure the speedier movement of goods across national borders, the Single European Act introduced the Single Administrative Document in January 1988. This document replaces the many different forms previously used for transporting goods within Europe.

A single Community patent has also been introduced and a single Community trade mark. Previously, each member state had its own national patent system. Any inventor who wished to obtain patent protection across the whole Community had to apply for a patent in each country individually, and the procedures involved tests to establish what is patentable. This was a formidable task, considering the differences in standards regulations between member states. The Single Community Patent Convention was signed in December 1989, making it possible to obtain patent protection in some or all of the Community to which it applies through a single application. As far as trade marks are concerned, prior to the Single European Act there were ten separate systems for registering trade marks in the European Community. This meant that anyone wishing to protect a trade mark throughout the EC had to meet the criteria laid down by each of the separate national systems. Against this, the Commission has proposed that there should be a Community trade mark. This would operate in parallel with national systems, and would enable business to secure Community-wide protection through a single application to a Community Trade Mark Office set up for this purpose. A Community trade mark now confers the same rights in all member states. Member states would also designate some of their courts as Community trade mark courts. A Community trade mark owner who considers that another business is infringing its trade mark in other member states would be able to go to one of these courts and obtain a judgment valid for the whole of the EC.

While efforts were being made to remove physical barriers to trade with the Community, issues of health and agricultural products were also raised. The Community introduced harmonized changes for health inspection for both red meat and poultry on 1 January 1991, which stipulated that all meat produced in the EC will have to be inspected in accordance with common rules. The Commission issued a single standard of structure, hygiene and supervision on all red meat slaughterhouses, cutting premises and cold stores across the Community. Regarding plant health, the Commission produced in 1987 a paper proposing a plant health strategy for the Single Market. The Commission proposed the development of common plant health standards, the introduction of a plant passport which would replace the old plant health certificates and the systematic phasing out of existing controls at the Community's internal borders. A Community Plant Health Inspectorate was subsequently established.

The removal of technical barriers

The removal of technical barriers affects both the free movement of people and of goods.

Free movement of people   Even with the removal of physical barriers and the freedom to work anywhere in the Community, Community citizens' movement may still be restricted due to the following factors. Academic qualifications of students or vocational training and professional qualifications are not always equally recognized in all member states. Professionals often have to re-qualify before they can pursue their profession in other member states. Accountants, for example, would have to spend nearly 50 years to qualify and re-qualify in order to be qualified to audit throughout the Community (Department of Trade and Industry, 1991a, p. 3).

To overcome these difficulties, the Commission put forward proposals on the mutual recognition of academic diplomas and the mutual acceptance of vocational training qualifications for apprentices. This led to the introduction of a European 'Vocational Training Card' which aims to provide proof that the holder has reached a generally accepted standard. The Commission also put forward a proposal, in 1985, for a single system of mutual recognition that could be applied to all professions. According to this system, provided that professional people met certain minimum requirements of qualification, experience and supervised training, their qualifications would be recognized in all member states and they would be allowed to practice without any further restriction. This proposal was put forward in 1985, agreed by the Council in December 1988, and implemented with effect from 4 January 1991. The directive clearly stipulates that if an EC citizen is fully qualified in one member state, he or she has a right to be recognized as a professional in another member state including the right to use to the relevant professional title or designatory letters. The directive also allows a professional from one member state to become a member of the equivalent profession in another without having to re-qualify, based on the principle of mutual recognition. This directive applies only to professions whose practice is regulated by law or administrative rules. So far, the greatest progress has been achieved in the health sector. Doctors, nurses, dentists, veterinarians and midwives have had all their basic training harmonized, and now have the right of establishment and the right to practice in all Community countries.

Free movement of goods   The idea here is that any product which can be sold in any member state, should also be freely marketable in all other parts of the Community, unimpeded by different national rules, standards, tests or certification practices. To achieve this, all technical barriers to the free movement of goods in the Community must be removed, including differences in national industrial standards, differences in national regulations and differences in testing and certification procedures (*European File*, 1988b). Furthermore, the existence of different national production standards and regulations meant that many products had to be separately manufactured to separate standards for each separate country. The Community has been trying for many years to eliminate these barriers through the harmonization and adjustment of national regulations to conform to an agreed Community standard. This has proved difficult and complex.

The new approach adopted to the harmonization of technical conditions and standards was adopted on 7 May 1985 (Department of Trade and Industry, 1991b). It stated that once minimum standards in respect of safety and compatibility are reached, individual variations can be tolerated. A Joint European Standards Institution was consequently established to produce European Standards essential for safety in use, health, consumer protection and the environment. Products complying with these requirements will be issued with an EC mark which will guarantee them free access to all markets in the Community.

The removal of fiscal barriers

Fiscal barriers include restrictions on capital movements as well as differences between tax levels and excise duties. According to the Commission, businesses in the Community should have access to efficient financial services. They should be able to choose the services most appropriate to their requirements, which are also the most reliable and the least costly. In addition, business firms should be able to exercise their activities throughout the Community without having to fragment their financial dealings, which can be caused by disparate national regulations. The view of the Commission is that an integrated financial market cannot be achieved without the full liberalization of capital movements.

In 1988, a directive for the full liberalization of capital was adopted, requiring member states to implement it. The main features of the directive are the following. First, all restrictions on the transfer of cash are to be abolished. Second, discriminatory measures such as the taxation of certain types of investment, must also be eliminated. Third, consumers in one area should have access to the full range of insurance, unit trusts, banking, mortgage and securities options available in all member states.

A second Banking Coordination Directive was adopted in 1988. It provided the right of a credit institution which is authorized in any one member state to provide services and to establish a branch in any other member country, without having to obtain further authorization. This directive also put forward the idea of a single banking licence valid throughout the European Community, and a proposal for the creation of an integrated European securities market. The main objectives of the establishment of the European securities market was to make it easier for companies to treat the Community as a Single Market for the issue of shares and bonds, and for obtaining stock exchange listing. The Directive for a full liberalization of activities and services in transferable securities was adopted in 1985, and came into force in 1989. According to this directive, unit trusts, too, which are authorized by their own member state, will be allowed to market their units to investors in any other member state. Financial services and banks can now offer the full range of their services throughout the entire Community, and set up branches in another member state as easily as in their own country. Insurance too can be bought, and is valid throughout the Community (*European File*, 1988a,c).

The liberalization of competition

Physical, technical and fiscal barriers were originally erected to protect national markets from external competition. Their removal consequently opens up those markets to such competition. A rigorous competition policy is therefore essential to the development of a Single European Market.

The Commission believes that a strong competition policy is necessary to ensure that the freedom for trade provided by the creation of an internal market is not constrained by anti-competitive practices, whether initiated by governments or by enterprises. Competition rules seek to prevent enterprises from distorting trade rules or abusing their power in the market place (Department of Trade and Industry, 1989, 1992b). EC competition policy is designed to ensure that trade between member states takes place on the basis of free and fair competition, and that state barriers to trade between member states, when dismantled, are not replaced by private barriers which might fragment the single market. Article 85, for example, prohibits all agreements which have as their object or effect the prevention, restriction or distortion of competition within the EC, such as agreeing to fix prices, sharing markets, discriminating against third parties to their competitive disadvantage, or imposing territorial restrictions which might partition the Common Market. Article 86 prohibits the abuse by one or more firms of a dominant position within the EC. Establishing and maintaining a dominant position itself is not prohibited, but the abuse of a dominant position by such means as predatory pricing, limiting production, markets or technical development, refusal to supply or the imposition of discriminatory trading conditions to the competitive disadvantage of others, is no longer unconstrained.

However, Articles 85 and 86 made no specific provision for control by the European

Commission of concentrations or mergers within the Community. The EC therefore adopted a European Merger Regulation which came into force on 21 September 1990. This meant in general that mergers involving parties with a combined worldwide turnover of more than 5 billion ECU should be subject to the control of the European Commission, provided that the EC turnover of each of at least two companies involved exceeds 250 million ECU and that the companies concerned do not have at least two-thirds of their EC turnover from the same member state.

Today, mergers with a Community dimension must be notified to the European Commission and suspended for at least three weeks. The Commission will examine the consequences of the merger and decide within a month whether to initiate proceedings within four months, to declare it compatible with the Common Market, or to declare it incompatible and thus prohibited.

THE SOCIAL CHARTER

Much has been said and written about the Social Charter. Former British Prime Minister Margaret Thatcher has been known on numerous occasions to have called it 'Socialism by the back door' (Mazey, 1989). For Jacques Delors, President of the EC Commission, on the other hand, this social dialogue and collective bargaining are essential pillars of democracy.

The Community Charter of Fundamental Social Rights for Workers was adopted at a meeting of the European Council in Strasbourg on 8 and 9 December 1989 by the heads of state or governments of the EC, with the exception of the UK (*European Business Review*, 1989, p. 4; *European File*, 1990).

The aims of the Community Charter of Fundamental Rights are:

1. To combat unemployment and reduce the inequality of its impact. Unemployment in the Community is 11 per cent of the working population (16 million Europeans). Unemployment is also unevenly distributed. For example, the unemployment rate among those under 25 years of age is 20 per cent, which is more than double that of other workers (Venturini, 1988).
2. To ensure growth and greater job opportunities, and to reject all forms of discrimination or exclusion.
3. To promote improvements in living and working conditions.
4. To increase the economic and social cohesion of the 12 members of the Community.

To achieve these aims the Social Charter of Fundamental Rights comprises a set of rights:

1. *Freedom of movement*   According to the Social Charter, each citizen of the European Community should have the right to freedom of movement throughout the territory of the Community, subject to restrictions justified on the grounds of public policy, public security or public health. The right of freedom of movement enables any citizen to work in the EC country of his or her own choice, and to engage in any occupation or profession in the Community under the same terms as those applied to nationals of the host country, subject to the provision of Community law. This includes, for example, equal opportunities. Wages and social benefits applied in the host country must be granted to workers in another EC state. The right also ensures that social protection is extended to all citizens of the Community in gainful employment in a country other than their country of origin, on terms identical to those enjoyed by workers of the host country.
2. *Employment and remuneration*   A principal objective of the Social Charter is to ensure fair remuneration for all employment in the Community, which means establishing a 'decent'

wage or 'fair' remuneration. The Charter states that all employment shall be 'fairly' remunerated and that all employees should be able to earn 'equitable' wages which allows them a decent standard of living. The Commission regards the setting of such 'fair' wages to be up to the national governments and the prevailing national systems.

3. *Improvement of living and working conditions*   This relates to the organization of work, with emphasis on flexible working time arrangements and the establishment of a maximum duration of working hours per week, a weekly rest period and annual paid leave. The minimum employment age is set at 16 years.

4. *Social protection*   Every worker in the EC, according to the Social Charter, should have a right to adequate social protection and enjoy an adequate level of social security benefits. The unemployed should also receive sufficient subsistence benefits and appropriate social assistance.

5. *Freedom of association*   This right provides every worker in the Community with the opportunity to belong freely to any professional or trade union organization of his or her choice. This general right also includes the freedom to negotiate and conclude collective agreements and the right to resort to collective action, including the right to strike.

6. *Vocational training*   The Social Charter also declares that every European should have the opportunity to continue vocational training. Every European should have the right to enrol for occupational training courses, including those in universities and technical colleges, on the same terms as those enjoyed by the nationals of member states, and in the country of which the course takes place.

7. *Equal treatment of men and women*   Equal opportunities must also be developed with regard to access to employment, remuneration, working conditions, social protection, education, vocational training and career development.

8. *Information, consultation and participation of workers*   This is one of the most controversial areas of the Social Charter. It is discussed later in this chapter.

9. *Health protection and safety at the workplace*   According to this right, every worker must enjoy satisfactory health and safety conditions in his or her working environment. This means that health and safety measures need to be significantly improved in some member states. Minimum standards of fire prevention, lighting and ventilation are being instituted, as well as stricter guidelines for the use of machinery and protective equipment. The technological dimension is particularly highlighted, in so far as it involves changes in employees' working conditions, the restructuring of the company arising from mergers, collective redundancy procedures and when policies of the parent company affect trans-frontier workers.

10. *Elderly persons*   According to this right each member of the Community, in retirement, should be entitled to receive a minimum income giving him or her a decent standard of living and suitable medical and social assistance.

11. *Disabled persons*   Measures should be taken to ensure the fullest integration of the disabled into working life through vocational training, professional reinsertion and readaptation, and social integration by means of improving accessibility, mobility, means of transport and housing.

Problems and barriers of implementation

Four major problems have been identified for implementing the Social Charter (Venturini, 1988).

The first major problem is that the full implementation of the Charter remains the responsibility of individual member states. It is their task to ensure that all resources, legislation or collective agreements are being used to implement fully the social measures mentioned above. It is, however, doubtful whether all members are pursuing the implementation of those rights fully. Article 189 of the Treaty clearly stipulates that although 'a directive shall be binding as to the result to be achieved, upon each member state to which it is addressed, the choice of form and method for achieving the desired results shall be the responsibility of national authority'.

The second problem with implementation is the lack of legal muscle of the EC and the difficulty of converging national laws to meet the requirements of the internal market. In other words, establishing one basic set of social rules which can be adapted to the entire Community is difficult to develop and sustain.

The third barrier is the lack of political support. Member states do not seem convinced that Community development of this kind is a vital element in their national interests. Hence the failure to provide Community institutions with adequate resources and the political authority to promote and proceed with the development process. In the UK, for example, it is argued that parts of the Social Charter go beyond what is acceptable to the British Government, which still has memories of the strikes and disputes of the 1970s and is not keen to see them re-emerge (Goodhard, 1992). The Social Charter, it is further asserted, might help trade unions to regain an influential role in bargaining and worker participation, and might boost the unions by restoring an ideological climate favourable to unions. The Thatcher government, during the 1980s, re-moved most of the laws on collective bargaining, replacing them with a system based on local level or individual bargaining in relation to the market conditions in the area (Wedderburn, 1990).

Finally, the fourth major problem of implementing the Social Charter is the great diversity of existing social systems within the 12 member states. There is a great disparity in the resources, standards of living and of the structures of social security schemes between one member state and another. The payment of unemployment benefits at the German level, for example, would encourage people in Portugal never to work again (Welford and Prescott, 1992, p. 105).

The implementation of the Charter will furthermore impose costs for businesses which are forced to implement some aspects of it (Welford and Prescott, 1992, p. 109). Against this, the Commission believes that if all firms are expected to implement the same directives, then no firm will be at a disadvantage. The problem here is that firms are beginning from different bases. German firms, for example, have a long history of worker participation and involvement, and are unlikely to be faced with the same transaction costs of implementing key directives as, say, a firm in Greece (*European Industrial Relations Review*, January 1992). Firms in Southern Europe may be worried that if implementation of the Charter does cost them a significant amount of money, via increased wages and benefits and tougher health and safety procedures, they might as a result lose some of their relative competitiveness (Welford and Prescott, 1992, p. 109). In the UK, where nearly 4.5 million people work part-time, and where its legislation does not require equivalent treatment of part-timers and full-timers, the implementation of the Social Charter might create additional expense for employers.

EUROPEAN MONETARY UNION

The first steps towards monetary union were made in 1969 with the Barre Plan, which required member states to consult before making changes to their domestic economic policy. Early attempts at linking currencies were unsuccessful. In 1977, Roy Jenkins, then president of the Commission again raised the issue of monetary union. In 1988, Jacques Delors was asked by the

Council of Finance Ministers to investigate more closely the process of monetary policy links and the issues involved in achieving European Monetary Union.

Business firms, as shown in Part One, are influenced by the economic environment in which they operate. The government's economic, industrial and competition policies have an impact upon interest rates, inflation, taxation and economic growth. The creation of a European Monetary Union will affect every business in the European Community, and outside.

THE EUROPEAN MONETARY SYSTEM: STRUCTURE, FUNCTION AND OPERATION

Monetary union, simply stated, is an agreement between member states in terms of which internal exchange rates are permanently fixed, and with no institutional barriers to the free movement of capital or to the circulation of currencies. The dynamics behind a closer European Community are not simply a response to internal changes within the Single Market after 1992. Several factors operating at the global level have influenced this recent push towards a greater monetary integration in the European Community. These are clearly illustrated in Figure 13.1.

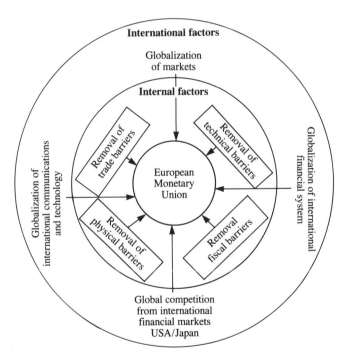

Figure 13.1   Dynamics behind European Monetary Union

The European Monetary System (EMS) was created in 1979. It is a system of fixed but adjustable exchange rates, designed to create a zone of monetary stability in Europe. The main objectives of creating the EMS were described in *The European Monetary System: Origins, Operation and Outlook* (European Perspectives Series, 1985):

- To attain and ensure a zone of internal and external monetary stability, with both low inflation and stable exchange rates

- To improve economic policy coordination, and therefore ensure a high level of employment and boost in growth
- To provide a pool of stability in world currency markets

The European Monetary System is based on three main elements: the ERM, the ECU and the financial support mechanisms and agreement to coordinate monetary policy.

The Exchange Rate Mechanism (ERM)

The ERM was introduced in 1979. The main impetus for the ERM was the general dissatisfaction with the floating exchange rate system which came to replace the fixed rates of the Bretton Woods System in the early 1970s. There was a general concern in the Community with the high level of exchange rate volatility, which prevented European business from reaping the full benefits of the Common Market. The ERM is the exchange rate pegging arrangement by which bilateral exchange rates between member countries are stabilized (Emerson and Huhne, 1991).

Under the ERM, each currency has a central rate against the ECU (this will be discussed in the next section) called the 'central rate'. Membership of the ERM obliges each country to keep its exchange rate against other currencies within 2.25 per cent above or below a pre-determined central target rate (6 per cent to 15 per cent for new members for a transitional period). The ERM is a flexible system of exchange cooperation where the central rate can be changed allowing a currency to depreciate or appreciate against other currencies within the mechanism (subject to the mutual agreement of all members). There were no realignments in the ERM from January 1987 to mid-September 1992 (Portes, 1993, p. 1). Until then, all currencies were included in the ERM with the exception of the Greek drachma and the Portuguese escudo. However, in the beginning of September 1992, a currency crisis in Europe led to several realignments within the EMS, which led to the partial disintegration of the ERM. The United Kingdom and Italy were forced to leave the ERM; Spain devalued twice; and Portugal devalued once. The French franc escaped devaluation in September and managed to stay in the ERM, after drawing down half its reserves and receiving massive German assistance to prop up the franc (Goldstein, 1992–93, pp. 117–32).

The Danish krone has also been threatened in part because Finland, Sweden and Norway have had to cut loose their unilateral pegs to the EMS; and the Irish punt is very weak (Portes, 1993, pp. 1–15). This recent near collapse of the ERM shows how difficult it will be to achieve European Monetary Union and puts into question the desirability or even viability of such a plan.

The European Currency Unit (ECU)

The second main element of the EMS is the European Currency Unit (ECU). The ECU is a basket of all the Community member states' currencies (*The ECU*, European Documentation Series, 1987). This basket is composed of fixed proportions of Community currencies. The ECU has no independent value on its own. Its value is calculated from the value of all 12 currencies, each reflecting its economic and financial strength and the relative economic importance of each member state within the Community. The value of the ECU is revised every five years, or on request if the external value of a currency has changed by 25 per cent in accordance with Section 2.3 of the European Council Resolution of 5 December 1978.

The ECU is the official unit of account of Community institutions. It has gradually displaced the European Unit of Account (EUA) created in 1975 as a replacement for the gold-based budgetary unit of account, and in 1980 was substituted for the European Unit of Account (EUA) in Community texts. The EC budget is now drawn up in ECUs and all accounts are in ECUs. Financial aid and Community loans are also all expressed in ECUs. The Commission uses the ECU for billing and as an instrument of payment.

The ECU has also developed a 'private' market. It has recently become a major currency unit, an important instrument for international financial transactions in Europe, the USA, Japan and the Far East. It is also being used increasingly for settling international transactions. A growing number of companies are now invoicing and carrying out their international accounting in the ECU (Drew, 1992, p. 174). The benefits of the ECU and its impact on business, as well as arguments put forward for and against a single currency in Europe, will be discussed later in this chapter.

The Financial Support Mechanism

Finally, the third element of the EMS is the Credit Mechanism, or Financial Support Mechanism, which was intended to provide short- and medium-term support for member states with balance of payments difficulties via the granting of credit. However, this system was not used since 1979.

FROM THE EMS TO EMU

Although the EMS did provide a useful framework for monetary stability, exchange rates under the system were still permitted to fluctuate within 2.25 per cent of the target rate, which meant that monetary policies and inflation rates consequently could still diverge significantly in the short-term. Since central rates could also be periodically realigned, exchange rate uncertainty still remained. In June 1988, at the Hanover Summit, EC Heads of State directed the Commission to prepare a report into how an economic and monetary union could be achieved. The EC President, Jacques Delors, with the assistance of Europe's central bankers and some independent monetary experts, proposed a three-stage transition to full European Monetary Union (EMU) which was to become known later as the 'Delors Plan' (Delors, 1989).

EMU is an irrevocable commitment to fix bilateral exchange rates against each other by eliminating exchange rate uncertainty and transaction costs. According to the Delors Plan, the transition from the ERM to EMU is achieved through three stages.

Stage 1 came into force in July 1990, and required that all national currencies join the ERM on equal 'terms'; which meant that all currencies should respect the 2.25 per cent band. The main objective of Stage 1 was the convergence of economic performance of member states, by providing greater economic and monetary policy coordination between them, the removal of fiscal barriers and the free flow of capital movements within the Community.

Stage 2 is the setting up of a system of European Central Banks to run EMU. The ESCB or EUROFED would supervise and harmonize national monetary policies. The second stage accordingly will require three main actions. First, national monetary policies would be executed in accordance with the general monetary orientation set up for the EC as a whole. Second, a proportion of the foreign exchange reserves will have to be pooled and used by ESCB to intervene in exchange markets and a Central Bank System. Third, the ESCB would supervise and harmonize national monetary policies (Welford and Prescott, 1992).

Stage 3, planned for 1997 at the earliest, involves the move to irrevocably fixed exchange rates by locking together the national currencies, and the replacement of national currencies by a single European currency to facilitate the management of the Community and to avoid the transaction costs of converting currencies. This common currency could then be transformed from a basket of currencies into a genuine single European currency.

The second and third stages cannot be implemented without modification to the Treaty of Rome, because they would require institutional changes within the EC. An inter-governmental conference was held in Rome in December 1990, charged with drawing up concrete proposals to turn the Delors Plan into reality. At Maastricht in the Netherlands in December 1991, the heads of state of the European Community initiated the Treaty on European Union. The treaty laid out a plan – complete with deadlines and institutional blueprints – for a common central bank and a single currency, the European Currency Unit (ECU). (The structure and content of the treaty proposal will be discussed in detail at the end of this chapter.)

The Delors Plan raised various arguments and heated debates. The UK, mostly worried about an unaccountable European central bank, proposed that instead of gradually locking the EC's currencies and handing over control of monetary policy to a European central bank, as suggested by the transitional Stage 2 of the Delors Plan, the transition should take a different form through the issuance of a completely new currency, the hard ECU. This would circulate through the EC alongside existing national currencies. Private citizens could then take or leave the common currency as they chose. Its widescale adoption would then depend upon a central bank's success in making it attractive to EC citizens, by preserving its real purchasing power better than other nationally issued currencies (Healy, 1991, p. 108).

Germany expressed its opposition to this UK concept of 'parallel currencies' and is clearly committed to a clear switch from national central banks to an independent European central bank. The French, Belgian, Dutch and Italian governments desired a greater voice in EC monetary policy. As they saw it, a European central bank would give them more say than they had in an EMS dominated by the Bundesbank (Sandholtz, 1993, p. 38).

In order to achieve unanimity, a right to opt-out was granted to the two most sceptical states, Denmark and the United Kingdom. The UK, not prepared to commit itself to a single currency was entitled to postpone its decision to participate until a later date. The opt-out clause for Denmark allowed it to reverse its present decision of participation. A right entitling any member state to opt-out, such as initially proposed by the UK was, however, firmly rejected by all the other member states.

The treaty proposal was finally signed by all hardline member states' foreign and finance ministers on 7 February 1993. (Article R of the Treaty of European Union provides that it is to be ratified by its signatories in accordance with their respective constitutional requirements.) It was originally hoped that the Treaty would enter into force on 1 January 1993, but this has not proved possible. (For a detailed commentary on the process of ratification see *European Law Review*, June 1993, pp. 228–53.) As of June 1993 ratification has been completed in ten member states. Denmark and the UK are still behind the other countries in this process.

Benefits of EMU and its implications for international business

It is important to consider what specific benefits business firms can realistically expect from EMU. Debates over EMU are still continuing. What follows is a brief outline of the main arguments presented, and their implications for international business.

The EC report 'One Market, One Money' presents the Commission's view of the benefits of EMU for business. A brief list of the benefits it identifies in the report includes:

- The elimination of transaction costs for firms when they exchange one currency for another
- The disappearance of bank commission and of the exchange margin or spread, by which a bank sells a currency more expensively than it purchases it
- The elimination of exchange rate uncertainty
- Reduced inflation
- A reduction in the rate of return expected by shareholders

Additional benefits identified by Ernst & Young are:

- Greater scope for sourcing materials and components for production
- Improved access to finance
- Companies in more than one EC country will be able to centralize and possibly shrink their treasury functions
- Similar accounting procedures all over Europe will be established. It will consequently be possible to achieve economies of scale in accounting procedures.

As far as the benefits of the adoption of the ECU are concerned, Michael Emerson and Christopher Huhne argue that first, business people would be able to quote to provide goods and services in the same currency, knowing that what they receive in cash would be exactly what they had planned, rather than a different amount determined by the movements of foreign exchange rates (Emerson and Huhne, 1991). Traders, they also argue, could take advantage of price differences to buy and sell much more easily and make profits, because goods and services would be priced in the same currency. They would be able to notice price differences more easily, which would encourage trade and competition. Bankers, in their view, would also benefit from the adoption of a single currency in Europe. They would be able to borrow and lend throughout the Community in a much easier way. The ECU would also assist investors in avoiding the risk of a sharp rise in currency, and in avoiding the risk that exchange rate changes might wipe out the value of their future profits (Emerson and Huhne, 1991, Ch. 2).

THE SINGLE EUROPEAN MARKET: WINNERS AND LOSERS

In 1986, on behalf of the European Commission, Lord Cockfield, Commission Vice-President responsible for the internal market, invited Mr Cecchini, special advisor to the Commission, to organize a comprehensive enquiry into the likely economic impact of completing the action programme set out in the 1985 White Paper on the internal market, and to evaluate the costs and benefits of the proposed Single Market (Cecchini, 1992). A large number of independent economic experts, consultants and research institutions contributed to this project. The main conclusions of the study are summarized as follows. 'The completion of the European internal market planned for the end of 1992 will help generate industry and services; it will give a lasting boost to the prosperity of all Europeans with savings of some 200,000 million ECU for firms, and in the medium term 2 to 5 million new jobs as well as 5 to 7 per cent extra non-inflationary economic growth'.

The Cecchini Report concluded that the economic gains of EC market integration in the short term would trigger a major relaunch of economic activity, adding on average 4.5 per cent of GDP for the Community as a whole. It will also simultaneously cool the economy by deflating consumer prices by an average of 6.1 per cent. This will lead to a relaxation of budgetary and external constraints, thus improving the balance of public finance by an average equivalent to

2.2 per cent of GDP, thus boosting EC employment and reducing unemployment by 1.5 per cent by creating 1.8 million new jobs (Cecchini, 1992, p. 97).

The long-term benefits of the removal of trade barriers, according to the report, will be improved conditions of supply by industry, lower unit production costs and therefore lower prices, thus ensuring long-term job creation. The opening up of public contracts will result in cuts in public deficits and a general cooling of inflationary pressures.

According to the Cecchini Report, consumers will benefit from a Europe without frontiers in several ways. They will be able to pay similar prices for the same item and items will be cheaper because they will be produced in the cheapest way. Finally, there will be greater consumer choice, due to market integration and increased internal competition (Cecchini, 1992, p. 73).

Companies too will have greater opportunities for success. Competition, the report argues, will lower input cost by removing non-tariff barriers, thus leading to direct reductions in the cost and price of goods and services for final consumption. Consequently, companies will be able to cover their basic requirements of labour, capital, plant and components more cost effectively. Competition will also trigger increased efficiency and innovation. EC integration will offer management the opportunity to optimize existing resources, modernize plant, and promote new activities and new ways of organizing work, and introduce new business processes and products (Cecchini, 1992, p. 74).

FROM THE SINGLE EUROPEAN ACT TO THE MAASTRICHT TREATY

In the light of current debates on the desirability of pushing beyond the Single European Market towards increased political union, it is important to have an overall view of these issues.

While the removal of barriers across Europe is designed to promote increased business, cost savings and greater efficiency, liberalization of this kind would be impossible without considering the political requirements and implications involved. Reconciling economic gains with political considerations is essential to the successful development of the Single European Market.

European integration is not solely about economic transactions, or a single integrated economic market, but is simultaneously about the nature of political and social relations between states and people. This is reflected in the various and sometimes conflicting views of heads of state in their original aspirations for political union, which conflicts with the 1990s debates of movement towards a purely economic union, not involving political union. For example, Walter Hallstein, first President of the EC Commission said 'We are not in business at all, we are in politics'; or George Thomson, the UK's first Commissioner in 1975, who said, 'the EC was not to make capitalism more efficient, it was to make war unthinkable'.

In contrast, and more recently, the European Community for Margaret Thatcher should be considered purely as a customs union between sovereign states, which would facilitate the free flow of goods and services, and capital and labour, between member states. The EC, in this view, should be seen as a means of raising levels of economic efficiency, wealth and living standards of individual citizens, while member states retain their different systems of governance and economic and social institutions (Burkitt and Braimbridge, 1989). The Single European Market should not be seen as an attempt to create a federation of Euro-states, but as an attempt to put the European economy back on its feet, to restore European competitiveness in the global political economy, and to raise European incomes. By signing the Single European Act, argues V. C. Price, governments have committed themselves to behaving like any profit-making firm, that is, to take the best offer, irrespective of the nationality of the bidder (Price, 1988, p. 12).

On the other hand, Jacques Delors sees the Community not only as an instrument to promote economic ends but as 'a stepping stone to the creation of a democratic socialist European superstate, that will enable it to maintain the cultural identity of European civilization against capitalist threats from the US, and Japan'. The EC in this view is considerably more than a 'market' – it is a struggle for world power (Galtung, 1981).

Debates before and after the Maastricht Treaty signing of December 1991 reflected these competing visions of Europe. While the Single European Act represents precise guidelines on how to achieve the Single Market, including a timetable for implementation, the Maastricht Treaty ended up as 250 pages of amendments and additions to the three founding treaties, most significantly to the Treaty of Rome of 1957 and the Single European Act itself.

The main features of the Maastricht Treaty

The major difference between the Single European Act and the Maastricht Treaty is that in the Maastricht Treaty there is greater scope for views about what the EC is or should be concerned with. The new Treaty does not restrict itself to the Treaty of Rome's ten activities, which were mainly economic and designed to promote closer relations between states. It cites just about every goal and policy with which a modern national government should concern itself. The Maastricht Treaty deals for example with joint foreign and security policy and common defence policy, health, education, the environment, industrial policy and consumer protection, cooperation on immigration policy, the establishment of common law for the treatment of workers, economic and monetary union, the future role of the European Central Bank in continuously assessing the economic policy of each member, and so on (*Economist*, 11 July 1992, pp. 12–39).

Aims and objectives of the Treaty on European Union

The aim of the Treaty is to unify key elements of Europe's strengths:

1. Convergence of monetary and fiscal policy among the EC hardline member states and a common European currency by 1999 at the latest.
2. Political union with more rights for the European Parliament and the introduction of a common foreign and security policy.
3. New rights for European citizens (with people being citizens of the European Union).
4. A new strategy regarding the future enlargement of the EC with the eventual admission of a dozen new nations, including members of the European Free Trade Association (EFTA) – Austria, Switzerland and Scandinavia – Mediterranean nations – Turkey, Malta and Cyprus – and members of the Visegard Group in Eastern Europe: Hungary, Poland and Slovakia and the Czech Republic.
5. The European Community's field of responsibility is to expand to cover increased consumer protection, public health policy, the issuing of visas, the creation of major transport, telecommunications and energy infrastructures (Trans-European networks), development cooperation, industrial policy, education, and increased activities in the field of environmental protection, research and development and social policy (except in the UK), and cooperation on domestic and criminal policy.

Additionally, the word 'economic' is dropped from the new Treaty. The making of joint foreign policy and cooperation in policing border controls forms part of this new view of the union. However, negotiations as to the nature and future development of the Community are kept out of the Commission and restricted to the Council of Ministers. The Commission's right to initiate policy and law-making, which it possessed in all the community activities, does not extend to this new political area. Maastricht gave more power to the Council of Ministers than to the Commission, to such an extent that it was referred to as 'the Government of the member states, by the member states, for the member states' (*Economist*, 11 July 1992, p. 13). According to the Treaty, the collapse of the Berlin Wall, the reunification of Germany, and changes in Eastern and Central Europe present challenges and new problems urging closer European integration. The Commission is excluded from participation in EC foreign policy formulation.

REVIEW QUESTIONS

1. What factors have stimulated the recent push towards greater economic and political integration in the European Community?
2. Why was a Single Market seen as necessary for Europe?
3. What is meant by 'Europe without Frontiers'? Briefly explain the philosophy behind the creation of a Single Market in Europe.
4. What are the economic benefits of the Single Market for business according to the Cecchini Report? Do you agree with all of them?
5. Should the Single European Market be simply considered in economic terms, as a market to restore European competitiveness and raise European income, or as a 'Fortress Europe' in order for Europe to re-assert itself as a world power, at the level of the USA, Russia and Japan?
6. Can the view of the Social Charter, seen as 'Socialism by the back door' be sustained, or is it to be welcomed for positive entrepreneurial reasons as well as social responsibilities?
7. 'The Social Charter is a laundry-list of tired political nostrums' (John Banham, Director General of the Confederation of British Industry). Do you agree?
8. What is the structure and purpose of the European Monetary System, and how does it work?
9. Briefly discuss why the Maastricht Treaty caused such controversy among Heads of State.

EXERCISE 13.1: The Single European Market and international business

Aim   This exercise is designed to illustrate the complexity of the Single European Market and its implications for international business. It aims to improve students' skills in conducting a debate, in choosing the main issues to be discussed, and in reaching an acceptable position between the different points of view involved.

Assignment   The class is divided into two groups.
Each group has a specific assignment:

- *Group 1*   The protagonist view of 1992. This group should explain the benefits of European economic and political integration and its positive contribution to international business development.
- *Group 2*   The antagonist view of 1992. This group should argue against European economic and political integration, highlighting its negative implications for business, the economy, national identity and sovereignty.

Each group should develop arguments to present to the class, and seek to persuade them either of the benefits of the single market or of its negative implications.

Format   The discussion should proceed as follows:
1. Each group will have 15 minutes to discuss its position internally and develop its arguments into a coherent and presentable form. One person should be selected to present the group's views.
2. Group 1 will present their views in no more than 10 minutes.
3. Group 2 will present their views in no more than 10 minutes.
4. Each group will then have an opportunity to discuss the other group's views. The debate duration should not take more than 20 minutes.
5. Recapitulation and conclusions reached.

FURTHER READING

Cecchini, P., *1992: The European Challenge. The Benefits of a Single Market. The Cecchini Report*, Willwood House, Aldershot, 1989.

Department of Trade and Industry, *The Single Market. The Facts*, 7th edn, 1992.

El Agraa, A. M., *Economics of the European Community*, Phillip Allan, London, 1992.

Emerson, M. and Huhne, C., *The ECU Report. The Single European currency and what it means to you*, Pan, London, 1991.

European File, *The Removal of Technical Barriers to Trade*, Commission for the European Communities, European Documentation, 1988.

European File, The Community Charter of Fundamental Social Rights for Workers, Commission for the European Communities, European Documentation, May 1990.

Treaty on the European Union, Maastricht, 7 February 1992, Office for Official Publications of the EC, Luxembourg, 1992.

Venturini, P., *The Social Charter. 1992. The European Social Dimension*, ECSC, Brussels, 1988.

FOURTEEN

STRATEGIES FOR THE SINGLE EUROPEAN MARKET

In the previous chapter we discussed the economic benefits and business opportunities of the Single European Market. Community firms may find their current business threatened by the changes in customs and supply practices or changes in technical regulations (Department of Trade and Industry, 1991b). Their own national and European markets could be threatened by the arrival of new competitors, not only from within the Community but also from foreign firms. American and Japanese multinational firms, attracted by the harmonized market, are now rushing to expand across the Community. These giant multinationals are realizing the importance of securing a presence in Europe in order to maintain their international competitive advantage against their global rivals. Business opportunities and threats within the EC are thus equally affected by aspects of the increasingly global political economy and the position of the EC within it. John Owens, Deputy Director General of the Confederation of British Industry, warned in January 1989 that nearly 10 000 UK companies were sleepwalking towards 1992, and that many of them would go out of business in the 1990s unless they started preparing now for the complete abolition of trade barriers within the EC (Walker, 1989).

This situation demands a major rethink of how firms can survive increased competition in the Single Market and take advantage of the opportunities available to them. There is, however, no 'magic' formula for this.

Tugul Atamer and Gerry Johnson conducted a survey of five major industries in Europe (breweries, retailing, book publishing, retail banking and the automobile industry) to see what strategies companies were developing in order to deal with the new competitive situation in Europe. Nineteen researchers of eight nationalities were involved in this research. Managers from 90 companies in seven member states were interviewed. The overall message and conclusion from the study was that managers cannot expect to maintain strategic success in Europe by a reliance on the 'proven strategic formulae of the past'. Europe is developing in ways which challenge managers to understand and cope with the nature of this complexity, and to review their management systems to cope with it (Calori and Lawrence, 1991, p. 229).

To address this issue, business managers need to formulate a Single Market strategic plan of action. This chapter aims to offer guidance to business managers and to students of international business in formulating business strategies for the Single European Market.

LEARNING OBJECTIVES

- To introduce the various steps involved in the formulation of a strategic plan for the Single European Market

- To develop an understanding of the homogeneity/diversity paradox of contemporary Europe
- To provide a brief introduction to the various strategies appropriate for doing business in the Single Market
- To learn how to organize, plan and market in the Single Market
- To offer guidance on how to implement change, and how to overcome resistance to change

A STRATEGIC PLAN FOR THE SINGLE EUROPEAN MARKET

Although there is no one single Strategic Plan that can be universally valid for doing business in the single European environment, there is a general model that can operate as a basis for the development of a specific strategic plan. Figure 14.1 provides a comprehensive model for constructing a strategic plan for the Single European Market. This has six general stages.

Stage 1: Defining corporate mission/corporate objectives

The starting point in designing a strategic plan for the Single European Market is to identify what business the company is in and clearly state its mission and its objectives. The corporate mission includes corporate purposes and intentions. For example, these could be increasing profits, capital growth or achieving a prestigious market leader position.

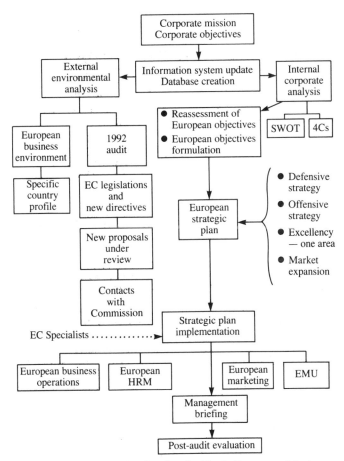

Figure 14.1   Strategic plan for the Single European Market

Stage 2: Information systems/database creation

Designing a strategic plan for the Single European Market requires comprehensive and up-to-date information on what is happening in the Single Market. With increased European competition, business firms must have the relevant information necessary for the conduct of their business. A company must first determine how much information it will require and assess its information system. It might consider the benefit of using commercially available information services, such as electronic data interchange, electronic mail and access to databases. It must decide whether its present information system is capable of meeting the growth in demand from the wider European market, and whether it is sufficiently flexible to cope with these new demands. It is also important in evaluating the present system to check new suppliers of hardware and software and their products, and to evaluate public telecommunications, services and tariffs, comparing them with what is availabe from privately managed network providers. The company at this stage should also ensure that someone is responsible for monitoring the changes in European telecommunications regulations (Department of Trade and Industry, 1992).

Stage 3: Analysing the contemporary European business environment

The main issue here is to find out what changes, threats or opportunities the Single Market has brought, and how they might affect the business. Questions such as 'Is there a European opportunity?', 'What is the size of that opportunity?', 'What are our competitors doing in that market?' 'Who are their major competitors, suppliers and customers?' and 'Where are they located?' are important. There is no simple procedure for dealing with this. The company will take some months of research before resolving this issue.

The process involved here requires first developing a 'Single Market Readiness Audit' (Gibbs, 1990). This includes obtaining clear and up-to-date information on what is happening. A company needs to know whether there are any current trade barriers affecting its business which are due to be dismantled by Community actions, or on which it would like to seek action. Events are moving all the time in Brussels, and this action might need to be repeated several times in order to keep up with the latest developments. There are many sources of information covering the whole of the Single Market programme, with various levels of detail (Drew, 1992, pp. 253–353).

Heavy fines could be imposed for negligent infringements of Community legislation. Business managers should be aware of the latest Community legislation and its precise relation to the business they are involved in. It is also important to keep up to date with new proposals being drafted in the Commission or debated in the Parliament to determine whether there is a need to try to influence legislation to protect the company's interests.

If there is any piece of legislation that a company wishes to influence, the first thing that needs to be done is to decide whether to approach Brussels directly or indirectly, by working with others in the same trade. In either case, the first step is get a list of key contacts in the Community institutions and get to know which are the relevant Directorates General and EC Commissioners dealing with the issue of particular concern to you. Since the Commissioners' task is to propose legislation for industry in particular, it might be useful to contact them. A company may either write to them and present its case, or go to Brussels and meet them. MEPs can also be particularly helpful if quick action on urgent matters is needed. MEPs not only know what is going in the Community, but can speak on behalf of a company or group in the Parliament.

Once the 'Single Market Readiness Audit' is completed, a general environmental assessment of the European business environment is needed. This can be developed by studying and reviewing various country profiles of EC member states prepared by the OECD and some financial institutions. There are a number of ways of looking at potential markets in Europe (Drew, 1992, p. 94). Major surveys, although general, might provide a base to start from. Banks are particularly active in providing information on countries and markets in the EC. Banque Nationale de Paris has a special division, BANEX, for that purpose (Dudley, 1990, p. 152). The task, then, is to shortlist the countries reviewed to two or three, and develop more detailed individual country profiles through specific market research. The services of international market research agencies may be used. They may have offices in the member states concerned or a local agency which employs its own local staff to do the research. Information on competition in member states is usually available from individual company annual reports. Extel Financial Service provides financial data on European companies, while McCarthy has newspaper and magazine cuttings containing recent information about companies and markets.

Finally, it is important to note in the analysis that despite the removal of trade barriers and the creation of a Single European Market, Europe still consists of countries with different languages, cultures, histories and customs, not to mention different tastes and preferences, levels of wealth and bodies of legislation. Europe is a diverse geographical, cultural and market entity (Calori and Lawrence, 1991, p. 224). J. Van der Merwe recounts a conversation he overheard in the departure lounge of Heathrow Airport that highlights in a small way the problematic nature of the Single Market (Calori and Lawrence, 1991, p. 3)

The discussion is between an American, an Englishman and a German manager, all working for the same American company.

American: 'We just spent three days at Headquarters in Colorado. Fantastic! The Board revealed a fully integrated European strategy for our business over here. What is more, further penetration into the German market is a priority.'

Englishman: 'That is very nice. When you discussed the European strategy, how exactly did you define Europe?'

American: 'Hell, you ought to know, you are European.'

Englishman: 'Well, I am English actually. I come from Hereford.'

American: 'Sure, but don't you think that many problems will be resolved by 1992, with the United States of Europe?'

Englishman: 'Not exactly. Europe will remain what it is, a collection of countries each with different customs, sometimes even within a particular country. Jolly hard to build a fully integrated European Strategy.'

German: 'And there are other questions. You implied that Europe is the EC, but it now also includes the former Eastern Bloc countries. As to the further penetration of the German market, you must recognize that it is both a mature and a fragmented market, with regional differences as well. The characteristics of distribution in Schleswig-Holstein differ importantly from those in Bavaria. Then we don't even speak about the completely different situation on the East German market.'

Englishman: 'Also, you must take account of the entirely different conditions we face in the premium and middle-range segments of the market, where the internal cultural differences will be more critical.'

American: 'You Europeans sure want to make everything complicated.'

This story clearly illustrates the different perceptions of Europe that exist. The US view of Europe is quite different from Europe's view of Europe (Calori and Lawrence, 1991, p. 216). However, the countries of Europe have a number of broad features in common. For example, most have good transport systems, good retailing systems, effective media, and a considerable degree of technological and financial development. They may, therefore, appear to be similar on the face of it, apart from language and social differences. Differences between countries in Europe will continue to persist, despite the efforts in Brussels to create a homogeneous market through increased harmonization and common legislation. The existence of cultural differences in Europe cannot be denied (Mole, 1990; Randlesome *et al.*, 1990). Differences in business practices, managerial philosophies, culture, tastes and attitudes are all different in Europe and will remain different (Mole, 1990). These differences must be taken properly into account for the development of an appropriate strategic plan for Europe.

Stage 4: Internal corporate analysis

The ability of a company either to expand into Europe or to protect its domestic market depends to a great extent on its competitive advantages in comparison to its competitors. Methods for analysing a company's internal position to 'international' position, international business operations and competitive analysis have been thoroughly covered in Chapter Eleven. Peter Drucker has identified eight performance areas critical to the long-term success of a company (Drucker, 1974b) which might be particularly useful in assessing corporate competitiveness and capability for Europe. These are:

- Market standing
- Innovation
- Productivity
- Physical and financial resources
- Profitability
- Management performance and development
- Workers' performance and attitude
- Public responsibility

Finally, in analysing competition in the Single Market it is important to look briefly at the features of principal potential competitors and their characteristics, and to analyse their impact on the Single Market as well as their overall effect on global competition from North America, the Pacific Rim and Japan (Dudley, 1990, pp. 62–84).

North American multinationals existed in Europe long before the single market was established. They played a major role after 1945, for example, in the European reconstruction efforts. The single market offers them great opportunities for expansion due to the harmonization of products and freedom of movement for goods across borders. Acquisitions have so far been the method adopted by most American multinational firms for entering the Single Market because of their interest in a quick return on their investment and their fear of a 'Fortress Europe' developing. Pacific Rim countries, such as Korea, Taiwan, Singapore, Hong Kong, Indonesia, Thailand and Malaysia, are all slowly awakening to the potential of global competition, offering cheap labour and technology (Kotler *et al.*, 1986). Japan has displaced the former West Germany and the USA as leaders in world trade in the 10 years between 1975 and 1985, and has become the second largest economic force in the world. Japanese companies are currently under pressure to source outside Japan. The Single Market provides them with many opportunities for components and service suppliers. These suppliers will have to meet the Japanese total quality and services standards to survive. Another serious impact of Japanese competition on the Single Market is the quality of marketing of Japanese companies, which spend heavily on advertising, price aggressively, provide high levels of customer support, and are prepared to wait for long periods before getting a return on their investment. Japanese operations in the Single Market so far have been established mainly through joint ventures and informal collaboration agreements.

Stage 5: Formulating strategies for the Single Market

At this stage, a company needs to reassess its objectives on a pan-European basis, reformulate its objectives and redefine its Single Market objectives, in order to decide what it should do *vis-à-vis* the changes introduced in the Single Market.

In choosing a strategy for the Single Market the company has four alternative choices: it could adopt a defensive or offensive strategy, decide to achieve excellence in one area, or expand into the Single Market and benefit from economies of scale.

Defensive strategies A defensive strategy is a 'concerted and unified set of missions targeted on competitors to make it expensive and difficult for them to establish a foothold in the domestic home market' (Dudley, 1990, p. 127). It is important to research competitors and their products, to find out, for example, what competitive advantage they will bring to the market in terms of cost, uniqueness, broad market capacities or narrow niches; to review their marketing promotion to find out whether their existing promotional message is sustainable against competition laws, for example; and to investigate their customers' behaviour and response to their activities.

There are three main aspects to defensive strategies. The first is to find a strong position behind which to defend the home market, and to force up a competitor's costs of entry (Lynch, 1990, p. 256). The company needs to be clear about what precisely it is defending, its position in the market, its customers and distribution networks. It is important to decide whether the company's intention is to defend everything it owns, especially in the case of larger companies with a portfolio of many products, or whether some small businesses must be disposed of because, although viable now, they will no longer be able to survive. Philips NV of the Netherlands, for example, decided in 1989 to sell its defence companies in France, Belgium, Holland, Switzerland and Germany when it realized that these interests were no longer defendable at reasonable cost due to growing concentration in an increasingly competitive industry and the steep cost escalation in developing new defence systems (Lynch, 1990, pp. 258–9).

The second aspect of a defensive strategy is the decision to deny those segments and customers to competitors upon which their market entry strategy will depend for success. The company here needs to look after its established customers and not allow new entrants to become established.

Finally, the third aspect is to attack competitors' weaknesses in terms of service, product range and so on. New entrants are usually vulnerable in the early stages. This is the time to hit back before they gain a foothold. The company here might reinforce its domestic market by matching its advantages to foreign company needs through collaboration with local firms to increase domestic competitive position (Dudley, 1990, p. 127).

Offensive strategies These involve attacking competitors in their own market. There are four main possibilities for attack, developed from military strategy: head-on attack, flanking manoeuvres, occupying new territory or guerilla warfare.

A head-on strategy is when the firm decides to attack its main competitor's market leader in another country head-on. It is a very expensive process, needs resources for a sustained campaign to be successful, and takes a long time, perhaps several years for branded goods, or more than 6 years for capital goods. Sony, Hitachi and Toshiba have all taken the European TV industry head-on, but for European companies this strategy might be too costly and risky to undertake.

Flanking manoeuvres refer to an attack on a specific part of the leader's franchise that is relatively undefended, or currently holds little interest to the major multinational firm. This requires investment for some years before gaining a foothold and then to keep it and prevent others from getting in. Great attention and care should be given to pricing, performance and service in a flanking operation. This is also known as a 'loose-brick' approach, by which an entrant exploits the weak strategic position of a European business or business sector. For example, the weak point of the European car industry in the UK, with problems of quality, manpower and manufacturing, has allowed the Japanese market to penetrate the UK by exploiting this weakness and gap in the market (Hamel and Prahaland, 1985, pp. 139–48).

Occupying totally new territory requires the creation of a totally new sector or 'niche' market, choosing a small area that the leaders are simply not interested in or geared to handle. Prices play a major role here. A company will need to operate at a premium price, and launch on a modest scale in specialized outlets where the targeted group is located. Innovation is the key to success in this strategy, while improving existing products would lead nowhere.

The guerilla approach refers to when a company decides to produce one-off machinery designs or limited-run fashion products, launched to take advantage of a gap left by market leaders. Guerilla tactics need reliable, up-to-date information, and the ability to respond to market opportunities quickly, regardless of location. The company should also be prepared to withdraw rather than to stand and fight if a large company moves in. For this strategy to be successful in the Single Market, the removal of trade barriers is not enough. The infrastructure is not yet in place for many companies to move fast enough to fully exploit opportunities across the Community.

Achieving excellency in one area   This may be adopted as an alternative strategy. This concept concentrates on achieving total quality in one particular area of the business (Dudley, 1990, pp. 128–9).

Firms are faced with the decision of which mode of entry to employ in order to secure a competitive position in the Single Market. While the effects of 1992 and the creation of the Single European Market are likely to vary from firm to firm, a simple prescription for future expansion method into Europe is impossible. Various international business operations can be adopted (*The Director*, January 1992, pp. 41–2). These have been discussed in greater detail in Chapter Eleven.

Market expansion   Finally, a company may decide to expand its operations into other member states to take advantage of the economies of scale of the Single Market. Various international business operations can be adopted here, such as franchising, joint ventures, licensing and so on.

Stage 6: Strategic plan implementation

The strategic plan implementation includes organizing and planning for the European operation and European marketing.

EUROPEAN HUMAN RESOURCE MANAGEMENT

The success of any European business venture depends on its ability to recruit, select and develop highly qualified managers for its European operations. Because every business has different strategic and operating requirements it is difficult to prescribe an ideal approach to human resource management for the Single European Market. However, attention must be given to the following factors:

- Working conditions
- Different employment laws and the Social Charter
- Cultural differences
- Training, language and new skills needed for Europe

Personnel managers should also be aware of the impact of new European legislative and cultural changes on employment at a strategic level. While it is undoubtedly true that the priority for most companies is to investigate the Single Market implications for sales and marketing, and for products or services, human resource implications are also important, and need to be considered seriously.

Mark Pinder identifies clearly the major issues to be addressed by the personnel manager in relation to the Single European Market (Pinder, 1990, pp. 76–95). First, the changing needs of the company must be taken into consideration. Companies in the Single Market will undergo fundamental structural and cultural changes as a result of wider and more intense competition, whether they are seeking to improve their market position or pooling their resources through joint ventures, mergers or acquisitions. They will either need to 'buy in' the talents of new managers with the cross-cultural skills necessary to create a competitive advantage, or to develop such skills within their existing cadre of managers. The second major concern relates to the attitudes of the present managers themselves. The Single Market creates a very competitive employment market. Those companies who cannot and do not offer a pan-European career structure to their talented employees will be likely to lose them to rivals with more attractive European career structures. The third concern is the attitudes of those who will become the managers of the future, as illustrated below.

CASE STUDY 14.1: Who is the Euro-executive?

A London-based headhunter published a survey entitled 'The Search for the Euro-Executive', in which the following description is offered (Pinder, 1990, p. 78):

… he or she – is a rare, exotic beast. Fluent in at least one other community language, of greater importance is the exposure to a diversity of cultures stemming both from family background – he or she is likely to have a mixed education, a multi-cultural marriage and parents of different nationalities – and working experience. In terms of career, the Euro-Executive will have graduated from an internationally oriented business school, have gained line management experience in a foreign culture company, and have obtained experience, through various career moves, of different skills, roles and environments.

The survey even extends to a commentary on clothes, job pressures and lifestyle.

Readily adaptable to living and working in different European capitals, the Euro-manager is likely to be unobtrusively but expensively dressed, to enjoy eating well, and above all to have the ability of assimilating rapidly the subtleties and values of different cultures. He or she must be capable of absorbing the pressures of a stressful lifestyle, which will involve extensive travel and disruption to social life.

The European business manager should have the following characteristics:

- Adaptable and cosmopolitan
- An understanding of change processes, and the ability to cope with a rapidly changing environment
- The ability to operate across cultural boundaries
- The ability to cope with a demanding lifestyle, with frequent travel, relocation and disruption of family life

There are other additional attributes, such as general technical and managerial competence, that would also be expected of professional staff operating in a non-international environment.

Sources
Pinder, M. *Personnel Management for the Single European Market*, Pitman, London, 1990, pp. 78–9.
Vineall, T., What is European Management? How can it be developed?, *Personnel Management*, October 1981.

The Single Market also introduces a new role for the personnel manager, which is different from performing the traditional function of human resource management at the domestic level (Pinder, 1990, pp. 119–20). In addition to the normal functions and duties the European personnel manager must keep up to date with the timing and content of Community legislation related to social policy and employment, for this will be crucial to the personnel manager's role. Some of the changes might affect the company's personnel policies directly and require specific measures. Personnel managers need to know for example about the extent to which mutual recognition of qualifications is achieved for certain positions, or what EC initiatives or funding areas are available to organize and assist the company's language and cultural training programmes. Other issues include equal opportunity for women, the harmonization of child care and maternity leave standards, vocational training for women, pension entitlements, health and safety measures at the workplace, part-time and temporary contractual rights, employee involvement in decision-making, and information for and consultation with employees.

A decision must also be made whether to re-deploy or relocate part of the company's operation in order to be closer to the new market, to reduce employment costs, or to tap new sources of labour. A feasibility study needs to be conducted, reviewing the cost of relocation, the cost to the company of the loss of key staff, availability of labour, local workforce skills, employment standards and norms of the country where relocation is to take place.

The personnel manager also needs to identify the demand for foreign nationals, and then decide how and where to advertise in Europe, how to organize recruitment campaigns, and how to determine the level of pay and conditions that will be attractive to foreign candidates. There is also a need to decide on effective lines of communication and control between managers operating in different countries. Decisions are to be made on whether the company should adopt a decentralized or a centralized approach, and which mobility policy is most appropriate for the company. ICL provides a good example of how a company has adopted a European approach in its overall strategic operations. ICL established a 'Europe 1992 Group' based at Putney in London. The group has some staff based in Brussels and Luxembourg who produce a regular 'Letter from Brussels', giving up-dated information on the progress of the Single Market legislation at the European Commission. This group reports directly to the European Strategy Board, and carries out the bulk of research work. The group also produces 'Europe sans Frontières' and circulates it to staff to create an awareness and interest in general European affairs. ICL has also recently established an ICL Euro-Graduate Programme (for more examples, see Pinder (1990, pp. 217–59)).

EUROPEAN MARKETING STRATEGIES

Although Community Directives clearly stipulate that member states must give access to goods accepted as fit for sale in other countries, opinion of what is tasteful still varies immensely from one Community member to another. Physical taste changes too, as well as the precise use to which a product is put. It is also very important to keep up to date with Commission regulations and standards.

Given that previous fragmentation of the European market, arising from the existence of national regulations and non-tariff barriers, has in the past discouraged companies from operating in more than one country, the removal of trade barriers, physical, technical and fiscal, between the 12 member states might lead some companies to consider a pan-European marketing approach to exploit market economies (Guianluigi, 1991, pp. 23–33).

It is, however, unrealistic to expect the 320 million consumers to be 'suddenly transformed into 320 million Euro-clones drinking Euro-beer, eating Euro-wurst and watching Euro-soaps on Euro-satellite television' (Guianluigi, 1991, p. 24). But it is still possible to adopt a pan-European strategy (Martin, 1988). According to a research developed in Geneva by S. Van der Merwe and M. L'Huillier, the Euro-market is reasonably homogeneous in six major 'clusters', having similar demographic and economic characteristics which cut across cultural and national boundaries (Kossoff, 1988, pp. 43–4; Van der Merwe and L'Huillier, 1989, pp. 34–40). These geographical clusters are: the UK and Ireland; France and Switzerland; Spain and Portugal; North Italy and Austria; South Italy and Greece; and West Germany, Luxembourg, The Netherlands and Denmark.

Another basis for a general pan-European strategy is to distinguish four distinct segments, or social groups, across the Community with similar interests, tastes and attitudes: young people, trend-setters, European business people and old people.

Implementing the Strategic Plan – Management briefing

Implementing a European Strategic Plan does not only depend on the Chief Executive. Input from other departments and from across all functions and all levels of management is necessary for successful implementation. A 'Cascade of Management Briefings' needs to be organized. The cascade approach (Drew, 1992, pp. 78–84) is recommended in order to tailor briefings to the interests of each business function, business unit, department or team. The significance of the Single Market must be imparted to key managers, and they must in turn take responsibility for implementing the necessary changes.

A senior management review of the Single Market must first be organized where there is a need to explain exactly what the Single Market is, and why it is important, how it might affect the business, and to show opportunities and threats by highlighting the increased competition in traditional markets from other European markets. There is likely to be considerable resistance from management, particularly the national managers of subsidiaries, who may be reluctant to change old habits and may not be attuned to working with colleagues in other countries (*The Director*, January 1992, pp. 41–2). Regular briefings should therefore be introduced, as well as articles in the house journal.

Implementing a European strategy can involve considerable change within the organization. Successful implementation requires not simply having a good strategic plan, but the cooperation of the people involved. A major obstacle for any successful implementation of change can be the resistance of members of the organization; alternatively, their readiness and willingness to accept change can enhance the implementation possibilities (Bedelian, 1989, pp. 257–60; Lawrence, 1969).

It is therefore crucial to identify the possible sources of resistance to change. Change is rarely received without protest. Resistance to change is a common human reaction. The most common reasons for resistance are lack of understanding and trust, uncertainty about the causes and effects of change, parochial self-interest and unwillingness to give-up existing benefits, different assessments of the situation, and low tolerance for change.

- *Lack of understanding and trust*   People tend to resist when they do not understand the intended purpose of a planned change. People do not resist change *per se*, only the uncertainties that change can bring. Employees might, for example, resist because they are worried about how their work and living will be affected by the proposed change. It is therefore crucial for a Euro-executive to clearly explain in advance to all employees why a change is needed and how it will affect them.
- *Unwillingness to give up existing benefits*   Individuals might resist change if they feel that they might lose something of value to them as a result. Individuals often focus on their own self-interest and only incidentally on the firm's overall good. Some of the factors which almost inevitably provoke resistance include: power, prestige, salary, professional competence, convenience and job security (Kotter and Schlesinger, 1979, pp. 107–9).
- *Different assessment*   People might resist change because they have different assessments of the situation. Resistance to change frequently occurs when employees receive inadequate information concerning the proposed change, or when their evaluation of the likely costs and benefits of a proposed change is different from that of top management (Bedelian, 1989, p. 259).
- *Low tolerance for change*   Opposition to change may result from an employee's low personal tolerance for change or from anxiety and apprehension, for example when an employee is unable to develop the new skills and behaviour demanded by unfamiliar circumstances associated with the new plan.

Overcoming resistance to change

Various methods for dealing with resistance to change have been proposed.

1. *Education and communication*   Resistance to change is based largely upon misinformation or poor communication. There is a responsibility to explain the need for, and the logic of, change to individuals, groups or the entire organization very clearly. A great effort must be made to eliminate misunderstanding due to incorrect or incomplete information, and to resolve different points of view through discussion. This can be achieved through the use of mass media educational campaigns, one-to-one discussion, memos, group presentations or reports (Bedelian, 1989, p. 261).
2. *Participation and involvement*   By asking members of the organization to help design the change, resistance may be overcome, on the assumption that 'people will support that which they help to create' (Ash, 1984, p. 73).
3. *Facilitation and support*   This involves offering retraining programmes, emotional support and understanding. This method is most successful when the resistance to change is a result of fear, insecurity and lack of self-confidence.

4. *Negotiation and agreement*   Negotiating with potential resisters to reach a potential agreement might sometimes be an effective way of overcoming resistance to change.
5. *Manipulation and co-optation*   This simply means giving key persons a desirable role in designing or implementing the change process.

Support at the top level is crucial to success. New product launches and new structures are expensive and disruptive and it is important that senior managers are clearly accountable so that people can see how expenditure and progress are being controlled (Carnall, 1990, pp. 164–5).

REVIEW QUESTIONS

1. Why should domestic firms be at all concerned with the latest developments in the Single European Market?
2. What is the difference, if any between a Single European Market strategic plan and an international business plan?
3. What are the various strategies that firms can adopt to survive the increasingly intense competition created by the Single European Market?
4. To what extent, if at all, does the creation of the Single European Market contribute to the homogeneity of the market?
5. In what ways does the Single European Market change the traditional role of personnel managers and their functions?
6. Compare and contrast the characteristics of the Euro-executive with those of the globalists (discussed in Chapter Nine).
7. Identify the need for change in an organization known to you and show how you would introduce that change. What resistance do you expect and how would you overcome it?

EXERCISE 14.1: Strategic planning for the Single European Market

Aim   The purpose of this project is to give students an opportunity to apply the theories and material covered in the book regarding international and European business to a realistic situation. The project involves substantial outside work. Students should be given at least two to three weeks to prepare for it.

Assignment   Each group will be assigned a local company wishing to expand its operations, sales, production or service into Europe. Each group is asked to decide which market it wishes to enter and how it proposes to enter, taking into consideration the Single European Act and the changes introduced by the single market.

The presentation of the class should take the form of a Single European Market strategic plan, presenting the findings to a top management group. Each group will also prepare a written document to back up its oral presentation.

Format   Students may use the model illustrated in Figure 14.1, a strategic plan for the single market, as a guide.

EXERCISE 14.2: How to do business in . . .

Aim   This exercise is intended to familiarize students with the various ways of doing business in the European community, taking into consideration the cultural diversity of each member state.

Assignment   As part of its 'Single Market Awareness Programme' the Department of Trade and Industry is recruiting business graduates to contribute to its research programme on 'Doing business in . . .'. Choose a particular country of interest to you within the European Community, study the various elements of its culture, and analyse their implications for doing business in that country, including your advice and recommendations. Be ready to present your findings to the group responsible for this project and prepare a booklet ready for publication on 'How to do business in . . .'.

Format   Students are expected to work in small groups on this assignment. The presentation to the class should not take more than twenty minutes. Originality and creativity should be encouraged. Students may use visual aids, video recording, television clips, slide projections or any other means which they feel would make their presentation interesting, and capture the attention of their audience.

Note: Make sure your 'strategic plan' includes any latest developments in the Single European Market relevant to your business.

Sources

Drew, J., *Doing Business in the European Community*, 3rd edn, Whurr, London, 1992, Chapter 24, pp. 253–353, contains a list of names and addresses of organizations and a comprehensive source of publications and explanations on how to use them and how to interpret them.

The Command Paper on Developments in the EC is a six-monthly publication which includes a regular update on single market developments.

The *Official Journal* publishes full texts of newly adopted Community measures and is available at any European Documentation Centre.

Euro Info: a monthly bulletin providing information on Community initiatives.

The European Report is a twice weekly news publication.

Extel Financial Services provides financial data on top European companies.

OECD Economics Survey for country profiles.

Price Waterhouse: guide to doing business in various countries.

Economist Intelligence Unit publishes annual country profiles and quarterly reports.

Gibbs, P., *Doing Business in the European Community*, Kogan Page, London, 1990, contains a country by country guide to the cultural, social and economic differences that exists in each of the 12 member states. It also provides detailed guidance on how to make an appointment, conduct a meeting, entertainment, working hours, marketing and so on.

FURTHER READING

Carnall, A., *Managing change in Organizations*, Prentice-Hall, Hertfordshire, 1990.

Danton de Rouffignac, P., *How to sell to Europe*, Pitman, London, 1990.

Drew, J., *Doing Business in the European Community*, 3rd edn, Whurr, London, 1992.

Mole, J., *Mind your manners, Cultural clash in the European Single Market*. The Industrial Society, New York, 1990.

Pinter, M., *Personnel Management for the Single European Market*, Pitman, London, 1990.

Randlesome, C., Brierly, W., Burton, K., Gordon, C. and King, P., *Business Cultures in Europe*, Heinemann, Oxford, 1990.

FIFTEEN

DOING BUSINESS IN CENTRAL AND EASTERN EUROPE

Recent developments in Eastern and Central Europe represent the biggest change in Europe since the Second World War. They offer increased opportunities for trade with the East, and the West must expect a change in the direction of Eastern European trade. Providing guidance on doing business in Eastern and Central Europe at a time of constant and dramatic change means that certain kinds of information need continuous updating. Furthermore, despite the process of liberalization and marketization taking place within Eastern and Central Europe today, business people should not only be aware of the potential opportunities, but they also must take account of the many problems involved in trading with these countries.

The aim of this chapter is therefore to help business managers obtain some understanding of the changes occurring in Eastern and Central Europe, and how these might affect opportunities for business development in the 'New Europe' of the 1990s and beyond.

LEARNING OBJECTIVES

- To provide a general overview of the recent changes being introduced in Eastern and Central Europe
- To identify potential business opportunities in those regions
- To provide guidance on how to enter those markets, and how to overcome the many problems that may be encountered

ECONOMIC REFORMS IN CENTRAL AND EASTERN EUROPE

Economic reforms on a massive scale are being introduced in Eastern and Central Europe to facilitate the process of liberalization. Multinational firms are attracted towards tapping this vast new potential market of approximately 393 million consumers. With the majority of the state-owned business being auctioned to the private sector, a frenzy of business activity is currently taking place. This has attracted a great deal of attention, both from scholars and practitioners of international business, as well as governments, throughout the world.

Central and Eastern European countries are currently experiencing a 'seemingly' dramatic transition from centrally planned systems to free market economies. In November 1990, for instance, the Council of Ministers of the Russian Soviet Federative Socialist Republic approved the setting up of the first 'free-trade zone area' in the USSR to increase foreign economic cooperation, promote foreign investment and to serve as a laboratory for developing new economic forms during the period of transition (Torbet, 1991, pp. 16–18).

The 'Shatalin Plan' or the 500 day plan for installing capitalism, represented another drive by Mikhail Gorbachev for the full restoration of market relations in the USSR. The Shatalin Plan included:

- The slashing of the budget deficit from 100 billion roubles to 5 billion roubles in 100 days
- The establishment of a stock exchange
- The privatization of 40 per cent of industry (including 50 per cent of construction and 60 per cent of the food industry) by the 400th day
- The sale of collective farms to peasants, and the elimination of state subsidies on many foods and properties
- The deregulation of prices
- The recognition of trade unions, and the opportunity for the workforce to 'buy out' their factories via share issues, and to operate them as private companies (Hibbert, 1991; Lindsay, 1989).

Market-oriented policies are also being fiercely pursued in Central and Eastern Europe, particularly in the Czech Republic, Slovakia, Hungary and Poland. According to Czechoslovakia's (as it then was) Minister of Economics, Vladimir Dlouhy 'For Eastern Europe to have a market economy, the government must get out of the way' (Donlon, 1991, pp. 60–76).

Consequently, state industrial assets estimated at $148.7 billion have all been put up for privatization. Vouchers or coupon books were issued in October 1991 and distributed to Czechoslovakian citizens to allow them to buy equity in the companies that appealed to them (Ash, 1991, pp. 511–14). Reforms introduced since 1991 include the total liberalization of foreign trade. Under a law adopted on 1 January 1989, Czechoslovakian entities could form a joint venture only with prior government approval. The law guaranteed repatriation of profits and salaries, but only to the extent that the joint venture generated foreign currency. The new Joint Venture Act of 1991 now allows 100 per cent ownership of companies by foreigners (Tormarchio, 1991, pp. 12–18), internal convertibility of the currency and full price liberalization (Alperowicz, 1991, pp. 38–40; *Chief Executive*, July/August 1991, pp. 50–2).

The new Hungarian government's main goals include the privatization of half the current 90 per cent state-owned enterprises within four years (Szegedi, 1989–90, pp. 109–20), the demonopolization of foreign trade (Newbery, 1991, pp. 571–80), and a three-year reform programme including the development of new laws on banking, insurance, mutual funds and bankruptcy, and full liberalization of foreign trade by the end of 1992 (Jones, 1991, pp. 34–9).

In Poland, the government also intends to transform the Polish economy to a market economy. This process is to be accompanied by a gradual change in the pattern of ownership towards that which prevails in countries with advanced economies (Nuti, 1991, p. 62). The new Mazowiecki government, determined to achieve a full-fledged market economy, introduced in January 1990 a series of provisions which could be called, because of their extreme austerity, a shock treatment to stabilize the economy, bring about market equilibrium and to lower inflation (Adam, 1992, p. 55). This stabilization package introduced to achieve a free market includes the abolition of subsidies and the reduction of the budget deficit to 1 per cent of GNP (down from 8 per cent in the previous year), an increase in real interest rates, almost complete price liberalization, trade liberalization, 32 per cent devaluation of the zloty (made convertible and held at 9500 zlotys per dollar (Nuti, 1991, p. 61)), and the setting up of a stock exchange where Polish state assets could be sold and re-traded (Grosfeld, 1990).

The privatization of some companies (over 7000) started in September 1990. Under the new Polish law of privatization, approved in July 1990, foreign investors can freely purchase state company shares, subject to an overall ceiling of 10 per cent. The dividends and the proceeds of subsequent shares sales may be repatriated abroad without special permits (Grosfeld, 1990, p. 63). All of these economic reforms, the reinstatement of private enterprise, 100 per cent ownership, Joint Venture Acts, price liberalization, the removal of trade restrictions and so on have made it possible for the general belief to develop in the West that the potential exists for a 'capitalist renaissance' in Eastern and Central Europe.

WESTERN BUSINESS ACTIVITIES IN CENTRAL AND EASTERN EUROPE

The Bush Administration and now the Clinton Administration have actively encouraged US companies to expand trade of non-strategic goods, such as health care products, with Eastern European countries. Johnson & Johnson, Dow Chemicals, Du Pont, Pfizer and Eli Lilly International are among the US health care companies that have opened offices in Poland, and are looking for further opportunities in Hungary, the Czech Republic and Slovakia (Reihn, 1991, pp. 47–51). US hoteliers are also competing fiercely for deals and properties in the Eastern and Central European Markets. Hotel groups such as Marriott, Hyatt International Group, Sheraton and Hilton are all establishing hotels in that region (Persmen, 1990, pp. 46–7). The Moscow Sheraton, for example, cost an estimated $75 million and the Sheraton group is currently looking at projects in Poland, the Czech Republic, Slovakia, Hungary and Romania. Negotiations are also taking place within the Baltic states of Estonia, Latvia and Lithuania (Niemeyer, 1990, pp. 72–4). The food industry is making headway in Eastern and Central Europe too. The USSR's first McDonald's restaurant opened in Gorky Street in January 1990 with 200 seats outdoors, 700 more inside and 27 cash registers. It is the largest and the busiest of the nearly 12 000 McDonald's restaurants worldwide (Hume, 1990, pp. 16–51), serving 40 000–50 000 people a day. To service them, McDonald's had to build a 100 000 square foot distribution centre that included a meat plant, a bakery, a potato plant, a dairy and quality assurance laboratories, at a cost of $50 million (Foster, 1991, pp. 51–65).

The potential of these markets is obviously considerable. Eastern and Central European countries offer more than 393 million consumers (Siren and Shaw, 1991, pp. 30–3) which have been deprived of most Western consumer goods for 45 years (Korabi and Grieve, 1990, pp. 23–5), apart from black market purchases. A great potential exists for Western investment, especially in the areas of construction, property, medical supplies and professional services (de Bendern, 1990, p. 27). There are also huge growth possibilities for foodstuffs, natural foods and fresh products, and especially for semi-luxury goods and branded goods (Barber and Montag-Girnmes, 1990, pp. 121–2). Pepsi-Cola in April 1990 signed the biggest ever trade agreement between the USA and Russia. The $3 million barter agreement enables Pepsi to add 26 new plants to the 24 already operating throughout Russia (Holden and Peck, 1990, p. 29). In return for the new plants, the company will now receive double the present quantity of vodka per year and ten 25 000–65 000 tonne freighters and oil tankers. Estée Lauder opened its first Soviet outlet in November 1989. Situated in Moscow's Gorky Street, and with all goods priced in roubles, the merchandise has been hugely successful. During the first month of trading, crash barriers were erected to keep a permanent queue of up to 200 people off the road (Holden and Peck, 1990, pp. 26–31). Littlewoods had a similar success too in its early opening days and had to issue vouchers limiting purchases to five products per customer. Adidas sold its whole stock of famous striped sport shoes in one morning. In the first three months of its operation Lotus Development

Corporation sold more than 1000 copies of its Lotus 1–2–3 personal computer software (Crummey, 1991, p. 25).

PROBLEMS AND DIFFICULTIES OF DOING BUSINESS IN CENTRAL AND EASTERN EUROPE

The euphoria that followed the dramatic changes since 1989 towards the establishment of a free-market economy, is now slowly dying down and we are beginning to see the challenges that lie ahead in the reconstruction of the Eastern and Central European market economies. In Russia, for example, the greatest obstacle resulting from the liberalization of trade and privatization lies within the factories themselves, which are now left to operate on a self-accounting basis, and able to negotiate commercial contracts directly with Western firms without approval from Moscow ministries. This dramatic transition has caused, and still is causing, serious problems in adopting democratic and Western business practices. Until the recent movements towards privatization, over 90 per cent of all orders to factories were placed, priced and distributed by the state (de Bendern, 1990, pp. 26–30). The state also chose suppliers and determined prices and wage levels. S. De Bendern of Ernst & Young summed up the general situation in the area as follows (de Bendern, 1990, p. 27)

> The East European countries who are now embracing the politics of the free market have been used to central planning for the past four to five decades. In a planned economy, state enterprises are used to receiving allotments of raw materials and funds, and have to produce enough goods to fulfil the plan that is imposed by a State Planning committee. If they fall short of the plan, state subsidies are increased to help boost the output. If they surpass the plan, the surplus is reabsorbed by the state. Concepts such as profit, loss, cost accounting and marketing played no role in the functioning of the state enterprise. Whatever the end results, the status quo within the enterprise remains the same.

Consequently, Russian managers have no concept of competitive markets, quality control or workers' participation in decision-making. A recent USSR-based study demonstrated that 35 per cent of managers questioned had no knowledge of world standards, and only 52 per cent had a minimal knowledge. A third of executives polled thought their products were competitive with world standards, but knew little of international market standards (Hibbert, 1991).

Management training in Western business practices has become a high priority for Eastern and Central European managers. They are now seeking practical solutions to the problems facing them as they struggle towards a free market (Storm, 1991, pp. 40–3). Some of the problems faced by these companies include overmanning, technical backwardness, management shortages, lack of capital and debt (Pearce, 1990, pp. 43–7). Eastern and Central European firms need technical advice on how to structure their internal organization, how to create new departments such as procurement, finance, personnel and marketing, and how to introduce new technology (de Bendern, 1990). During his business trip to Eastern Europe in April and May 1991, Sir John Harvey Jones reported for example that at Krosno – the first company to be privatized in Poland – one of its seven factories was still maintaining the same level of glass production despite the lack of demand for its product. The unsold glassware was simply stacked in a large warehouse, costing the company around $1 million in interest charges. The factory was overmanned, and management simply not allowed either to slow down or even stop production. In Hungary, following the collapse of the market with Russia, Ikarus, the largest bus factory, is now facing bankruptcy. With a serious drop in contract supply to the Russian Government from 78 000 buses to a mere 2000, an over-staffed workforce, and 80 per cent bank interest charges, the company needs large investments in new technology and marketing strategies to survive.

When asked about their costing systems, both companies had no record of their profit and loss accounts, but kept a simple record of their stock inventory (Harvey Jones, 1991).

Universities, colleges and management consultancies from all over the world have developed considerable plans to offer management and marketing education in the countries of Central and Eastern Europe, based on the general belief that, without knowledge of Western practices, market economies and democratic regimes in Eastern and Central Europe can neither be successfully introduced nor developed, and that even if capital is available, most of the new public companies will need Western management and technology to succeed (Brademas, 1991, pp. 432–5; Nelson-Horchler, 1991, pp. 52–6; Marer, 1991, pp. 4–10; Ash, 1990, pp. 145–8). As a result, management schools are springing up throughout Eastern Europe, with the establishment for example of the Moscow International Business Management School, the US Business School in Prague and the Sofia School of International Management (which has signed a contract with Cranfield School of Management to educate Bulgarian managers). At Moscow State University, crash courses in Western accounting methods have been introduced since April 1990 as part of a plan set up by the UN Center for Transnational Corporations (Aurichio, 1991, pp. 54–6). The MBA Enterprise Corps, a sort of Peace Corps for the finance and marketing set, was formed in 1990 by a 16-school Consortium headed by the University of Carolina's Kenan–Flagler Business School. In August 1991, the Corps sent 41 members of its first intake to Czechoslovakia, Poland and Hungary to spend at least a year working for government agencies and newly privatized businesses. At the newly formed US Business School in Prague, set up under the auspices of the Czech Technical University and the Rochester Institute of Technology, visiting professors from the USA are teaching a brand of free market economics called the Chicago School, which is considered far to the right even in the West (Siller, 1991, pp. 78–9).

ECONOMIC AND SOCIAL PROBLEMS OF TRANSITION

This particular focus on the mechanics of introducing privatization by simply concentrating on the techniques and tools needed for a successful implementation of privatization has neglected consideration of whether or not the infrastructures do in fact exist for privatization to succeed in Central and Eastern Europe, for example the lack of capital, money markets, technology, know-how and so on. As a result, the adoption of Western business ethics and business models in Central and Eastern Europe, contrary to the general expectations and experience of the workforce, have so far failed to improve the local economy. It has instead caused disastrous economic and social consequences at a tremendous human cost in growing unemployment and increased poverty (Pearce, 1990, pp. 43–7). All the economies of Central and Eastern Europe that are currently in transition from a command economy to a market-based system are, according to a recent study in the OECD observer, experiencing a rapid deterioration in economic performance and standards of living (Marer, 1991, pp. 4–10). In Yugoslavia, for example (prior to the civil war), reforms were accompanied by bankruptcies, unemployment and increased poverty. In the first half of 1990, bankruptcy proceedings were started against 523 companies employing 306 000 people (*Euromoney*, September 1990, pp. 13–16) Even in the then Czechoslovakia, which had one of the most developed command economies in Eastern Europe, open unemployment emerged in the economy in 1990, after 40 years of full employment (Kapl *et al.*, 1991, pp. 199–210). Most of the existing companies have no chance of surviving in a free market. The functioning of the labour market in socialist economies was characterized by over-full employment, inefficient allocation of labour, low levels of productivity and a lack of competitiveness. The lack of incentives for innovation and productivity were largely due to the remote possibility of firing an employee for non-performance. After completing their education, most

Soviet citizens were assigned to a job for three years, from which they could not be fired, with little possibility of promotion or salary increase. This tended to reflect tenure only, and rarely kept up with inflation (Ubelhart, 1991, pp. 38–42).

The state-run economies have instilled in people a specific behaviour and work culture, radically different from that in the West (Reinsch, 1991, pp. 13–14). The productivity and commitment of workers is often quite low due to a lack of incentives (Fairlamb and Slavinskis, 1991, pp. 29–30). According to Frederick P. Feger of Krupp Stahl AG, a major steel company in the former West Germany: 'The East Germans simply lost all their incentives to work because there were no consumer goods to buy, and no incentive to earn money' (Rohan, 1990, pp. 66–9). Lutz Maz of Wissenschaftszentrum Berlin, describes the experience of a former East German cable and wire company covering the period before and immediately after German unification as follows:

> and then it happened. Within nine short months we were all torn out of our familiar environment and flung into a completely new one. We fell into a 'black hole'. We were completely disoriented. In the new situation all that we had for years been taught to believe became useless and irrelevant. Most of us could not even perceive this new environment and its requirements. . . . Instead of permanent supply shortages, there was now potentially over abundance, instead of bureaucratic control we were thrown into market anonymity, cost pressures, international competition, and individual responsibility. We had to act and think independently. New theories, professional knowledge and new laws replaced the old ones and the new corporate environment became a whirlpool (Maz, 1991, p. 8; Warner, 1990, pp. 20–38).

In the former Czechoslovakia transition to a market economy is also imposing a tremendous strain on all Czechs and Slovaks. Fundamental changes in business attitudes are taking place. Under the old system, there was no need to take any responsibility. There was always a government procedure. People are now finding themselves transposed to a system where the emphasis is on decisions and taking risks, which they were never exposed to before (CBI, 1992, pp. 20–1). Despite all this counter evidence, a hardly questioned belief still remains in Eastern Europe that the free market, in other words privatization and deregulation, will improve the domestic economy and benefits will ultimately trickle down to the poorer members of society. What is interesting and intellectually puzzling here is, first, what it is that explains the tacit public acceptance of privatization and economic liberalization and deregulation, despite the obvious deterimental effects it has on the poor, and second, what it is that explains in spite of the huge differentiation between Eastern and Central European states in terms of economic development, education, culture and political history, the simultaneous huge convergence of state decision-makers around the norms of privatization, marketization and trade liberalization. Part of the answer may be found by relating the recent trends of privatization and marketization in Eastern and Central Europe to the current changes in the global political economy. These include, for example, the transnationalization of the economy, hegemony and order in the international system, and the global articulation of a dominant business ethic and its mediation through public international organizations, such as the IMF, the World Bank and the ITU, and more recently UNESCO. Analysis of the problems of transition in Central and Eastern Europe, from centrally planned economies to free market systems, needs to be related more explicitly to the current changes in the global political economy rather than being restricted simply to the European regional and domestic level. Business activities can no longer be evaluated and understood in terms of economics only, or international finance, but increasingly need to be related to the way in which the world is politically organized, for example the nature of capital, problematic relations between states and markets, and the underlying structures and dynamics of information technology (El Kahal, 1992, p. 14).

HOW TO DO BUSINESS IN CENTRAL AND EASTERN EUROPE

Despite the gloomy picture presented in the previous section, there is considerable potential for Western business in Eastern and Central Europe as has so far been testified by Japanese and American multinational firms and international financial institutions, which are attempting to move into the area in a substantial way. There are many ways in which international business managers can take advantage of the opening up of the Eastern and Central European markets, provided they bear in mind the underlying difficulties and problems of transition outlined briefly in the previous section.

A Western company considering taking an industrial venture in Eastern and Central Europe must first identify quite clearly where and how improvements can be made and how to increase productivity in terms of costs and product quality. This cannot be done easily by just thinking about the product, but includes different functions such as research and development, purchase of raw materials, processing assembly, packaging, control of activities within the factory, marketing, sales and distribution (Watson and Frazer, 1991, pp. 17–22). There is also a need to carry out an 'improvement audit', not only to determine the current competitive position of the industry, but also to discover the potential if they are assisted by Western technology, management and marketing (Pitt-Watson and Frazer, 1991, p. 22).

Conducting an 'audit' of business opportunities in Eastern and Central Europe consists of the steps described below.

The first step is to understand the political behaviour of each of the Eastern European nations considered. Information needs to be extracted about whether reforms will continue and if so in what direction. Although there have been multi-party elections in a number of Eastern and Central European countries, some still have a substantial Communist component in their governments. Romania and Albania are such examples, although the Romanian government has changed its name (Pinder, 1991, p. 2). The opposition within these countries is still too weak to offer any real opposition at the present time. Bulgaria has a coalition government, which includes some former Communists, although not in the key positions of President or Prime Minister, which the opposition insisted should be non-Communist (Pinder, 1991, p. 2).

In Russia, although many of Boris Yeltsin's government are reformists, many of the Parliamentary Deputies, elected under the old system in 1990, will have been Communist Party members. The Parliamentary Deputies have, for example, recently blocked reforms to implement a bankruptcy law, which forced Yeltsin to issue a Presidential decree in an attempt to get the provision implemented (*Economist*, 20 June 1992, pp. 95–6). At the time of writing, President Yeltsin is involved in a major internal power struggle with former Communist Party members who are now Parliamentary deputies. This has worried Western governments to the extent that with the initiative of the Clinton Administration, loans of $1.6 billion have recently been granted to Russia.

The second step is to find out whether the organizations with which you want to do business are likely to be competitive on an international basis.

The third step consists of assessing the difference which technology transfer can make to an Eastern European organization, which activities it can affect and what values this will add. Transport and telecommunications infrastructures within Eastern Europe are a major problem area for many western investors. Although there are extensive rail networks within the region, a large proportion is single track, very little is electrified and the rolling stock is of poor quality (Commission of the EC, 1991, pp. 75–6). Additionally, many rail links are inadequate. Telecommunications are also in a very poor state due mainly to a lack of technology, which causes unreliable services, particularly overseas (Commission of the EC, 1991, p. 76).

As a fourth step, it is important to establish the sources of raw materials. Distribution problems and the failure of the centralized systems produced chronic shortages of raw materials. Western manufacturers may have to import their own raw materials if the requirements cannot be met in the local markets. The best way to find out is by making an initial visit as a member of a trade mission. Details of trade missions and joint visits can be obtained from the Chamber of Commerce or from the Eastern European Trade Council.

The fifth step relates particularly to dealing with the local language. Language is proving to be a greater barrier than anticipated in Eastern and Central Europe. Excellent translators are available, but the problem is that in the Slavic languages the vocabulary needed to describe many of the new concepts of business simply does not exist. Trying to explain the significance of branding, for example, is extremely difficult, especially when the Russian word for brand is exactly the same as the Russian word for product (Holden and Peck, 1990, p. 30).

The sixth step in making decisions about investing in Eastern and Central Europe is for investors to be aware of the levels of debt that exist between Eastern European companies, particularly in Russia. It has been estimated that in recent months, debt between Russian companies, resulting from IOUs being written, amounts now to 1 trillion roubles, about $10 billion (*Economist*, 2 May 1992, p. 129). Rather than cutting output when demand fell, Russian enterprises have been writing IOUs to each other to keep output well above demand.

Before making any investment decisions, Western investors need therefore to have reliable financial information. They will have to spend a great deal of time and effort finding out about the credit-worthiness of some companies (*Export Today*, September/October 1990, pp. 47–8). The availability of such information is furthermore a problem in itself.

Finally, potential investors must be aware of the lack of legal protection for their goods and investments in Eastern and Central Europe. Under the old planned economies, there was no protection of property, for example (Houda, 1991, pp. 66–72). The former Czechoslovakia, in particular, has no adequate legal protection of ownership rights. The protection of intellectual property rights is also inadequate compared to that in the West. Eastern and Central European countries are signatories of the Paris Convention of 1883 regarding the protection of industrial property, and the patent systems provide roughly the same sort of protection as in the West. There exists a system, for example, of protection in the form of a certificate of inventorship which protects the investor from unauthorized use by private individuals. But this same certificate allows the state the right to use the invention (Danton de Rouffignac, 1991). These certificates, furthermore, although similar to patents, are only available to nationals (Danton de Rouffignac, 1991).

REVIEW QUESTIONS

1. What are the main differences between Eastern and Central European countries and the Western world as far as international business is concerned?
2. What are the major types of products exported from the West to the East?
3. Explain how Western firms might market their products and services to Eastern European customers?
4. Many argue that the current reforms in the former Eastern Bloc countries provide the greatest opportunity to improve East–West business relations, which the West must not waste. Others see the developments in Central and Eastern Europe as welcome but no reason for euphoria. The results so far of the limited reform programmes in Central and Eastern Europe are uncertain, and serious setbacks are inevitable. Discuss the issues involved in these different views.

5. What are the major problems of trying to do business in Eastern and Central Europe? What factors should be taken into consideration before making decisions concerning trade and investment within this area?
6. In the light of the problems and opportunities of doing business in Eastern and Central Europe which business techniques or methods would you recommend as most appropriate, and why?

EXERCISE 15.1: Doing business in Eastern Europe

Aim   The aim of this exercise is to familiarize students with the political, economic and social structures of various Eastern and Central European countries, and to enable them to choose the most appropriate business operations and methods that can be used in conducting business in Eastern Europe.

Assignment   Choose a local company of your choice, and design a strategic plan for its expansion into Eastern and Central European markets. Advise the company of the problems that you think the company might encounter, and how to overcome them.

Format   Each group should choose a particular country in Eastern or Central Europe, and conduct an environmental analysis of the country before developing their strategic plan.

The presentation to the class should include:

1. A brief country profile.
2. A company profile.
3. Identification of business opportunities in the chosen country and why you think the company should expand its operations in that particular country.
4. An overview of the problems that might be encountered and how to overcome them.

FURTHER READING

Due to the rapidly changing events occurring on a daily basis in Eastern and Central Europe, students are advised to consult recent issues of the following journals, which are known to publish interesting articles related to the latest developments in business in that area. Some of these are:

- *Journal of European Business*
- *Export Today*
- *The Economist*
- *Institutional Investor*
- *The Banker*
- *The Director*
- *OECD Observer*
- *Euromoney*
- *European Business Review*

absolute advantage   According to the theory of absolute advantage, since countries have different national or acquired advantages they should concentrate on the production of those goods in which their country has an absolute advantage and acquire or purchase from abroad those goods that it cannot produce domestically as cheaply or efficiently.

animism   The oldest religion on Earth. It is often associated with spirit worship, magic, casting spells, ancestor worship, taboos and fatalism.

anti-trust laws   These are used to prevent foreign business firms from engaging in anti-competitive practices.

arbitrage   This occurs when a currency is purchased in one market, where it is cheaper, and sold in another market, where it is more expensive, in order to make a profit from the differences in spot exchange and price quotations.

arbitration   A method of resolving commercial disputes where both parties are required to submit the documents relevant to the case to an outside agency for an independent judgement, and to accept that judgement.

bank draft   Similar to a Bill of Exchange, except here the bank is the drawee instead of an individual or a company.

barter   The exchange of goods and services without money.

Berne Convention   The oldest treaty for the protection of copyright and artistic works.

Bill of Exchange   A written order to pay a certain amount of money specified in the bill to a specified person or company.

boycott   A form of embargo carried out on the basic agreement among several countries to prohibit trade either partially or totally with a particular country.

Bretton Woods system   The purpose of the Bretton Woods Conference was to put an end to the collapse of the international financial system and to create a new stable and internationally acceptable monetary system.

broad line global strategy   When a firm competes worldwide in the full product line of the industry.

buy-back or compensation trading   An agreement to sell the technology, the construction of an entire project, the licensing of patents or trade marks in return for agreeing to buy part of the output as payment.

cable transfer An order transmitted by one bank to another bank in a foreign country with instructions to pay a specific amount to a designated person or account.

cash in national currency Payment made in the national currency, such as bank notes.

Chaebol The South Korean equivalent of the Japanese *Keiretsu*, representing a combination of large companies, centred on a bank or a holding company, usually dominated by founding families.

code law Law established by arbitrary methods and constituting a comprehensive set of codes which clearly spells out the laws applicable in all possible legal situations.

common law A legal system broadly based on previous court decisions, precedents or past practices.

comparative advantage According to the theory of comparative advantage, if one country could produce each of the goods more efficiently than another, it should specialize in and export that commodity in which it is comparatively more efficient.

confiscation Similar to expropriation but without the compensation payments.

counter-purchase or parallel barter This occurs when two parties agree to exchange products that are delivered now for goods to be delivered in the future from a list mutually agreed upon by the two parties.

counter-trade A process which links imports with exports and can take the following forms: single barter, buy-back, counter-purchase, switch trading or clearing arrangement.

currency swaps An arrangement between two firms or a firm and a central bank or commercial bank to exchange one currency for another at a certain time in the future, and at exactly the same amount of the original currency that was exchanged at the time of the swap.

deposits in commercial banks Monetary payments made through transferring ownership to bank deposits from one company to another.

domestication This is also known as pre-arranged disinvestment and occurs when a multinational enters into an agreement with the host government to relinquish ownership and/or managerial control of its facilities in that country within a set period of time.

embargoes Complete bans on trade exports to or imports from a particular country.

Eurobond market A bond capital market through which funds are raised on a long-term basis via the marketing of debt securities.

Eurobonds Bonds issued in one or more countries as long-term securities in currencies other than the local ones, and payable in currency other than that of the country of the issuer of the bond.

Eurocurrency   A currency deposited outside the country of its origin. Eurocurrencies are also referred to as 'stateless money'.

Eurocurrency market   An international monetary market in which funds are deposited and borrowed from commercial banks. The Eurocurrency market deals with major world currencies.

Eurodollar market   An international monetary market which started in the 1950s dealing with US dollars deposited outside the USA.

European Commission   – European Commission headquarters are in Brussels. It is mainly responsible for the initial preliminary designing of Community policies, proposals and legislation.

European Court of Justice   A court that sits in Luxembourg and rules on the interpretation and application of Community Law.

European Currency Unit (ECU)   A monetary unit representing a basket of all the Community member states' currencies.

European Monetary System (EMS)   Created in 1979, this is a system of fixed but adjustable exchange rates, designed to create a zone of monetary stability in Europe.

European Monetary Union (EMU)   An agreement between member states in terms of which internal exchange rates are permanently fixed, and with no institutional barriers to the free movement of capital or to the circulation of currencies.

European Parliament   The European Parliament sits in Strasbourg. Its main function is to debate European legislation received from the Commission and recommendations from the Council.

Europe without frontiers   An idea based on the achievement of four freedoms of movement: free movement of goods, free movement of people, free movement of services and free movement of capital.

ethnocentric management   This occurs when a firm considers the home country's management practices to be superior to those of other countries, and where all key executives of the subsidiary are recruited from home country nationals.

Exchange Rate Mechanism (ERM)   Introduced in 1979, this is an exchange rate pegging arrangement by which bilateral exchange rates between member countries are stabilized.

exporting   The oldest form of entry into international markets, where a firm decides to maintain its production facilities at home and export its products to foreign countries. In direct exporting, export tasks are carried out directly by the firm itself. In indirect exporting these tasks are delegated either to agents or to export firms.

export management company   A company which acts to some extent as the export department of many manufacturers. It provides advice on overseas markets and helps in marketing the company's product.

expropriation   The physical take-over and control of foreign assets by the host government, usually accompanied by some kind of compensation or reimbursement to the firm, the value of which is decided by the host government. *Creeping* expropriation is when foreign firms are subjected to demands to relinquish a large amount of ownership and management control of the business to the government and nationals of the country in which these businesses are located.

factor endowment   According to the factor endowment theory, a country should specialize in the production and export of goods which uses its productive factors more abundantly.

Federalist theory of integration   According to the Federalists, the aim of integration is to create a political community based upon strong rule-bound central political institutions, superimposed upon autonomous nation states to keep order and control among them.

flanking   A strategic attack on a specific part of the market leader's business that is relatively undefended.

foreign bonds   Bonds issued by foreign borrowers in a nation's domestic capital market, and denominated in the nation's domestic currency.

foreign currency options   Under foreign currency options, the buyer has the opportunity and also the right to buy and sell the foreign currency at a pre-agreed exchange rate in the future, if this is to the buyer's advantage, but without any obligation to do so.

foreign exchange futures   Also known as currency futures, these are agreements to buy or sell at a fixed amount of foreign currency for delivery at a fixed future date and at a fixed price.

foreign exchange market   A market where financial institutions, commercial banks, firms, governments or their central banks, and individuals, tourists, speculators or investors buy and sell foreign currencies.

foreign exchange rates   The prices at which different national currencies are traded for one another in the foreign exchange markets.

foreign freight forwarder company   A company specializing in the export/import of goods across national borders.

forward contract market   A market in which two parties agree to exchange one currency for another at some future date at a fixed rate mutually agreed upon.

Functionalist theory of integration   According to the Functionalists, there is a concrete distinction between activities that are political and those that are economic or technical ones. The aim of integration is to increase technological cooperation, which will lead to political cooperation.

General Agreement on Tariff and Trade (GATT)   Created in 1945, GATT's original purpose was to combat the worldwide restrictions and protectionism that contributed to the post-Second World War economic recession.

geocentric management   This occurs when a firm considers the nationality less important than the particular skills and experience of the employees.

global branding   An international marketing strategy which consists of establishing a world brand identification for a certain product.

global capability   The ability to use rapidly productive human resources, technological and financial resources at the right time and the right place.

global environment analysis   The systematic identification and analysis of the domestic, foreign and international environments that may face a business firm in its international activities.

global focus strategy   This occurs when a firm targets a particular segment of the industry for competing worldwide.

globally standardized production   An international marketing strategy which consists of producing one product and selling it in the same way everywhere in the world with the same specification and characteristics.

guerilla strategy   A strategy in which a company decides to produce one-off machinery designs or limited-run fashion products, launched to take advantage of a gap left by market leaders.

hedging   A way of managing foreign exchange risk by eliminating the need to borrow funds or tying up a certain amount of money for a period of time.

home country nationals   Citizens of the country where the firm has its head office.

host country nationals   Citizens of the country where the firm has its own subsidiary.

International Bank for Reconstruction and Development (IBRD)   Better known as the World Bank, this is the largest international lending institution in the world, which began its operation in 1946.

International Center for the Settlement of Investment Disputes   An organization used when the contract being disputed between two firms involves investments in foreign markets.

international compensation package   People performing relatively similar jobs in different countries may receive different amounts and forms of compensation. An international compensation package consists of a basic salary and overseas allowances depending on which country the expatriate is assigned to.

International Monetary Fund (IMF)   An international financial institution created in 1945 with the overall aim of facilitating the growth of world trade by providing loans to those countries that were unable to earn enough foreign currency to pay for the imports they needed.

international trading company   A company which is usually the major supplier of foreign goods in its home market.

Islamic Law   A legal system derived entirely from the precepts of the Koran, which governs all aspects of life, individual behaviour, and social and economic relations.

joint ventures   Business partnerships created under local laws and jointly owned by two or more firms, multinationals or governments, or by multinational and local business persons.

Keiretsu   A combination of 25 to 50 different industrial companies centred on a large trading company or bank, predominant in Japan.

Letter of Credit   A document issued by a bank upon the request of an importer, declaring that payment should be made to an exporter regarding a specific shipment of commodities upon the presentation of shipment documents.

licensing   The process in which one firm—the licensor—provides certain resources, for example technology, brand name use, the right to use certain patents and copyrights, or trade marks, to another firm – the licensee – in exchange for a fee or a royalty or any other form of payment.

litigation   The most expensive and time-consuming method of resolving international commercial disputes.

localization   The placing of local national managers in all key managerial positions by a multinational firm operating in that country.

location theory   According to this theory, the location of industry is determined first by transportation and labour costs and second by location factors.

Madrid Union   Ensures automatic trade mark protection for all members.

management contract   An agreement by which a business firm provides managerial assistance to another firm by training its personnel to assume managerial positions in return for a fee for providing such assistance.

mediation   A method of resolving commercial international disputes where the assistance or help of a third party, known as the mediator, is used.

Most Favored Nation Clause (MFN)   All members of GATT must adhere to the MFN Clause, which stipulates that if a country grants a tariff reduction to one country, it should grant the same concession to all other members at the same time.

nationalization   The transfer of the whole industry from the private sector to public sector.

Neo-functionalist theory of integration   According to this theory, the end result of integration is the creation of a new political community, superimposed on the pre-existing ones, thus leading to the development of a new supranational state.

oligopoly   Limited competition between a small number of firms.

organizational structure   The arrangement and interrelationship of the component parts and positions of a company. It clearly shows the division of work activities and functions within the firm and their relationships.

organization chart   To show the organization structure, a chart is usually drawn indicating the various departments, functions and activities within the firm and their relationships.

Paris Convention   Also known as the International Union for the Protection of Intellectual Property, provides, for all members, protection of their trade marks, patents and property rights.

piggy-back exporting   Occurs when a manufacturer in one country distributes its products in another country through an already established distribution network.

Pluralist theory of integration   The main purpose of integration for the Pluralists is the attainment of peace and security in the international system through peaceful settlement of conflicts.

political risk analysis   Analysis of the risk of loss of assets, earning power and managerial control due to events or actions that are politically biased or politically motivated.

polycentric management   This occurs when a firm regards all countries as different and hard to understand, and where all key personnel in the subsidiary are recruited locally on the assumption that they are more familiar with the local culture and business ethics and have better relations with the host country.

privatization   Generally defined as primarily an economic, technical and administrative problem-solving concept consisting of the rolling back of the activities of the state and its replacement by the market.

product differentiation   Also referred to as product adaptation, this occurs when a company realizes the need to introduce some modifications to its product in various foreign markets due to different lifestyles, tastes, religion, habits, language or other cultural elements, legal requirements, physical differences and different infrastructures.

product extension   An international marketing strategy which consists of selling exactly the same product in foreign markets as in domestic markets.

product life cycle   The assumption that certain products go through a life cycle composed of four stages: introduction, growth, maturity and decline, and that the location of production varies internationally depending on the stage of the cycle.

quotas   Quantitative restrictions and limitations set by a government on either imported or exported goods.

recruitment   The process of identifying and providing the firm with a sufficient number of candidates for a particular job, large enough to allow the firm to select the most suitable employees it needs.

remote environment Consists of economic, political, legal, sociocultural, technological, physical, geographical and natural factors.

selection The selection process involves evaluating all the job applications received, conducting initial interviews, testing skills or the ability to learn on the job, gathering references, checking the truthfulness of applicants' résumés, conducting physical examinations, and finally making the job offer, specifying the salary and benefit packages.

Social Charter Also known as the Community Charter of Fundamental Rights, this was signed on 8 and 9 December 1989 by the Heads of State of governments of the European Community, with the exception of the United Kingdom. The Social Charter comprises set of rights for workers in Europe.

speculation Requires speculators to purchase a foreign currency in either the spot or forward markets using their own money, or to borrowing it with the intention of selling it at a later date at a high future spot rate.

spot exchange market A foreign exchange market where the exchange of currencies in the form of cheques drawn on different currency-denominated bank accounts bearing an immediate delivery or value or in the form of cash where payment of one currency into the other is completed on the same day.

strategic diamond model Introduced by K. Ohmae, this model attempts to explain the relationship between governments and multinational firms in the global political economy.

subsidies Low-cost loans or tax breaks granted by governments to domestic producers to assist them in competing against foreign goods.

tariffs Taxes imposed by governments on imported and exported goods.

task environment Consists of customers, suppliers, resources, competitors, market conditions, creditors and labour markets.

third country nationals Also known as cosmopolitan expatriates, these are citizens of a country other than the parent or host country.

triangular diplomacy Recently developed by J. Stopford and S. Strange. According to this theory, governments in the 1990s, as a result of the increasing global competition and globalization of business, no longer merely negotiate among themselves, but are increasingly pushed to negotiate with foreign firms.

turnkey operation An agreement by which a business firm agrees to construct an entire manufacturing plant or production facility, equip it and prepare it for operation and then turns it over to the new owners when it is ready for operation.

White Paper Published in June 1985 by the European Commission, this identifies all existing physical, technical and fiscal barriers and sets out proposals for their removal.

SELECTED NEWSPAPERS AND JOURNALS

The following publications are among those useful for continual study of international business.

Across the Board
Advertising Age
Columbia Journal of World Business
Euromoney
European Business Review
Export Today
Foreign Affairs
Fortune
Harvard Business Review
Institutional Investor
International Affairs
International Organizations
International Marketing Review
Journal of European Business
Journal of International Business Studies
Journal of Marketing
Lloyds Bank Review
Long Range Planning
Sloan Management Review
The Banker (London)
The Director
The Economist
The Wall Street Journal
The World Economy

REFERENCES

Adam, J., The possible new role of market and planning in Poland and Hungary, in *Market Socialism or the Restoration of Capitalism* (ed. Anders, A.), Cambridge University Press, Cambridge, 1992.

Adams, D., The monkey and the fish: cultural pitfalls of an educational advisor, *International Development Review*, **2**(2), 1969.

Adler, N., How they educated their companies, *Across the Board*, February 1988.

Alperowicz, N., Czechoslovakia: big changes, emerging opportunities, *Chemical Week*, **148**(27), 24 July 1991.

Anderson, A., Manager's journal: Why there are so few lawyers in Japan, *The Wall Street Journal*, 9 February 1981.

Argy, V., *The Post-War International Monetary Crisis: An Analysis*, George Allen & Unwin, London, 1981.

Ash, M. K., *Mary Kay on People Management*, Warner Books, New York, 1984.

Ash, N., The privatization dilemma, *Euromoney*, September 1990.

Ash, N., Czechoslovakia. Fulfilling the new state plan, *Euromoney*, June 1991.

Asheghian, P. and Ebrahimi, B., *International Business: Economics, Environment and Strategies*, Harper Collins, New York, 1990.

Aurichio, K., Western accounting principles head East, *Management Accounting*, **23**(2), August 1991.

Aylen, J., Privatization in developing countries, *Lloyds Bank Review*, Issue 163, 1987.

Ayres, R. L., *Banking on the Poor: the World Bank and World Poverty*, MIT Press, Cambridge MA, 1983.

Bairy, M. (ed.), *Japanese Ways in Doing Business in Japan*, Sophia University, Tokyo, 1967.

Baldev, R. N., *National Communication and Language Policy in India*, Frederick A. Praeger, New York, 1969.

Bank of America, *Information service ranking of 100 nations according to economic risk*, 1986.

Barber, F. and Montag-Girnmes K.-D., Everyone knows the Lilac Cow, *Director* **44**(4), November 1990.

Bassivy, G. R. and Hrair Dekmejian, R., MC4NC's and the Iranian revolution, an empirical study, *Management International Review*, **25**, 1985.

Beamish, P. W., Killing, J. P., Lecraw, D. J. and Crookell, H. (eds.), *International Management: Text and Cases*, Irwin, Homewood IL, 1991.

Bedelian, A. G., *Management*, 2nd edn, Dryden Press, New York, 1989.

Behrman, J. and Grosse, R., *International Business and Governments: Issues and Institutions*, University of South Carolina Press, 1990.

de Bendern, S., Eastern Europe towards the millenium. Economic miracle or Weimar Year 2000?, *Economic Situation Report*, *CBI*, **21**(3), Summer 1990.

Bergsten, F. C., Keohane, R. O. and Nye, J. S., International economics and international politics: a framework of analysis, in *World Politics and International Economics* (eds F. C. Bergsten and C. G. Frause), Brookings Institute, Washington, 1975.

Biger, N. and Hull, J., The valuation of currency options, *Financial Management*, Spring 1983.

Bird, G., Developing countries' interests in proposal for international monetary reform, in *Adjustment and Financing in the Developing World. The Role of the IMF*, 1984.

Black, J. S. and Gregersen, H. B., The other half of the picture. antecedents of spouse cross-cultural adjustment, *Journal of International Business Studies*, Third Quarter, 1991.

Bleeke, J. and Ernest, D. The way to win cross-border alliances, *Harvard Business Review*, November–December, 1991.

Boddewyn, J., The global spread of advertising regulations, *MSU Business Topics*, Spring 1981.

Boddewyn, J., Barriers to trade and investment, in *Advertising. Government Regulation and Industry Self-Regulation in 53 Countries*, Advertising Association, New York, 1989.

Brademas, J., A moment to seize. Management training and market economics education in Central and Eastern Europe, *Vital Speeches*, **57**(14), 1 May 1991.

Bradley, F., *International Marketing Strategy*, Prentice-Hall, Englewood Cliffs NJ, 1991.

Brash, J., Export Management Companies, *Journal of International Business Studies*, **9**(1), Spring/Summer 1978.

Brewster, C. and Tyson, S., *International Comparison: Human Resource Management*, Pitman, London, 1991.

Brooke, M. Z., *International Management. A Review of Strategies and Operations*, Stanley Thornes, Cheltenham, 1990.

Brooke, M. and Remners, H. L., *The Strategy of Multinational Enterprise*, Longman, London, 1970.

Buckley, A., *The Essence of International Money*, Prentice-Hall, Englewood Cliffs, NJ, 1990.

Budd, S. A. and Jones, A., *The European Community. A Guide to the Maze*, 3rd edn, Kogan Page, London, 1989.

Burkitt, B. and Braimbridge, R., What 1992 really means. Single market or double cross, Britain anti-Common Market Campaign, 1989.

Burton, F. N. and Hisashi, I., Expropriation of foreign owned firms in developing countries. A cross-national analysis, *Journal of World Trade Law*, September–October, 1984.

Calori, R. and Lawrence, P., *The Business of Europe. Managing Change*. Sage, Beverly Hills CA, 1991.

Campbell, D. (ed.), Comparative law, *Yearbook of International Business*, **12**, 1990.

Carnall, C. A., *Managing Change in Organizations*, Prentice-Hall International, Hemel Hempstead, 1990.

Cateora, P. R., *International Marketing*, 7th edn, Irwin, Homewood IL, 1990.

Carusgil, T., Yavas, U. and Bykowicz, S., Preparing executives for overseas assignments, *Management Decision*, 30, MCB University Press, 1992.

CBI, The birth of a new work ethic. Czechoslovakia. A special report, *CBI Initiative. Eastern Europe*, March 1992.

Cecchini, P., *1992: The European Challenge. The Benefits of a Single Market. The Cecchini Report*, Wildwood House, Aldershot, 1989.

Cerami, C. A., Boomtime for the Middle East, *Across the Board*, **28**(5), May 1991.

Chakravarthy and Perlmutter, *Columbia Journal of World Business*, Summer 1985.

Chandler, A. D., *Strategy and Structure*, MIT Press, Cambridge MA, 1962.

Chapman, C., *How the Stock Exchange Works*, 3rd edn, Hutchinson Business Books, London, 1991.

Crummey, S., Adventures in the Soviet market place, *Computer World*, **25**(18), 16 May 1991.

Chidomere, R. C. and Amyansi-Archinbong, C., Expansion strategies for global competition, *Advanced Management Journal*, **54**(3), Summer 1989.

Cocks, R., Towards a Marxist theory of European integration, *International Organization*, Winter 1980.

Commission of the European Community, *Completing the Internal Market*, European Doc, 1989.

Commission of the European Community, *European Community. The Regions of the 1990s*, Commission of the European Community, 1991.

Copland, L. and Criggs, L., *Going International*, Random House, New York, 1985.

Daniels, J. D. and Radebaugh, L. H., *International Business. Environments and Operations*, 6th edn, Addison-Wesley, Reading MA, 1992.

Danton de Rouffignac, P., *How to sell to Europe*, Pitman, London, 1990.

Danton de Rouffignac, P., *Doing Business in Eastern Europe. A Guide for the 1990s*, Pitman, London, 1991.

Darlin, D., Japanese advertisements take earthiness to levels out of this world, *Wall Street Journal*, 30 August 1980.

Davidson, W. H., The role of global scanning in business planning, *Organization Dynamics*, Winter 1991.

Delors, J. *EC Commission on Economic and Monetary Union in the European Community*, European Commission, 1989.

Department of Trade and Industry, *Merger Control in Europe. The Main Provisions of EC Legislation*, No. 40, 64/89 DTI Publications, 1989.

Department of Trade and Industry, *Europe open for Professionals*, 2nd edn, DTI Publications, 1991a.

Department of Trade and Industry, *Testing, Certification and Inspection*, 3rd edn, DTI Publications, 1991b.

Department of Trade and Industry, *Brussels. Can you hear me? Influencing decisions in the EC*, DTI Publications, 1992a.

Department of Trade and Industry, *The Single Market. The Facts*, 8th edn, DTI Publications, 1992b.

Department of Trade and Industry, *Monopolies and Mergers. Commission Function and Operation of Commission and how the Commission handles a monopoly reference*, 4th edn, DTI Publications, 1992c.

De Vries, M., The IMF: 40 years of challenge and change, *Finance and Development*, September 1985.

De Vries, T., Jamaica or the non-reform of the International Monetary System, *International Organization*, Autumn 1973.

Dicken, P. and Lloyd, *Location in Space: Theoretical Perspectives in Economic Geography*, 3rd edn, Harper & Row, New York, 1990.

Dickens, P., *Global Shift. Industrial Change in a Turbulent World*, 2nd edn, Paul Chapman, London, 1992.

Donlon, J. P., The hard work begins, *Chief Executive*, Issue 69, July/August 1991.

Douglas, C., Nestlé's latest killing in bottle baby market, *Business and Society Review*, No. 26, Summer 1978.

Douglas, S. P. and Yoram, Y., The myth of globalization, *Columbia Journal of World Business*, Winter 1987.

Dowling, P. J. and Schuller, R. S., *International Dimensions of Human Resource Management*, PWS Kent, Boston, 1990.

Doz, Y., Strategic management in multinational companies, *Sloan Management Review*, **21**(2), 1980.

Dressler, D. and Carn, D., *Sociology. The Study of Human Interaction*, Alfred A. Knopf, New York, 1969.

Drew, J., *Doing Business in the European Community*, 3rd edn, Whurr, London, 1992.

Drucker, P., New templates for today's organizations, *Harvard Business Review*, January–February 1974a.

Drucker, P., *Management*, Harper & Row, New York, 1974b.

Drucker, P., The changed world economy in global strategic management, in *Global Strategic Management. The Essentials*, 2nd edn (eds. H. V. Wortzel and L. Wortzel), Wiley, New York, 1990.

Dufey, G. and Giddy, I., *The International Money Market*, Prentice-Hall, Englewood Cliffs NJ, 1978.

Dudley, J. W. *1992: Strategies for the Single Market*, Kogan Page, London, 1990.

Dunning, J. H., Towards an eclectic theory of international production. Some empirical tests, *Journal of International Business Studies*, **11**, 1980.

Dunning, J. H., The eclectic paradigm of international production. A restatement and possible extensions, *Journal of International Business Studies*, **10**, Spring 1988.

Dymza, W. A. *Multinational Business Strategy*, McGraw-Hill, New York, 1972.

Economist, 8 February 1986, p. 86.

ECU, The, European Documentation Series, (**31**), 1987

El Agraa, A. M., *Economics of the European Community*, Phillip Allen, London, 1992.

El Kahal, S., International business and international relations: a case of mutual neglect, *British Academy of Management Newsletter*, (13), July 1992.

Emerson, M. and Huhne, C., *The ECU Report*, Pan, London, 1991.

Euromoney, October 1987.

Euromoney, September 1989, p. 206.

European Business Review, **1**(4), 1989.

European File, A European financial area: the liberalization of capital movements, Commission for the European Communities, European Documentation, June/July, 1988a.

European File, The Removal of Technical Barriers to Trade, Commission for the European Communities, European Documentation, November 1988b.

European File, Towards a big internal market in financial services, Commission for the European Communities, European Documentation, November 1988c.

European File, Community Charter of Fundamental Social Rights for Workers, Commission for the European Communities, European Documentation, May 1990.

The European Monetary System: Origins, Operation and Outlook, European Perspective Series, 1985.

Fairlamb, D. and Slavinskis, G., Making it in the Soviet Union, *Institutional Investor*, **25**(5), May 1991.

Ferguson, C. H., Computers and the coming of the US *Keiretsu, Harvard Business Review*, August 1990.

Ferrieux, E., Hidden Messages, *World Press Review*, July 1989.

Foster, P., McDonald's excellent Soviet venture, Canadian Business, **64**(5), May 1991.

Fraser, R. and Wilson, M., Privatization: The Experience and International Trends, *Keesing's International Studies*, Longman, London, 1988.

Freedman, A., Advertising, *Wall Street Journal*, 25 April 1989.

French, W. L., *The Personnel Management Process*, 5th edn, Houghton Mifflin, New York, 1982.

Friedman, S., War spurs interest in political risk, *National Underwriter* (Property/Casualty/Employees Benefits), **95**(23), 10 January 1991.

Frobel, F., Heinricks, J. and Kreye, O., *The New International Division of Labour*, Cambridge University Press, Cambridge, 1980.

Galtung, J., *The European Community. A Superpower in the Making*, Allen & Unwin, London, 1981.

Garland, Farmer, Taylor, *International Dimensions of Business Policy and Strategy*, 2nd edn, PWS Kent, Boston, 1991.

George, S., *How the Other Half Dies*, Penguin, Harmondsworth, 1976.

Gibbs, P., *Doing Business in the European Community*, Kogan Page, London, 1990.

Giddy, I. H., The demise of the product life cycle in international business, *Columbia Journal of World Business*, Spring 1978.

Giddy, I. H., Foreign Exchange Options, *Journal of Future Markets*, Summer 1983.

Gill, S. and Law, D., *The Global Political Economy. Perspectives, Problems and Policies*, Harvester Wheatsheaf, Hertfordshire, 1988.

Glover, K., Dos and taboos. Cultural aspects of international business, *Business America*, 13 August 1990.

Goldstein, Europe after Maastricht, *Foreign Affairs*, Winter 1992–93.

Goodhard, D., Opting out and crashing in, *Financial Times*, 28 February 1992, p. 16.

Goold, M. and Campbell, A., *Strategies and Styles*, Ashbridge Management Center, 1989.

Graham, J. L., Campbell, N. A., Jobbert, A. and Meissner, H. Marketing negotiations in France, Germany, the United Kingdom and the United States, *Journal of Marketing*, April 1988.

Grosfeld, I. Propspects for privatization: Poland, *European Economy*, No. 43, Brussels, March 1990.

Grosse, R. and Kujawa, D., *International Business. Theory and Managerial Applications*, 2nd edn, Irwin, Boston MA, 1992.

Griffiths, B., *Morality and the Market Place. Christian Alternatives to Capitalism and Socialism*, Hodder & Stoughton, London, 1982.

Guianluigi, G., Implementing a Pan-European Marketing Strategy, *Long Range Planning,* **24**(5), 1991.

Guillaum, C., Culture and cultures, *Culture*, **6**(1), 1979.

Gunter, D. and Giddy, I., *The International Money Market*, Prentice-Hall, Englewood Cliffs NJ, 1978.

Guy, V. and Mattock, J., *The New International Manager – An Action Guide for Cross-Cultural Business*, Kogan Page, London, 1991.

Habib, G. M. and Burnett, J. J., An assessment of channel behavior in an alternative structural arrangement. The international joint venture, *International Marketing Review*, **6**(3), 1989.

Haendel, D. G., West T. and Meadow, R. G., *Overseas investment and political risk*, Philadelphia Foreign Policy Research Institute, 1974.

Hall, E. T., The silent language in overseas business, *Harvard Business Review*, May–June 1960.

Hall, E. T., *Beyond Culture*, Doubleday, Garden City NY, 1977.

Hamel, G. and Prahaland, C. K., Do you really have a global strategy?, *Harvard Business Review*, July–August 1985.

Hamel. G., Doz, Y. and Prahaland, C. K., Collaborate with your competitors and win, *Harvard Business Review*, January–February 1989.

Hamelink, D., *Finance and Information: A Study of Converging Interest*, Aplex, New York, 1983.

Harrigan, K., *Strategies for Joint Ventures*, Lexington Books, Lexington MA, 1983.

Harris, P. and Moran, T., *Managing cultural differences*, Gulf, Houston, TX, 1989.

Harrop, J., *The Political Economy of Integration in the European Community*, Edward Elgar, Aldershot, 1989.

Harvey, D., *The Limits to Capital*, Blackwell, Oxford, 1982.

Harvey Jones, J., *Troubleshooter in Eastern Europe*, BBC Video documentary, 1991.

Hayashi, E., Franchising fever: the growth business of the 1990s, *Export Today*, April 1989.

Hayter, T., *Aid Rhetoric and Reality*, Pluto, London, 1985.

Healey, N., From the European Monetary System to European Monetary Union: A guide to the debate, *Journal of European Business Education*, 1(1), 1991.

Hecksher, E., *Mercantilism*, George Allen & Unwin, London, 1985.

Heenan, D. A. and Perlmutter, H. V., *Multinational Organization Development: A Social Architecture Perspective*, Addison Wesley, Reading MA, 1979.

Heilbroner, R., Economic Prospects, 29 August 1983, p. 70.

Heller, J. E., Criteria for selecting an international manager, *Personnel*, **57**, May–June 1980.

Herbig, P. A. and Kramer, H. E., Cross-cultural negotiations: success through understanding, *Management Decision*, **29**(8), 1991.

Herskovits, M. J., *Man and His Works*, Alfred A. Knopf, New York, 1952.

Hibbert, N., *Soviet Managers*, European Training Agency, Coventry University, June 1991.

Hodgetts, R. and Luthans, F., *International Management*, McGraw-Hill, New York, 1991.

Hofstede, G., *Culture's Consequences: International Differences in Work-Related Values*, Sage, Beverly Hills CA, 1980.

Hofstede, G., Motivation, leadership and organization: do American theories apply abroad?, *Organization Dynamics*, No. 1, Summer 1980.

Hofstede, G., National cultures in four dimensions, *International Studies of Management and Organization*, Spring/Summer 1983.

Holden, L. and Peck, H., Perestroika, Glasnost, management and trade, *European Business Review*, **90**(2), 1990.

Holden, R. G., The global corporation, *Retail Control*, **58**(4), April 1990.

Houda, M., Czechoslovakia and foreign capital, *Journal of European Business Education*, 1(1), 1991.

Howard, R., The designer organization: Italy's GFT goes global, *Harvard Business Review*, September–October 1991.

Hume, D., *Of Money*, Essays Vol. 1, Green, London, 1912.

Hume, S., How Big Mac made it to Moscow, *Advertising Age*, **61**(4), 22 January 1990.

Huszagh, S. M. and Huszagh, F. W., Barter and countertrade, *International Marketing Review*, Summer 1986.

Hymer, S., *The International Operations of National Firms: A Study of Direct Foreign Investment*, MIT Press, Cambridge MA, 1976.

Ignatius, D., China frees 211 prisoners in move seen aimed at retaining Most Favored Nation Trade Status, *Wall Street Journal*, 11 May 1990.

Ingo, W. and Murray, T. (eds.), *Handbook of International Business*, 2nd edn, Wiley, New York, 1988.

Jacobs, L., Keorun, C., Worthley, R. and Ghymn, K. I., Cross-cultural colour comparisons: global marketers beware, *International Marketing Review*, **8**(3), 1991.

Jacques, L. C., Management of foreign exchange risk. A review article, *Journal of International Business Studies*, Spring/Summer 1981.

Jaeger, A. M., The transfer of organizational culture overseas: an approach to control in the multinational corporation, *Journal of International Business Studies*, **14**(2), Fall 1983.

Jensen, W. G. *Common Market*, Foulis, London, 1967.

Jones, C., Hungary: everything for sale, *Banker*, **141**(785), July 1991.

Kamerman, S. and Khan, A., *Privatization and the Welfare State*, Princeton University Press, Princeton NJ, 1989.

Kapl, M., Sojka, M. and Tepper, T., Unemployment and market-oriented reform in Czechoslovakia, *International Labour Review*, **130**(2), 1991.

Khambata, D. and Ajami, R., *International Business: Theory and Practice*, MacMillan, New York, 1992.

Khan, M. S., Islamic interest free banking, *IMF Fund Papers*, March 1988.

Khoury, S. and Hung Chan, K., Hedging foreign exchange risk: selecting the optimal tool, *Midland Corporate Finance Journal*, Winter 1988.

Killick, T. and Bird, G., *The IMF and the Third World (et al.)*, Heinemann, London, 1984.

Killing, P., How to make a global joint venture work, *Harvard Business Review*, May–June 1982.

Kluckholm, C., The Study of Culture in the Policy Sciences (eds. Lerner, D. and Lserwell, H. D.), Standford University Press, 1951.

Kobrin, S. J., Political risk – a review and reconstruction, *Journal of International Business Studies*, Spring/Summer 1979.

Kobrin, S. J., Foreign enterprise and forced disinvestment in LDCs, *International Organization*, Winter 1980.

Kobrin, S. J., Expropriation as an attempt to control foreign firms in LDCs. Trends from 1960 to 1979, *International Studies Quarterly*, **28**, 1984.

Korabi, T. and Grieve, D. G., Doing business in Eastern Europe: a survival guide, *Canadian Business Review*, **17**(2), Summer 1990.

Korner, P., *The IMF and the Debt Crisis: A Guide to the Third World's Dilemma*, Zed, London, 1986.

Kossoff, J., Europe: up for sale, *New Statesman and Society*, 1988.

Kotler, P., *Marketing Management: Analysis, Planning and Control*, 5th edn, Prentice-Hall, Englewood Cliffs NJ, 1984.

Kotler, P., Fahey, L. and Jatusripitak, S., *New Competition*, Prentice-Hall, Englewood Cliffs NJ, 1986.

Kotter, J. P. and Schlesinger, L. A., Choosing strategies for change, *Harvard Business Review*, March–April 1979.

Lall, S., Theories of direct foreign private investment and multinational behaviours, *Economic and Political Weekly*, **11**, pp. 31–3, 1991.

Lanier, A. R., Selecting and preparing personnel for overseas transfers, *Personnel Journal*, March 1979.

Lawrence, P., How to deal with resistance to change, *Harvard Business Review*, **47**(1) January–February 1969.

Lecraw, D. J., Managing export and import operations in *International Management: Text and Cases* (eds. Beamish, P. W., Killing, J. P., Lecraw, D. J. and Crookell, H.), Irwin, Homewood IL, 1991.

Lei, D., Slocum, J. W. Jr, Global strategic alliances: payoffs and pitfalls, *Organization Dynamics*, Winter 1991.

Levi, M., *International Finance. The Markets and Financial Management of Multinational Business*, 2nd edn, McGraw-Hill, New York, 1990.

Levitt, T., Marketing myopia, *Harvard Business School Review*, July–August 1960.

Levitt, T., The globalization of markets, *Harvard Business Review*, May–June 1983.

Liddle, J. and Joshi, R., *Daughters of Independence: Gender, Caste and Class in India*, Rutgers United Press Zed Books, London, 1986.

Lindsay, M., *International Business in Gorbachev's Soviet Union*, Pinter, London, 1989.

Litka, M., *International Dimension of the Legal Environment of Business*, PWS Kent, Boston, 1991a.

Litka, M., *Cases in International Business Law*, PWS Kent, Boston, 1991b.

Lutz, R., Perspectives on the World Court, the United States and international dispute resolution in a changing world, *The International Lawyer*, **25**(3), Fall 1992.

Lynch, R., *European Business Strategy: An Analysis of Europe's Top Companies*, Kogan Page, London, 1990.

MacBean, A. I. and Snowden, P. N., *International Institutions in Trade and Finance*, Allen & Unwin, London, 1981.

McCarthy, E. J., *Basic Marketing: A Managerial Approach*, 7th edn, Irwin, Homewood IL, 1981.

McKinnon, R. I., *The Euro-Currency Market: Essays in International Finance*, No. 125, Princeton University, December 1977.

Maclean, J., Interdependence. An ideological intervention in International Relations, in *Interdependence on Trial* (eds. Jones, R. B. and Willets, R.), Frances Pinter, London, 1986.

Maclean, J., Marxism and international relations: a strange case of mutual neglect, *Millenium*, **17**(2), Summer 1988.

Maddox, R. C., Terrorism's hidden threat and the promise for multinational corporations, *Business Horizons*, **33**(6), November/December 1990.

Magnier, M., Patience, dedication, key to succeeding in Japan, *Journal of Commerce*, 8 April 1988.

Main, J., How 21 men got global in 35 days, *Fortune*, 6 November 1989.

Marer, P., The transition to a market economy in Central and Eastern Europe, *OECD Observer*, April/May 1991.

Martin, J., Beyond 1992. Lifestyle is Key, *Advertising Age*, 11 July 1988.

Marubeni Corporation, *The Unique World of the Sogo Sosha*, Marubeni Corporation, Tokyo, 1979.

Maslow, A., *Motivation and Personality*, 2nd edn, Harper & Row, New York, 1970.

Mason, E. and Asher, R., *The World Bank since Bretton Woods*, Brookings Institute, Washington, 1973.

Matsuura, N., *International Business. A New Era*, Harcourt Brace Jovanovich, New York, 1991.

Maz, L., New Europe: New Germany. Analysis in times of upheaval, *Journal of General Management*, **16**(3), Spring 1991.

Mazey, S., European Community social policy: development and issues, *European Dossier*, Series No. 14, 1989.

Meerschwam, D. M., *Breaking Financial Boundaries*, Harvard Business School Press, Cambridge MA, 1991.

Melvin, M., *International Money and Finance*, 2nd edn, Harper & Row, New York, 1989.

Miles, R. H., *Macro Organization Behaviour*, Goodyear, Santa Monica CA, 1980.

Mole, J., *Mind your manners: Culture Class in the European Single Market*, The Industrial Society, New York, 1990.

Montgomery, D. B. and Weinberg, C. G., Towards strategic intelligence systems, *Journal of Marketing*, Issue 43, 1979.

Moran, T. H. and Maddox D. H., *Transnational Corporations in the Copper Industry*, UN Center on Transnational Corporations, New York, 1981.

Morden, T., 'Think Globally and Manages Locally', *Management Decision*, **29**(2), 1991, pp. 32–40.

Morgan Guarantee Trust, *World Financial Market*, New York, 1986–89.

Murray, F. T. and Murray, A. H., Global managers for global business, *Sloan Management Review*, **27**(2), Winter 1986.

Nathan, F. and Wells, L. T., Bargaining power of multinationals and host governments, *Journal of International Business Studies*, Fall 1982.

Nelson-Horchler, J., Desperately seeking Yankee know-how, *Industry Week*, **240**(5), 4 March 1991.

Newbery, D., Netherlands, *European Economic Review*, **35**(2,3), April 1991.

Niemeyer, E., Hotels chase travellers to Eastern Europe, *New England Business*, **12**(11), November 1990.

Noel, E., *The Institutions of the European Community*, Office for Official Publications of the EC, Luxembourg, 1988.

Noel, E., *Working Together. The Institutions of the European Community*, Office for Official Publications of the EC, Luxembourg, 1991.

Noreen, K., Searching the online globe. Best files for country profiles, *Database*, **14**(3), June 1991.

Nuti, M., Privatization of Socialist economies: general issues and the Polish case, in *Transformation of Planned Economies: Property Rights, Reform and Micro-Economic Stability* (eds. Bloommestein and Marrese, M.), OECD, 1991.

Nye, D., The female expatriates' promise, *Across the Board*, February 1988.

O'Brien, R., *Global financial integration. The end of geography*, Royal Institute of International Affairs, Pitman, London, 1992.

O'Brien, R., C. and Helleiner, G. K., The political economy of information in a changing international economic order, *International Organization*, **34**(4), Autumn 1980.

Ohmae, K., *The Mind of the Strategist*, Penguin, Harmondsworth, 1983.

Ohmae, K., *Triad Power: The Coming Shape of Global Competition*, Free Press, New York, 1985.

Ohmae, K., *The Borderless World. Power and Strategy in the Interlinked Economy*, Collins, London, 1990a.

Ohmae, K., Becoming a Triad Power, in *Global Strategic Management: The Essentials*, 2nd edn, (eds. Wortzel, H. V. and Wortzel, L. H.), Wiley, New York, 1990b.

Opack, J. H., Likeness of licensing, franchising, *Les Nouvelles*, June 1977.

Otis, L. H., Iraq crisis spotlights political risk, *Chubb Exec National Under-Writer (Property/Casualty/ Employee Benefits)*, **94**(50), 10 December 1990.

Oxley, A., *The Challenge of Free Trade*, Harvester Wheatsheaf, Hertfordshire, 1990.

Paliwoda, S., *New Perspectives on International Marketing*, Routledge, London, 1991.

Palmer, J., *Trading Places*, Mackays of Chatham Ltd, 1988.

Parson, T., *The Social System*, Free Press, Chicago, 1951.

Pearce, A., Globalization of networks: a capital question, *Network World*, **7**(8), 30 April 1990.

Pentland, C., *International Theory and European Integration*, Faber & Faber, London, 1973.

Perlmutter, H. V., The tortuous evolution of the MNC, *Columbia Journal of World Business*, No. 4, January/February, 1969a.

Perlmutter, H. V., The fortuitous evolution of the multinational corporation, *Columbia Journal of World Business*, No. 4, January/February 1969b.

Persmen, S., US hotels invade Eastern Europe on strength of their service and reputations, *Business Marketing*, **15**(10), October 1990.

Phatak, A. V., *International Dimensions of Management*, 2nd edn, PWS Kent, Boston, 1989.

Pinder, M., *Personnel Management for the Single European Market*, Pitman, London, 1990.

Pinder, J., *The European Community and Eastern Europe*, Royal Institute of International Affairs, Pinter, London, 1991.

Pirie, M., *Privatization*, Wildwood House, Aldershot, 1988.

Pitelis, C. N. and Sugden, R. (eds.), *The Nature of the Transnational Firm*, Routledge, London, 1992.

Pitt-Watson, D. and Frazer, S., Eastern Europe: commercial opportunity or illusion?, *Long Range Planning*, **24**(5), 1991.

Platto, C., *Obtaining Evidence in Another Jurisdiction. Business Disputes*, International Bar Association, Graham and Trotman, London, 1988.

Pomfret, R., *International Trade: An Introduction to Theory and Policy*, Basil Blackwell, Oxford, 1991.

Porter, M., *The Competitive Advantage of Nations*, The Macmillan Press, Basingstoke, 1990.

Porter, M., *Competitive Strategy: Techniques for Analyzing Industries and Competitors*, Free Press, New York, 1980.

Portes, R., EMS and EMU after the Fall, *The World Economy*, **16**(1), January 1993.

Poynter, T. A., Political risk: managing government intervention, in *International Management. Text and Cases* (eds. Beamish, P. W. *et al.*), Irwin, Homewood IL, 1991.

Prasad, S. B. and Shetty, K., *An Introduction to Multinational Management*, Prentice-Hall, Englewood Cliffs NJ, 1976.

Prayer, C., *The World Bank: A Critical Analysis*, Monthly Review Press, New York, 1982.

Price C. V., *1992: Europe's Last Chance: From Common Market to Single Market (Nineteenth Wincott Memorial Lecture)*, Institute of Economic Affairs, London, 1988.

Punnett, B. J., *Experiencing International Management*, PWS Kent, Boston, 1989.

Radharishnan, *The Hindu View of Life*, George Allen & Unwin, London, 1961.

Radice, H., *International Firms and Modern Imperialism*, Penguin, Harmondsworth, 1975.

Rahim, M., A model for developing key expatriate executives, *Personnel Journal*, April 1983.

Randlesome, C., Brierly, W., Burton, K., Gordon, C. and King, P., *Business Cultures in Europe*, Heinemann, Oxford, 1990.

Rangarajan, L., Politics of international trade, in *Paths of Political Economy* (ed. Strange, S.), George Allen & Unwin, London, 1984.

Redhead, K., *Introduction to International Money Markets*, Woodhead Faulkner, Cambridge, 1992.

Reed, B., Canning International management development, *Director*, 1992.

Reich, R., Who is us?, *Harvard Business Review*, **68**(1), January–February 1990.

Reich, R., Who is them? *Harvard Business Review*, March–April, 1991, p. 79.

Reihn, R., Bright prognosis for the health care industry in Eastern Europe, *Journal of European Business*, **2**(4), March/April 1991.

Reinsch, R. W., Doing business in the Soviet Union, *Europe*, No. 305, April 1991.

Ricardo, D., *Principles of Political Economy of Taxation*, Penguin, Harmondsworth, 1971.

Ricks, D. A., *Big Business Blunders. Mistakes in Multinational Marketing*, Irwin Dow Jones, Homewood IL, 1983.

Rohan, T. M., East Germany: another European comeback, *Industry Week*, **239**(18), 17 September 1990.

Root, F. R., Analyzing political risk in international business, in *The Multinational Enterprise in Transaction* (eds. Kapoor, A. and Grub, P. D.), Darwin Press, Princeton, 1972.

Rosecrance, C., *The Rise of the Trading State*, Basic Books, New York, 1986.

Rosen, B. N., Boddewyn, J. J. and Louis, E. A., US brands abroad: an empirical study of global branding, *International Marketing Review*, **6**(1), 1989.

Rosenau, J. N. and Czempiel, E.-O. (eds.), *Governance Without Government: Order and Change in World Politics*, Cambridge University Press, Cambridge, 1992.

Ross, F. H. and Hills, T., *The Great Religions by which Men Live*, Fawcett, Greenwich CT, 1986.

Rossman, M. L., *The International Business Woman*, Praeger, New York, 1986.

Rugman, A. M., Lecraw, D. J. and Booth, L. D., *International Business. Firm and Environment*, McGraw-Hill, New York, 1985.

Rweyemamu, J., Restructuring the international monetary system, in *Development Dialogue*, 1980, pp. 75–91.

Sanger, D. E., As Hong Kong's elite leave; investors from Japan arrive, *New York Times*, 29 May 1990.

Scheffer, R., Earle, B. and Augusto, F., *International Business Law and its Environment*, West Publishing, Minneapolis/St Paul, 1993.

Siller, J. F., Adam Smith goes to Czechoslovakia, *Business Week*, 13 May 1991.

Simon, J. D., Political risk assessment: past trends and future prospects, *Columbia Journal of World Business*, **XVII**(3), 1982.

Siren, M. and Shaw, D., Assessing the market and opportunities, *Directors and Boards*, **15**(2), Winter 1991.

Smithson, C. W., A Lego approach to financial engineering: an introduction to forwards, futures, swaps and options, *Midland Corporate Finance Journal*, Winter 1987.

Souter, G., Credit, political risk coverage to be used only as last resort, panelists advise, *Business Insurance*, **26**(15), 13 April 1992.

Spero, J. E., *The Politics of International Economic Relations*, 4th edn, Unwin Hyman, London, 1990.

Starr, P., The meaning of privatization, in *Privatization and the Welfare State* (eds. Kamerman, S. B. and Khan, A.), Princeton University Press, 1989.

Steers, R. M., Shin, Y. K. and Ungson, G. R., The *Chaebol*: Korea's new industrial might, 1989.

Stitt, H. J. and Baker, S., *The Licensing and Joint Venture Guide*, 3rd edn, Ministry of Industry, Trade and Technology, Toronto, 1985.

Stoner, J. A. F. and Freeman, R. E. *Management*, 4th edn, Prentice-Hall, Englewood Cliffs NJ, 1989.

Stopford, J. M. and Wells, L. T. Jr, *Managing the Multinationals*, Basic Books, New York, 1972.

Stopford, J., Strange, S. and Henley, J. S., *Rival States, Rival Firms. Competition for World Market Shares*, Cambridge University Press, Cambridge, 1991.

Storm, R., New dreams for old, *International Management*, **46**(4), May 1991.

Strange, S., The management of surplus capacity: or how does theory stand up to protectionism 1970s style?, *International Organization*, **33**, 1979.

Strange, S., An Eclectic Approach, in *The New International Political Economy* (eds. Murphy, C. M. and Tooze, R.), Lynne Rinner, Boulder, 1991.

Strange, S., Firms and world politics, *International Affairs*, **68**(1), January 1992.

Subhash, C., in *Global Strategic Management: The Essentials*, 2nd edn (eds. Wortzel, H. V. and Wortzel, L. H.), Wiley, New York, 1990.

Sumantra, G., *Environmental Scanning*, Doctoral Dissertation, MIT Sloan School of Management, 1985.

Symons, G. L., Coping with the corporate tribe: how women in different cultures experience the managerial role, *Journal of Management*, **12**(13), 1986.

Szegedi, Z., The economy and international business in Hungary, *Journal of Business Administration* (Canada), **19**(112), 1989–90.

Tandon, P., Maturing of business in India, *California Management Review*, Spring 1972.

Tavares, J., New political risk cover protects global profits, *National Underwriter*, **95**(24), 17 June 1991.

Taylor, P. *The Limits of European Integration*, Croom Helm, London, 1983.

Taylor, W., The logic of global business: an interview with ABB's Percy Barnevick, *Harvard Business Review*, March–April 1991.

Terpestra, V. (ed.), *The Cultural Environment of International Business*, South Western, Cincinatti OH, 1978.

Terpestra, V. and David, K., *The Cultural Environment of International Business*, South Western, Cincinatti OH, 1985.

Terpestra, V. and K. David, *The Cultural Environment of International Business*, 3 edn., Southweston Publishing Co., Cincinnatti, Ohio, 1991, pp. 80–81.

Terpestra, V. and Sarathy, R., *International Marketing*, 5th edn, Dryden, New York, 1991.

Theravaada, R. C. L., Buddhism in South-East Asia, University of Michigan Press, Ann Arbor, 1972.

Torbet, P., First Soviet Free-Zone will give firm access to Pacific Basin markets, East Asia, *Executive Reports*, **13**(3), 1991.

de la Torre, J. and Neckar, D. H., Forecasting political risk for international operations, *International Journal of Forecasting*, No. 4, 1988, p. 221.

Tormarchio, J. T., Joint venture law in Eastern Europe, *Journal of European Business*, **2**(5), May/June 1991.

Tsurmi, Y., *Sogosoha: Engines of Export Base Growth*, Montreal Institute for Research on Public Policy, 1980.

Tung, R. L., Selection and training of personnel for overseas assignments, *Columbia Journal of World Business*, Spring 1985.

Twitt, J. F., Expropriation of foreign investment. Summary of the Post World War II experience of American and British Investors in less developed countries, *Journal of International Business Studies*, Fall 1969.

Ubelhart, M. C., Compensation in the Soviet Union. Observations from Leningrad, *Benefits and Compensations International*, **21**(1), July/August 1991.

United Nations Center on Transnational Corporations, *Trends and Issues in Foreign Direct Investment and Related Flows*, United Nations, New York, 1985.

United Nations Department of Economic and Social Affairs, *Multinational Corporations in World Development*, United Nations, New York, 1973.

Van de Laar, A., *The World Bank and the Poor*, Vol. 6, Martinus Nijhoff, London, 1990.

Van der Merwe, S. and l'Huillier, M., Euro-consumers in 1992, *Business Horizons*, January/February 1989.

Venturini, P., *The Social Charter. Potential Effects of the Internal Market*, ECSC, Brussels, 1988.

Vernon, R., International investment and international trade in the product life cycle, *Quarterly Journal of Economics*, May 1966.

Vernon, R., Organizational and institutional responses to international risks, in *Global Strategic Management: The Essentials*, 2nd edn, (eds. Wortzel, H. V. and Wortzel, L. H.), Wiley, New York, 1990.

Vernon, R. and Wells, L. T. Jr, *The Manager in the International Economy*, 6th edn, Prentice-Hall, London, 1991.

Verzariu, P., *Countertrade, Barter Offsets*, McGraw-Hill, New York, 1985.

Viza Yakumar, K., Pratap, K.J. and Mohapatra, Environmental impact analysis, *Long Range Planning*, **24**(6), 1991.

Walker, P., *Taking Your Business into Europe*, Hawkmere, London, 1989.

Wall Street Journal, 27 January 1984, p. 19.

Walter, R. and Blake, D., *The Politics of Global Economic Relations*, 4th edn, Prentice-Hall, Englewood Cliffs NJ, 1991.

Waltz, K. N., *Theory of International Politics*, Addison-Wesley, Reading MA, 1979.

Warner, M., Management versus self-management in Yugoslavia, *Journal of General Management*, **16(2)**, Winter 1990.

Watchel, M., *The Money Mandarins. The Making of a Supranational Economic Order*, Pantheon Books, New York, 1986.

Watson, D. and Frazer, S., Make it here, sell it there. Eastern Europe: Opportunity or illusion?, *Long Range Planning*, **24**(5), 1991.

Weber, M., *The Protestant Ethic and the Spirit of Capitalism*, Allen & Unwin, London, 1952.

Wedderburn, Lord, *The Social Charter, European Company and Employment Rights: An Outline Agenda*, Institute of Employment, London, 1990, p. 68.

Weekly, J. K. and Aggarwal, R., *International Business. Operating in the Global Economy*, Dryden, New York, 1987.

Weisweiller, R., *Introduction to Foreign Exchange*, Woodhead Faulkner, Cambridge, 1983.

Welch, L. S. and Luostarinen, R., Internationalization: Evolution of a Concept, in *Global Strategic Management: The Essentials* (eds. Wortzel, V. H. and Wortzel, L.), Wiley, New York, 1990.

Welford, R. and Prescott, K., *European Business. An Issue-Based Approach*, Pitman, London, 1992.

Welt, L. *Trade without Money: Barter and Countertrade*, Harcourt Brace Jovanovich, New York, 1990.

Williams, J. Jr and Ryans, K. Jr, Attitudes towards advertising: a multinational study, *Journal of International Business Studies*, Winter 1982.

Williams, M. J., Women head the corporate game, *Fortune*, 12 September 1988.

World Bank International Development Association Annual Report, World Bank, Washington DC, USA, 1968.

World Bank Technical Papers no. 90, *Techniques of Privatization of State-owned Enterprises*, vols II and III, 1988.

World Christian Encyclopedia, Oxford University Press, New York, 1983.

Wortzel, L. H. Global strategies: standardization versus flexibility, in *Global Strategic Management: The Essentials*, 2nd edn (eds. Wortzel, H. V. and Wortzel, L. H.), Wiley, New York, 1990.

Wortzel, H. V. and Wortzel, L. H. (eds.), *Global Strategic Management: The Essentials*, 2nd edn, Wiley, New York, 1990.

Yugur, Y. and Tuncalp, S., Exporting to Saudi Arabia. The power of the Made-in-Label, *International Marketing Review*, Autumn/Winter 1984.

Zammuto, R. F., *Assessing Organization Effectiveness: Systems Change, Adaptation and Strategy*, Albany State University Press, New York, 1982.

Zysman, J. and Tyson, L. (eds.), *American Industry in International Competition. Government Policies and Corporate Strategies*, Cornell University Press, Ithaca, NY, 1983.

INDEX